Social Work Practice in the Criminal Justice System

George T. Patterson

Routledge
Taylor & Francis Group

LONDON AND NEW YORK

First published 2012
by Routledge
2 Park Square, Milton Park, Abingdon, Oxon, OX14 4RN

Simultaneously published in the USA and Canada
by Routledge
711 Third Avenue, New York, NY 10017

Routledge is an imprint of the Taylor & Francis Group, an informa business

British Library Cataloguing in Publication Data
A catalogue record for this book is available from the British Library

Library of Congress Cataloging-in-Publication Data
Patterson, George T.
  Social work practice in the criminal justice system / George T. Patterson.
    p. cm.
  1. Criminal justice, Administration of—United States. 2. Social work with
  criminals—United States. I. Title.
  HV9950.P38 2012
  364.4′04530973—dc23   2011038923

ISBN13: 978–0–415–78115–2 (hbk)
ISBN13: 978–0–415–78116–9 (pbk)
ISBN13: 978–0–203–12394–2 (ebk)

Typeset in Sabon
by Keystroke, Station Road, Codsall, Wolverhampton

Printed and bound in Great Britain by
TJ International Ltd, Padstow, Cornwall

To my parents, thank you for your gifts

Contents

Tables

Preface

The purpose of this book is to provide readers with introductory knowledge of the criminal justice system, and basic skills necessary for entry level practice in the criminal justice system. It is anticipated that such knowledge will enhance the education and training that social workers receive to better equip them for positions in the criminal justice system. I am also hopeful that this knowledge will prepare social workers who are employed *outside* of the criminal justice system (e.g., in outpatient mental health clinics and human service agencies without criminal justice service programs) to work with clients having criminal justice system involvement, and act as advocates for legislative and criminal justice reform efforts.

This book is intended primarily for social work instructors, students, and practitioners. In the criminal justice system, social workers are employed in law enforcement agencies, courts, correctional facilities, juvenile residential and detention facilities, and victim assistance agencies. They are police social workers, probation and parole officers, and members of Congress. Some law enforcement and correctional officers, as well as attorneys, also have MSW degrees. Social workers provide assessment and evaluations, counseling, referrals, monitoring, crisis intervention, case management, and advocacy in addition to numerous other services.

Instructors, students, and practitioners in other disciplines such as sociology and criminal justice who have an interest in practice in the criminal justice system will also find this book useful. Practice roles such as advocacy are not exclusive to the social work profession. Practice is also defined broadly at micro, meso, and macro levels, and includes clinical or direct services, research, and policy practice. Consequently, the many practitioners who are not social workers and who provide services to individuals with criminal justice involvement will also find this book useful.

This book is grounded in the need for social workers to balance public safety, a major goal of the criminal justice system, with the principles of the National Association of Social Workers (NASW) *Code of ethics*. The concept of public safety proposes that community residents should be protected from crime and victimization. A plethora of methods attempt to achieve public safety. Social workers have a responsibility to achieve public safety in an ethical manner. The social work profession adheres to ethical values such as social justice which must be considered in public safety efforts. It is important to point out that the NASW *Code of ethics* applies only to social workers who are members of NASW.

Balancing public safety with ethical responsibilities is not an easy task, particularly for social workers who are employed *within* criminal justice settings (e.g., correctional facilities, law enforcement, probation, and parole) because these are not social work settings. These are examples of host settings in which professional social work is not the dominate profession or mission of the agency.

Ideological differences between social workers and other practitioners employed in the criminal justice system are more than just differences in public safety and ethical ideologies. These differences are also rooted in job descriptions, political and personal beliefs, and worldviews regarding causes and best practices for addressing criminal behavior and treatment. Understanding these differences and having the skills and ability to resolve these differences can facilitate social work practice within the criminal justice system.

The U.S. criminal justice system is a complex system. Usually three components of the criminal justice system are described (law enforcement, courts, and corrections). This book will describe and review four components (legislation, law enforcement, courts, and corrections). Practitioners across these four subsystems include legislators, law enforcement officers, attorneys and judges, correctional officers, and probation and parole officers, among others. Each of the subsystems operates individually and yet is interdependent. These systems are also found at tribal, local, state, and federal levels.

This book is not intended to be an exhaustive review of the criminal justice system. Indeed, each of the chapters in this book could fill the pages of an entire book. It is a vast field to summarize. The field is comprised of multiple services, programs, and reform efforts that are both documented and undocumented. Numerous introductory books have been written as well as numerous specialty books that focus on specific components of the criminal justice system such as courts, corrections. or law enforcement. Additionally, some specialty books focus on critical or emerging issues within the criminal justice system. These issues include court and prison reforms, and police brutality and misconduct, among others. Encyclopedias have also been published that focus on police science, law enforcement, and race and crime, to mention a few.

Several features of this book should be noted. First, a summary of social work practice implications is provided in each chapter. In this way, the practice implications are highlighted relative to the chapter topic and do not become lost within an enormous amount of text. Second, a separate chapter explores pertinent issues for social work practice in the criminal justice system in greater detail. These issues include working within authoritarian and host settings, providing services to mandated clients, and recognizing individuals' rights to self-determination. Third, the application of evidence-based practice principles in criminal justice is discussed in a separate chapter. Fourth, only documented sources were used to describe issues in the criminal justice system and social work practice. As a result of using this approach readers should be able to locate the original source for further review. Readers also are encouraged to examine the Further Reading section at the end of each chapter to consider additional readings on the chapter topic.

The dilemma of including examples of criminal justice reform efforts and innovative programs is that, for every example included in this book, many more are inevitably excluded. Readers are encouraged to use the skills acquired from this book to seek additional information about reform efforts, services, programs, and critical issues that are not covered. Finally, a list of Key Terms used within each chapter is provided at the end of each chapter.

Many individuals who are involved in the criminal justice system experience social problems that are contributing factors to crime and criminal justice system involvement. Examples of these social problems include alcohol and substance use and abuse, mental illness and co-occurring disorders, juvenile delinquency, gang membership, child abuse, and domestic violence.

The issues facing the U.S. criminal justice system are plentiful. Large numbers of individuals are incarcerated, on probation, or on parole supervision; racial disparities exist in crime, sentencing, and incarceration rates; correctional facilities lack sufficient reentry services to prepare inmates adequately for release; and when inmates are released they often reenter communities that lack job opportunities, adequate housing, health care services, and evidence-based mental health, alcohol, and substance abuse treatments. This too often contributes to high recidivism rates. Moreover, crime legislation can have an adverse impact on certain demographic groups. Providing effective interventions in response to these situations requires that social work practitioners possess specialty practice skills and knowledge, as well as the ability to collaborate with other practitioners in criminal justice and other systems. This is in essence interdisciplinary social work practice.

Acknowledgments

Several individuals made this book possible. Numerous family and friends provided understanding, encouragement, and support during the writing process. Thank you to Dr. Jacqueline Mondros for your support and encouragement; Helen Williams for her assistance with permission to reprint portions of the NASW *Code of ethics*; Kara McCarthy of the Bureau of Justice Statistics (BJS) for her assistance with permission to reprint statistical tables. Thank you Grace McInnes, commissioning editor at Routledge, for your vision concerning the value of a comprehensive book on social work practice in the criminal justice system. Your vision helped to shape the concept for this book. I am also grateful to James Watson, editorial assistant at Routledge, for patiently addressing my numerous questions and managing the manuscript.

I appreciate the helpful comments from the anonymous reviewers who provided comments in response to the initial proposal. These comments were instrumental in helping me to determine which chapters should contain specific subjects. At times it seemed as though the subjects could be covered in several chapters. I would also like to thank the librarians at Silberman School of Social Work at Hunter College and John Jay College of Criminal Justice, both of the City University of New York, for your assistance with identifying, retrieving, and borrowing materials. I sincerely appreciate the invaluable comments from Ann Lewis, Carol Thomas, Charlene Robinson, and Aaron Smalley concerning the case examples, and I am grateful to Joy Luangphaxay for retrieving articles.

Finally, thank you to the many police officers whom I have met in the U.S. and U.K. You have embraced police social work practice and recognized the contributions of police social workers in community policing efforts, and the mental health needs of police officers. A special thank you to the Rochester Police Department and its members for your long-term commitment to police social work practice.

1 Introduction to the U.S. Criminal Justice System

Chapter Overview

The criminal justice system is comprised of complex organizations that interact with offenders and victims. However, the criminal justice system addresses much more than crime. It affects the daily lives of citizens in many ways. This chapter briefly describes and establishes the U.S. criminal justice system as a system comprised of interdependent subsystems. The four subsystems that form the criminal justice system are: legislation, law enforcement, courts, and corrections. The criminal justice system functions at local, state, and federal governmental levels. American Indian and tribal communities have established separate law enforcement agencies, courts, and correctional institutions. No uniform criminal justice system exists in the U.S. Each state has its own distinct laws that define criminal behavior as well as guidelines used to punish offenders. This chapter also provides an overview of criminal justice perspectives influencing the system, and of theories that explain criminal behavior and victimization; traces the early involvement of the social work profession in the criminal justice system; and examines the size and scope of the system. Finally, this chapter identifies the need to balance public safety concerns, a major focus of the criminal justice system, with ethical social work practice as articled in the NASW *Code of ethics*.

A Note on Terms Used Throughout the Book

At the onset of this book, it is important to distinguish between several concepts that will appear throughout the book. The term *social work practice* will be used often to refer to social work practice *within* the criminal justice system. Regarding social work practice in the criminal justice system, two types of practice are delineated. Social work practice *within* the criminal justice system is used to reference employment in the criminal justice subsystems that include the legislative arena, law enforcement agencies, the courts system, and corrections. Examples include social workers who are probation and parole officers, and police social workers. Practice *outside* of the criminal justice system involves employment in human service agencies that are not part of the criminal justice system. However, these agencies offer programs and services to individuals with criminal justice system involvement. Examples include community-based agencies that provide services or transitional housing for offenders reentering communities.

The term *individuals with criminal justice system involvement* refers to individuals who are on probation or parole supervision, those awaiting trial, individuals recently charged with a crime, crime victims, and formerly incarcerated offenders. A point is made that not all individuals are involved with the criminal justice system as a result of crime-related situations. The criminal justice system also intervenes in response to a variety of legal matters such as property issues, and family matters such as custody, guardianship, and divorce.

Four Components of the Criminal Justice System

Most often, three components of the criminal justice system are identified and described. These three components are law enforcement, courts and corrections (Albanese, 2008; Frase & Weidner, 2002; Young & Lomonaco, 2001; Wilson, 2010). Alexander (2008) described a fourth component of the criminal justice system, legislation. Alexander suggested that law enforcement has the responsibility of arresting individuals who commit crimes; the courts have the responsibility for bringing individuals to trial; corrections oversee incarceration, community-based supervision, and monitoring; and state legislatures and Congress have the responsibility for defining criminal acts and punishment guidelines. Ross and Gould (2006) also described four components although their components were courts, law enforcement, corrections, and juvenile justice. In subsequent chapters of this book, these four components will be examined as subsystems within the criminal justice system.

Public Safety and the NASW *Code of ethics*

This book is grounded in the need to balance public safety, a major goal of the criminal justice system, with ethical social work practice. *Public safety* refers to the efforts of law enforcement, public safety, security, and other officials to protect communities from crime and criminal behavior. The book is grounded in the NASW *Code of ethics* and the values of the social work profession. Indeed, a profession which has a central function to promote social justice can find many areas in the criminal justice system where the profession can be active. However, fulfilling this mission within the criminal justice system requires specialized knowledge and skills.

Size and Scope of the U.S. Criminal Justice System

Statistics help to contextualize the size and scope of the U.S. criminal justice system and populations with various types of criminal justice system involvement. Statistics are useful for understanding victimization rates, the numbers of incarcerated individuals, and how widespread an issue can be. Statistics also describe patterns and trends that change when compared over time. It is important to understand how data were collected and analyzed so that the strengths and limitations of the data can be assessed. As we shall see in Chapter 2, this is particularly useful when presenting an issue to legislators about the magnitude of a social problem or crime.

The size and scope of the U.S. criminal justice system and individuals involved with the system are quite impressive. The numbers include not only offenders and victims but also employees and governmental expenditures.

In 2007, family and juvenile courts processed approximately 1,666,100 juvenile delinquency cases, or about 4,600 cases per day. Juvenile delinquency court processing of cases increased by more than 300% between 1960 and 2007 (Puzzanchera, Adams, & Sickmund, 2010).

In 2009, more than 7.2 million individuals were either on probation or parole supervision, or incarcerated in jails or prisons. This figure represents 3.1% of the adult U.S. population or 1 of every 32 adults in the U.S. population. Through 2009, there were 4,203,967 adults on probation, and 819,308 on parole or mandatory conditional release from prison. Also through 2009, 1,613,740 adults were incarcerated in state or federal prisons (1,405,622 were incarcerated in state prisons and 208,118 in federal prisons). By midyear 2009, jails incarcerated 760,400 adults who were either awaiting trail or serving a jail sentence (Bureau of Justice Statistics, n.d.a).

Through June 30, 2009, nearly 1 in every 134 Americans was incarcerated in jail or prison. Black, non-Hispanic males were 6 times more likely to be incarcerated than white non-Hispanic males, and 2.6 times more likely than Hispanic males to be incarcerated. Among females, 1 in every 300 Black females was incarcerated, in contrast to about 1 in every 1,099 white females and 1 in every 704 Hispanic females (West, 2010). Approximately 650,000 individuals are released each year from state and federal prisons (U.S. Department of Justice, Office of Justice Programs n.d.). When these individuals reenter communities they are in need of a variety of community-based services such as substance abuse, health and mental health care, housing, and employment.

Recidivism rates among former offenders are relatively high. Langan and Levin (2002) used four outcomes to assess recidivism rates: rearrest, reconviction, a resentence to prison, and reincarceration either with or without a new sentence. In 1994, follow-up was conducted with approximately 300,000 inmates after their release from prison in 15 states. The data show that 67.5% of former offenders were rearrested within a three-year period. Within the same three-year period, nearly half (46.9%) committed new crimes that resulted in reconviction, 25.4% were resentenced to prison for committing a new crime, and 51.8% were returned to prison for a new sentence or a violation of their release conditions. These violations include failing a drug test, failing to keep parole appointments, or being arrested for committing a new crime.

The primary crimes that resulted in recidivism among former offenders were motor vehicle theft (78.8%), having or selling stolen property (77.4%), larceny (74.6%), burglary (74.0%), robbery (70.2%), and having, using, or selling illegal weapons (70.2%) (Langan & Levin, 2002). The authors reported lower rearrest rates for driving while intoxicated (51.5%), rape (46.0%), sexual assault (41.4%), and homicide (40.7%).

In general, the new crimes that were committed at higher rates are economic crimes. These crimes appear to provide some financial benefit for former offenders. The crimes also affect victims who are robbed or burglarized. Patterns in the types of new crimes that are committed, and how victims are impacted raise several questions. If more employment opportunities were provided for former offenders, would we observe a decrease in these new crimes? Would we observe a decrease in robberies and burglaries? What are the most effective approaches for assisting former offenders with financial needs? Certainly one's financial situation is tied to many other needs such as housing, food, and transportation.

Some crime and incarceration statistics have shown a decrease. For example, violent crimes, such as homicide, forcible rape, robbery, and aggravated assault, decreased by 6.2% during the first six months of 2010 when compared to the first six months of 2009 (Federal Bureau of Investigation, 2010). The number of inmates incarcerated in county and city jails decreased by 2.4% between midyear 2009 and midyear 2010 (Minton, 2011).

Criminal Justice Expenditures

Local governments spend more on criminal justice services than either state governments or federal government. Spending on law enforcement and judicial services (which includes civil and criminal courts, and corrections) has continued to increase since 1982. According to the Bureau of Justice Statistics (n.d.b), in 2007, all levels of government reported spending approximately $228 billion for law enforcement, judicial, corrections, and legal services. This figure represents a 1.3% increase over 2006 spending levels for these services. During 2007, federal, state, and local governments spent approximately $104 billion for police protection services, $50 billion for judicial and legal services, and $74 billion for corrections. Local governments spent $116 billion on criminal justice, whereas state governments spent $74 billion and the federal governmental spent $37 billion. To place criminal justice spending in perspective, this compares to $502.3 billion in Medicare spending, and $373.9 billion in Medicaid spending in 2009 (U.S. Department of Health & Human Services, n.d.).

Spending levels for criminal justice services clearly show that local governments spend more than state governments and the federal government combined. Although social workers provide a variety of criminal justice services within the federal and state governments, most services are provided at local governmental levels. These local governments overwhelmingly bear the responsibility for criminal justice services. Social workers are also more likely to be employed in local agencies and collaborate with local governmental agencies such as law enforcement agencies.

Criminal Justice Employment

In 2007, 2.5 million individuals were employed nationwide in local, state, and federal criminal justice systems. Among law enforcement services, 76% of employees worked within local government, 9.2% were employed at state levels, and 14% in the federal government. Judicial and legal services employed 53% of their workers at local levels, 35% at state levels, and 12% worked at the federal government level. Corrections employed 61% of their workers at the state level, 34% at the local level, and 5% at the federal level (Bureau of Justice Statistics, n.d.b).

As these employment figures show, with the exception of corrections, local governments employ more workers in the criminal justice system. As previously mentioned, local governments spend more for criminal justice services, and social workers are more likely to be employed in local agencies. In addition to employment within governmental agencies, social workers are also employed in private for profit and nonprofit agencies where they provide criminal-justice-related services.

Overview of the U.S. Criminal Justice System

"Criminal justice refers to the agencies that dispense justice and the process by which justice is carried out" (Siegel, 2010, p. 37). Siegel observed that the criminal justice system is "the loosely organized collection of agencies (police, the courts, corrections agencies, etc.) charged with protecting the public, maintaining order, enforcing the law, identifying transgressors, bringing the guilty to justice and treating criminal behavior" (p. 4). Frase & Weidner (2002) defined criminal justice as "a set of legal and social institutions for enforcing the criminal law in accordance with a defined set of procedural rules and limitations" (p. 371).

No universal criminal justice exists in the U.S., as each of the 50 states has its own criminal justice system (Frase & Weidner, 2002). American Indian and tribal criminal justice systems have separate law enforcement agencies, courts, and correctional institutions (Perry, 2005). This makes it impracticable to summarize all of the criminal justice systems. It also suggests that social workers within different jurisdictions will encounter different terminology, laws, and policies.

Despite the size and scope of the criminal justice system, Cole & Smith (2004) summarized numerous distinctive features:

- The U.S. criminal justice system is based on federalism. Governmental power is divided between federal and state governments. Criminal cases can be tried in federal courts (see Chapter 4) and federal prisons have been created (see Chapter 5).
- The U.S. constitution does not include criminal justice requirements, nor does it permit the development of a federal law enforcement agency. The power to develop law enforcement agencies is given only to states. However, the U.S. government is involved in law enforcement through the Federal Bureau of Investigation (FBI) (see Chapter 3).
- The majority of criminal justice services are performed at state government levels.
- During the 1960s the federal government assumed a large role in the provision of state and local criminal justice services. For example, funding provided to states to enhance the development and implementation of criminal justice initiatives focused on juvenile delinquency, violent crime, and terrorism, among other issues.

- The U.S. criminal justice system has a dual court system. This means that in addition to each state having a court system, a federal court is also located within each state.

As individuals are processed through the four components of the criminal justice system, they encounter a series of steps and are subject to a sequence of procedures. Siegel (2010) described this movement as a *process* which entails steps that begin with initial contact with a police officer and end in postrelease from a correctional facility. This is the "formal criminal justice process" (p. 13) which typically involves 15 stages. However, not all individuals who have criminal justice system involvement follow this formal process. Siegel referred to an "informal justice process" (p. 19) which involves informal processing procedures such as police officers making deals in exchange for cooperation and information, and defense attorneys and prosecutors making deals to obtain a lenient sentence.

It may seem surprising to most, but the majority of cases that come to the attention of the criminal justice system are settled by *plea bargaining*. Dripps (2002), also observing the criminal justice system as a process, reports that plea bargaining

> involves the prosecutor trading a reduction in the seriousness of the charges or the length of the recommended sentence for a waiver of the right to trial and a plea of guilty to the reduced charges. Both sides usually have good reasons for settlement. In a case in which the evidence of guilt is overwhelming, the prosecution can avoid the expense and delay of a trial by offering modest concessions to the defendant. When the evidence is less clear-cut the government can avoid the risk of an acquittal by agreeing to a plea to a reduced charge.
>
> (p. 368)

Table 1.1 Formal Stages in the Criminal Justice System

- Police contact
- Investigation by police
- Arrest by police
- Taken into custody by police
- Criminal charges made by police
- Preliminary or grand jury hearing
- Arraignment
- Detention and bail posted
- Plea bargain activities
- Trial phase
- Sentencing phase
- Appeal phase
- Incarceration
- Reentry
- Community-based supervision

Source: Adapted from Siegel (2010, pp. 12–19).

Approximately 80% of felony cases and more than 90% of misdemeanor cases are settled without having a trial (Siegel, 2010). An over-reliance on plea bargaining does not occur because too many cases come to the attention of the court system. It occurs because taking a case to trial involves risks for both the prosecutor and the defendant. These risks are associated with unanticipated trial outcomes such as the prosecutor losing the case or the defendant receiving a harsh sentence (Albanese, 2008). Victims or the general public may question whether this is actually justice in a system that does not bring to trial the majority of offenders. Or when they are brought to trial many times the criminal charges are reduced. If someone would like to see an offender "pay" for the crime that he or she committed, the offender may "pay", but for a crime based on plea bargaining and reduced charges. Indeed informal processing may frustrate those who perceive that justice is not being served.

Criminal Justice Agencies as a System

The criminal justice system has been described as a *system* comprised of numerous subsystems (Cole & Smith, 2004; Frase & Weidner, 2002). Viewing the criminal justice system as a system made up of numerous subsystems is consistent with systems theory and the ecosystems perspective which are both germane to social work practice.

The use of systems theory promotes social work assessment and interventions. In the *Social work dictionary*, Barker (2003) defined a *system* as

> A combination of elements with mutual reciprocity and identifiable boundaries that form a complex or unitary whole. Systems may be physical and mechanical, living and social, or combinations of these. Examples of social systems include individual families, groups, a specific social welfare agency, or a nation's entire organizational process of education.
>
> (p. 427)

Systems theory also posits that creating a change in one system will result in change in another system(s). Applying this theoretical framework, we would anticipate that a change in criminal justice legislation, such as the recent passage of the *Fair Sentencing Act* of 2010, will result in observable changes in other components of the criminal justice system. Because the law eliminates the mandatory minimum sentence that judges impose for possession of crack cocaine, less racial disparity should occur between individuals who possess powder cocaine and crack cocaine. As will be discussed in Chapter 9, social workers have an ethical obligation to monitor policies. Monitoring the *Fair Sentencing Act* of 2010 can yield information that demonstrates whether systemic changes have indeed occurred, and racial disparities been reduced.

Individuals not only interact with the various subsystems of the criminal justice system, they also interact with their families, communities, and other agencies. The *ecosystems perspective* utilizes concepts from the field of ecology and systems theory. This perspective posits that individuals engage in transactional interactions with their social and physical environments. The outcome of these interactions influences behavior.

In practice, social workers assess both individuals and environments, and provide interventions to individuals and their environments.

Taken together, viewing the criminal justice as a system requires not only that social workers assess and intervene with the various subsystems (legislation, law enforcement, courts, and corrections) but also that social workers assess and intervene within communities. Community-level factors that contribute to crime, such as unemployment, are also the focus of social work interventions.

Overview of Crimes

Siegel (2010, see p. 15) summarized three types of major crime:

1. *Violent crime* in which serious injury or death has occurred. Examples include homicide, intimate partner violence, gang violence, and hate crimes.
2. *Public order crimes* violate society's norms and morality. Examples include sex crimes such as prostitution, and drug and pornography trafficking.
3. *Economic crimes* provide an economic benefit to the individual committing the crime. Examples include property thefts such as stealing and burglary.

Crimes are also generally classified on the basis of the length of time spent incarcerated. A *misdemeanor* is a crime associated with a jail sentence of one year or less. Examples include petit larceny and assault. A *felony* is a category of crimes associated with a jail sentence of more than one year. These crimes include homicide and robbery. No uniform classification system exists among states to define which crimes are misdemeanors and which are felonies.

Measuring Crime Rates

As we have seen earlier in this chapter, statistics help to describe the size and scope of the criminal justice system. It is essential to have the skills necessary to assess the strengths and limitations of data. Such skills are useful for understanding how crime rates are measured in the U.S. The most common methods used to measure crime rates are the Uniform Crime Report (UCR) and the National Crime Victimization Survey (NCVS). Each method has some limitations. Despite the limitations each method remains an important indicator and source of crime and victimization in the U.S.

Uniform Crime Report (UCR) Program

The UCR Program collects statistics on crimes reported to law enforcement agencies operated by cities, universities and colleges, county, state, federal, and tribal law enforcement agencies throughout the U.S. Law enforcement agencies are not required to participate, and voluntarily submit statistics to the FBI UCR Program. The UCR describes incidences of "serious crimes" and "less serious crimes." Serious crimes, or

Part I offenses, reported to law enforcement include eight crimes: murder and non-negligent manslaughter, forcible rape, robbery, aggravated assault, burglary, larceny-theft, motor vehicle theft, and arson. Arson was added to the UCR Program in 1978. Less serious crimes, or Part II offenses, are made up of 21 crimes. Examples include driving under the influence and simple assault (FBI, 2009).

A limitation of the UCR is that not all crimes, such as embezzlement, are readily brought to the attention of law enforcement. Also, some serious crimes, such as kidnapping, occur infrequently. The UCR Program limits the reporting of offenses to the eight serious crime classifications because they are the crimes most likely to be reported and most likely to occur with sufficient frequency to provide an adequate basis for comparison (FBI, 2009). Nonetheless, the *Preliminary Semiannual Uniform Crime Report, January–June, 2010* shows a 6.2% decrease in violent crimes in the U.S. during the first six months of 2010 (FBI, 2010).

The National Crime Victimization Survey (NCVS)

The National Crime Victimization Survey (NCVS) is the largest yearly victimization survey, administered nationwide to a representative sample of approximately 135,300 individuals. The purpose of the NCVS is to obtain crime victimization information (victims of assault, household burglary, and motor vehicle theft, for example). The NCVS also assesses victimization rates among demographic groups such as women and the elderly, and by residential location (Bureau of Justice Statistics, 2011).

Theoretical Explanations of Crime and Victimization

Theories are statements that describe a relationship between concepts. Some theories that explain criminal behavior and victimization are criminological theories. Others are psychological or social theories. *Criminology* is the study of crime and criminal behavior. *Criminogenic needs* are factors that are associated with criminal behavior. These factors include: (1) antisocial personality; (2) procriminal attitudes; (3) a social environment that supports criminal behavior; (4) substance abuse; (5) poor family and marital relationships; (6) poor school and work performance; and(7) lack of appropriate recreational activities (Andrews & Bonta, 2010).

Theories are used to guide practice interventions and are tested as hypotheses in research studies. Research study results have implications for practice interventions. For example, examining Michael Gottfredson and Hirchi's self-control theory (social control theory posits that inadequate parenting results in adequate self-control), DeLisi, Hochstetler, Higgins, Beaver, and Graeve (2008) sampled 208 males on parole supervision. They argued that offenders with low self-control would exhibit negative behaviors while incarcerated such as substance abuse and negative interactions with correctional personnel. They found relationships between low self-control and negative behavior while incarcerated. Increasing levels of self-control have the potential to reduce negative behaviors, thereby reducing criminal justice system involvement.

In general, theories relevant to the criminal justice system emphasize individual factors, environmental factors, or the interaction between the individual and environment. Siegel (2010) summarized these theories into seven areas:

1. *Choice theory* assumes that individuals choose to commit crimes. A choice is made to either commit or not commit a crime after considering the risks of getting arrested or whether committing a crime is worth the effort.

2. *Biological theories* consider the influence of biochemical, neurological, and genetic factors on criminal behavior. Closely associated with biological theories are biosocial theories which recognize contributing factors such as biological, biochemical (hormonal imbalance), neurological (brain impairment), and genetic factors.

3. *Psychological theories* include psychodynamic theories which focus on internal psychic conflict, social learning theory which posits that individuals learn to commit crimes, and cognitive theory which identifies the affect of a cognitive problem on criminal behavior.

4. *Sociological theories* focus on the influence of environmental factors (e.g., poverty) to explain why individuals commit crimes. Examples include culture of poverty, social process theories, social structure theories, and disorganized neighborhood theories.

5. *Critical criminology* emphasizes economic and political factors as primary causes of criminal behavior. Critical criminology assumes that the criminal justice system is controlled by wealthy members of society who assert their moral beliefs on the poor.

6. *Developmental theories* explain why some individuals continue to engage in criminal behaviors throughout the life course, whereas others discontinue their involvement in criminal behavior. Theoretical examples include latent trait theory and life course theory.

7. *Theories of victimization* focus on the characteristics of crime victims as opposed to those who commit crimes. Examples include routine activities theory and lifestyle theory.

The most relevant theories for social work practice are those that consider the influence of both environmental and psychological factors, or biological, psychological, and social environmental influences. These are person-in-environment perspectives and are relevant to social work practice.

A major focus of the social work profession is an emphasis on environmental factors that shape behavior. Thus, central to the profession is the need to change these environmental conditions such as poverty, inadequate housing, unemployment, and inadequate access to alcohol and substance treatment, which are theorized to be a factor in criminal behavior.

Because social workers provide services to both offenders and victims, it is important for social workers to have an explanation of crime that can guide the provision of interventions. Such explanations also guide assessments and evaluations. For instance, a biopsychosocial assessment considers biological factors such neurological disorders, psychological factors such as cognitions, and poverty in the social environment.

Whereas practice interventions acknowledge the need to integrate environmental factors, research studies have not been guided by theories or rigorous methods that investigate how exposure to environmental factors influences criminal behavior (Wikstrom, Ceccato, Hardie, & Treiber, 2009).

Criminal Justice Perspectives

Several perspectives have had a major influence on the U.S. criminal justice system. The influence of these perspectives has affected the enactment of crime legislation, law enforcement policies and practices, and court and correctional reforms. These perspectives include: (1) the crime control perspective; (2) the rehabilitation perspective; (3) the due process perspective; (4) the justice perspective; (5) the restorative justice perspective; (6) the retributive justice perspective; and (7) the therapeutic jurisprudence perspective. These perspectives provide a framework for understanding policy and practice approaches within the criminal justice system. They are also linked to the goals of punishment (Cole & Smith, 2004).

Three perspectives are of most interest to the social work profession: the rehabilitation, restorative justice, and therapeutic jurisprudence perspectives. Social workers accept these perspectives more than the others. This has implications for social work practice as social workers interact with other criminal justice practitioners who may not hold similar views on criminal justice perspectives. Differential views on these perspectives can be a source of conflict between social workers and other practitioners, or result in the inconsistent treatment of individuals involved in the criminal justice system. For example, while adhering to a crime control perspective, criminal justice practitioners are likely to favor incarceration and deterrence strategies. Conversely, practitioners who adhere to the rehabilitation perspective will emphasize a variety of treatments and services for addressing social problems. Chapter 8 explores approaches for ethically resolving conflicts with colleagues.

Siegel (2010) summarized the crime control, rehabilitation, due process, justice, and restorative justice perspectives:

The *crime control perspective* focuses on controlling and preventing crime. This is achieved by imposing firm sentences and penalties such as the death penalty, police patrol, and incarceration, and by limiting technical issues that allow guilty offenders to go free of charges. In this perspective, firm and harsh punishment is intended to deter criminal behavior.

The *rehabilitation perspective* focuses on providing treatment and services to offenders. The causes of crime are seen as resulting from the lack of health and mental health care, education, and employment skills, for example. Rehabilitation approaches help offenders improve their functioning in these areas. Improved functioning should prevent future criminal behavior.

Rehabilitation is one of the criminal justice perspectives that most interests the social work profession. Rehabilitation not only centers on public safety issues but also ensures that individuals receive treatment, such as mental health and substance abuse treatment, or vocational training and services among others. Rehabilitation approaches provide opportunities for social workers to provide treatment and services. For example, within correctional facilities, because the majority of incarcerated offenders will reenter communities, it is important to prepare them for reentry through the provision of a variety of social services.

The *due process perspective* emphasizes treating individuals involved in the criminal justice system fairly according to their constitutional rights. It posits that due process should be given to each person involved in the criminal justice system. The goal of this perspective is to reduce bias resulting from characteristics such as race and social class, and inadequate legal representation. One way this goal is achieved is by providing fair and competent legal representation.

Somewhat similar to the due process perspective, the *justice perspective* emphasizes treating all individuals involved in the criminal justice in the same manner. One method for achieving this goal is to reduce *judicial discretion* (the power given to judges to use their own judgment when imposing harsh or lenient sentences). This perspective also suggests that offenders be tried based only on the current criminal charge. Charges related to past crimes, crimes committed in the past, or a person's propensity to commit crimes in the future are not considered during a trial pertaining to a current crime. *Truth-in-sentencing* laws (guidelines that require offenders to serve at least 85% of an original sentence) and *mandatory sentences* laws (guidelines that establish a preset amount of time that must be served for a specific crime) are included in the justice perspective. In sum, this perspective reduces the amount of judicial discretion afforded to judges and requires that judges adhere to pre-established sentencing guidelines.

The *retributive perspective* is a "traditional approach" (p. 408) to the criminal justice system. This perspective upholds the adversarial nature of the criminal justice system and the use of punishment as a means for retribution (Albanese, 2008).

The *restorative justice perspective* seeks to reduce the adversarial, harsh, and punitive nature of the criminal justice system. Instead of focusing only on offenders and victims, this perspective emphasizes the justice needs of victims, offenders, and communities (Van Ness, 2004). Restorative justice has been defined in many ways. Definitions range from the process used to reach consensus among victims, offenders, and communities, to finding solutions to crime that are restorative (Bazemore & Walgrave, 1999; Ward & Langlands, 2009). Bazemore & Walgrave defined restorative justice as "every action that is primarily oriented toward doing justice by repairing the harm that has been caused by a crime" (p. 48). Van Wormer (2009) defined restorative justice as "a non-adversarial approach usually monitored by a trained professional who seeks to offer justice to the individual victim, the offender, and the community" (p. 531).

Similar to the rehabilitation perspective, the restorative justice perspective is also of most interest to the social work profession. The perspective is congruent with social work values and ethics and has the capacity to increase social work involvement in the criminal justice system (Judah & Bryant, 2004). Moreover, restorative justice is tied to social justice (van Wormer, 2009). This is evident in Siegel's (2010) statement:

> This call for social justice has helped focus attention on the plight of the poor, women, and minority groups when they confront the agencies of the justice system. Programs that have been developed as a result include free legal services for indigent

offenders, civilian review boards to oversee police, laws protecting battered women, and shelters for victims of domestic violence.

(p. 117)

Finally, the *therapeutic jurisprudence perspective* was founded by David B. Wexler and Bruce J. Winick. Winick (1997) defined the perspective as

> the study of the role of law as a therapeutic agent . . . the exploration of ways in which, consistent with principles of justice and other constitutional values, the knowledge, theories, and insights of the mental health and related disciplines can help shape the development of the law. Therapeutic jurisprudence builds on the insight that the law itself can be seen to function as a kind of therapist or therapeutic agent. Legal rules, legal procedures, and the roles of legal actors (such as lawyers and judges) constitute social forces that, whether intended or not, often produce therapeutic or antitherapeutic consequences.

(p. 185)

Of all the perspectives outlined above, the crime control and justice perspectives are presently the major guiding perspectives that inform U.S. criminal justice policies and practices (Siegel, 2010). Siegel asserts that these perspectives are evident in tough on crime legislation, curtailing the rights of defendants, increased incarceration rates, and death penalty legislation.

Criminal Justice and Human Rights

The right to a fair criminal justice system is a human rights issue. According to the Universal Declaration of Human Rights adopted in 1948, Article 7, "All are equal before the law and are entitled without any discrimination to equal protection of the law. All are entitled to equal protection against any discrimination in violation of this Declaration and against any incitement to such discrimination" (p. 3). Article 8 states that "Everyone has the right to an effective remedy by the competent national tribunals for acts violating the fundamental rights granted him [*sic*] by the constitution or law" (p. 3) (*Universal declaration of human rights*, n.d.).

The Bill of Rights comprises amendments to the U.S. Constitution. There are ten amendments. Amendment VI of The Bill of Rights specifies:

> In all criminal prosecutions, the accused shall enjoy the right to a speedy and public trial, by an impartial jury of the state and district wherein the crime shall have been committed, which district shall have been previously ascertained by law, and to be informed of the nature and cause of the accusation; to be confronted with the witnesses against him [*sic*]; to have compulsory process for obtaining witnesses in his [*sic*] favor, and to have the assistance of counsel for his [*sic*] defence.

(*Bill of rights* transcript, n.d.).

Amendment VIII protects individuals accused of a crime from excessive bail and fines, and cruel and unusual punishment. Both the Universal Declaration of Human Rights and the Bill of Rights are in accordance with social work practice in the criminal justice system.

History of Social Work Practice in the U.S. Criminal Justice System

The social work professions' involvement in the criminal justice system began in the juvenile justice system. Alexander (2007) traced the involvement of the social work profession in the criminal justice system from its earliest beginnings. Fox (as cited in Alexander, 2007) states that social work played an important role in establishing the first juvenile court in Chicago, IL. Addams (as cited in Alexander, 2007) wrote that, after Hull House (a settlement house established in Chicago in 1889—settlement houses emerged to assist immigrants with transitioning to life in America) was established, its workers provided services to juvenile boys who were arrested and incarcerated. Later in 1903, social workers played a significant role in the juvenile court.

A worker at Hull House was employed in a police precinct near Hull House. She provided services to youth who were arrested and was described as the first juvenile probation officer. Five additional probation officers were hired one year later (Addams, as cited in Alexander, 2007). In 1898, the Flanner House, a settlement house in Indianapolis, IN, developed and implemented interventions to address juvenile delinquency within the African American community (Crocker, as cited in Alexander, 2007). During the same year, Hull House, the Illinois State Conferences of Charities, and the Chicago Bar Association formed a committee to enact changes impacting the treatment of juveniles within the criminal justice system. As a result of their efforts, the Illinois legislature passed *An Act to Regulate the Treatment and Control of Dependent, Neglected, and Delinquent Children*. The Act established the first juvenile court in the country located in Chicago (Abbott, as cited in Alexander, 2007). Presently, all 50 states have a juvenile court (Ellis & Sowers, 2001). The juvenile court was established on the principle that juveniles should receive treatment and rehabilitation instead of punishment.

In the 1920s, social workers were hired to work in juvenile correctional facilities. Social workers provided preventive services, assessment, and parent education (Schlossman & Pisciotta, as cited in Alexander, 2007). Not long after they were created, it appeared that juvenile courts were functioning poorly and not providing youth adequate services. Even social workers would not refer to the juvenile courts (Abbott, 1938, as cited in Alexander, 2007). The courts were poorly funded and operated by poorly trained judges who emphasized evidence and facts instead of treatment (Moran, as cited in Alexander, 2007). Finally, higher than expected recidivism rates were observed among juveniles processed in the courts (Abbott, 1938, as cited in Alexander, 2007).

Despite the development of a juvenile justice system, 14-year-old George Stinney, Jr. was executed in 1944 in South Carolina. He was a Black youth accused of murdering two White girls. No physical evidence placed him at the scene of the crime, his parents were not present during interrogation, and no records were maintained that documented his confession or conviction. He was the youngest person executed in the U.S. during the twentieth century. A movement is under way to exonerate George Stinney, Jr. owing to the lack of evidence justifying his execution (Smith, 2011).

Several individuals who were at the forefront of the social work profession were lawyers. Consequently, in the early period of the profession social work was more linked with law and the criminal justice system. Social work students completed field placements in many components of the criminal justice system including courts, corrections, law firms, and legal aid offices. Upon graduation social workers sought employment in probation, parole, and court settings. In fact, for the first 30 years of the social work profession, social work and the law were more linked than social work and mental health are at present. During the mid-1930s, the social work profession began to focus on poverty and mental health. This resulted in a shift towards mental health courses and field placements in mental health settings, denoting a shift away from criminal justice (Barker & Branson, 1993).

Social work remained influential in the criminal justice system until the 1980s when the profession's influence began to decline. Particularly during the 1990s, social work involvement continued to decline owing to: (1) lack of funding for treatment programs, (2) lack of funding for social work training, (3) the enactment of state legislation focused on punishment and incarceration instead treatment, and (4) professional social work organizations such as NASW not prioritizing criminal justice as an important area of practice, suggesting that practice settings which focused on punishment and social control were contrary to social work practice (Sarri & Shook, 2005).

Reamer (2004) also noted the decline of social work involvement in the criminal justice system. Reamer explains that the decline began during the 1960s when both the adult and juvenile justice systems shifted away from the rehabilitation perspective toward the retributive justice perspective. Because the later perspective is not consistent with social work values, the profession focused less attention on the criminal justice system.

Although declining involvement has been reported, the social work profession has played a role in both the adult and juvenile justice systems. Indeed, the social work profession was once much more influential in the criminal justice system than it is today. The numbers of social workers practitioners within each of the four components of the criminal justice system vary. Social workers are perhaps involved in the correctional system in the greatest numbers, followed by the court system, law enforcement, and finally legislation in that order.

In the NASW Center for Workforce Studies report titled *Social workers at work* Whitaker and Arrington (2008) reported that 1% of the NASW membership identified criminal justice as their primary area of social work practice. The authors reported that national membership is 80% female and 20% male. Women represented 78% of the workforce in juvenile justice whereas men represented 22%. Similarly, women represented 78% of the workforce in adult criminal justice settings and men 22%. NASW members were surveyed from August 2007 through November 30, 2007.

The NASW *Code of ethics*

The purpose of the NASW *Code of ethics* is to describe professional conduct for the social work profession. These ethical standards apply only to social workers who are members of the National Association of Social Workers (NASW, n.d.). Four sections make up the NASW *Code of ethics*: (1) the "Preamble" articulates the mission and core values of the social work profession (see Box 1.1); (2) the "Purpose of the NASW Code of Ethics" describes the purpose of the ethical standards and offers guidance for resolving issues that arise in practice; (3) "Ethical Principles" identifies the ethical principles that form the basis of social work practice; and (4) "Ethical Standards" summarizes ethical guidelines, some of which are associated with consequences for violations.

Box 1.1 NASW *Code of ethics* Preamble

The primary mission of the social work profession is to enhance human wellbeing and help meet the basic human needs of all people, with particular attention to the needs and empowerment of people who are vulnerable, oppressed, and living in poverty. A historic and defining feature of social work is the profession's focus on individual wellbeing in a social context and the wellbeing of society. Fundamental to social work is attention to the environmental forces that create, contribute to, and address problems in living.

> Copyrighted material reprinted with permission from the
> National Association of Social Workers, Inc.

Social workers face numerous challenges when practicing in the four components of the criminal justice system or in other settings that offer services to individuals who are involved in the system. Ethical issues are most likely to arise in relation to confidentiality, responsibilities to agencies and to clients, conflict with other professionals in the criminal justice system, and self-determination, among others. The NASW *Code of ethics* provides guidance for social work practice in criminal justice settings, although the code is clearer in its presentation in some areas than others. For example, whereas the code articulates that social workers have an ethical mandate to perform social change, the code does not provide specific guidance regarding how this ethical value should be achieved. Given that criminal justice populations experience a variety of issues that result from social conditions this omission is evident.

In sum, in spite of the code of ethics articulating social workers' ethical responsibilities, some forms of criminal justice practice may be difficult. For example, the NASW *Code of ethics* describes a professional value of dignity and worth of persons. Although this value is articulated relative to culture and ethnic diversity, some social workers may experience difficulty practicing this value or viewing the person as a troubled individual when the individual has committed a quadruple homicide of innocent victims or the homicide of children.

Case Example

The following case example illustrates the tasks performed by a social worker within each of the four components of the criminal justice system. These tasks are representative of those performed by social workers who are employed within criminal justice settings, as well as those performed by social workers who are employed within human service settings operated outside of the system. In a hospital setting a medical social worker might provide discharge planning and inquire about the referrals provided by the victim's assistance worker. These tasks exemplify how social workers can be employed in non-criminal justice settings yet still provide services to a crime victim involved in the criminal justice system. The example below illustrates the types of services that social workers provide to both crime victims and offenders. It also shows the types of services provided at each stage of the criminal justice system beginning with a law violation passed by legislatures and ending in post conviction. To illustrate how a social worker might intervene within each of the four components of the criminal justice system, consider the following case illustration.

Josef, a 22-year-old Mexican immigrant, was walking home from work during the early evening hours. He was approached by a group of White and African American men who began to shout and taunt Josef with ethnic slurs, suggesting that he go back to Mexico. The men accused Josef of taking their jobs. Josef was later found lying on the sidewalk by a passerby. Before he lost consciousness, Josef explained to the passerby that he was beaten with baseball bats, punched and kicked by the three attackers who shouted ethnic slurs. When police officers arrived a statement was taken from the passerby, who, although she did not witness the attack, recounted to the police what she was told by Josef. The police officers classified the attack as a hate crime. Josef was transported to the hospital where it was determined that he received several broken bones and required surgery. The police investigation revealed that the attack was captured on a video camera installed in a nearby parking lot. The video was shown during the evening news broadcast and a short time later a tip led to the apprehension of the three suspects. Approximately ten months later the three suspects were convicted and sentenced, and Josef continued to experience medical problems as a result of the attack.

Legislation

A social worker who is not employed in the legislative arena or a criminal justice setting supports hate crimes legislation. The social worker discovered from the NASW website that NASW also supports hate crimes legislation. Using the website to acquire a sample letter template and contact information for local representatives, the social worker prepared and sent a letter to the district Representative and Senator. The social worker is a member of a local social work practice group and encouraged other members via e-mail to also send letters in support of hate crimes legislation.

Law Enforcement

The police officers who responded at the scene contacted the police social worker who met with Josef and his family at the hospital. The police social worker provided crisis intervention, case status information regarding next steps that would be taken by the police department and a referral to the victim assistance unit. The police detective also provided Josef and his family with her contact information to receive updated information concerning the investigation.

Courts

The victim's assistance social worker provided emotional support, court accompaniment and transportation, and assistance with preparing a victim impact statement which Josef read during the sentencing phase of the trial. Court procedures were explained to Josef as needed. He also received assistance with filing a victim's compensation claim to pay for his medical bills, ongoing psychotherapy for the trauma he experienced as a result of the attack, and financial assistance due to lost wages. These services were paid by a crime victim's compensation fund acquired through fines and surcharges imposed on offenders. In his state Josef was eligible to receive unlimited paid medical expenses. All of these services were contingent upon Josef being an innocent crime victim and participating in court proceedings which he was willing to do.

Corrections

As a crime victim, Josef is not involved with the corrections component of the criminal justice system. The three offenders were sentenced to prison for committing a hate crime. One of the offenders experienced difficulty adjusting to the prison environment. The correctional social worker provided counseling focused on adjusting to incarceration and the prison environment.

Implications for Social Work Practice

Social workers are employed *within* criminal justice settings with the primary role of providing direct services to clients, although social workers perform other roles as well. Therefore social workers may have few, if any, opportunities to engage in social change efforts or to challenge social injustice in the larger criminal justice system. This can be difficult for social workers who can readily identify many areas for change. Social workers are obligated to perform their roles as described in a job announcement, but also adhere to the values and mission of the social work profession. This is not an easy charge. As described in subsequent chapters of this book, social workers have opportunities to engage in advocacy and other activities outside of their regular employment.

Social workers provide clinical or direct services to both victims of crimes and criminal offenders. Providing social work services to a crime victim is quite different from providing services to an offender. For many social workers, working with offenders requires a different skill set and they may not opt to work in a setting where they provide services to offenders. Providing services to a victim necessitates empathy. Social workers may find it easier to empathize with a crime victim. However, when working with an offender social workers may find it is more difficult to be empathetic particularly depending upon the type of crime committed. For example, a mitigation specialist conducting a social history in a case involving homicide is very different from one providing services to a victim of domestic violence. Although both situations involve violence still some social workers may prefer not to provide direct services in either of these situations. Social workers may have strong personal feelings and beliefs about homicide as well as how offenders should be punished. It may be more difficult, or impossible for some, to empathize with the reasons why an individual commits a crime and remain nonjudgmental.

It may or may not seem surprising, but social workers rank individuals who commit crimes "at the bottom of the list" (Young & Lomonaco, 2001, p. 479). Moreover, community-based mental health clinics, and social service and health care agencies, are often hesitant to provide services to offenders with criminal justice system histories (Primm, Osher, & Gomez, 2005).

While the criminal justice system may impose sanctions to punish the offender, and protect public safety, social workers can advocate for services to enhance well-being and social functioning, while at the same time sanctions protect public safety in terms of future crimes and victimization. Criminal justice perspectives that are congruent with social work values and the NASW *Code of ethics* can assist social workers with balancing public safety issues. The well-being of society recognizes the risks to public safety. Social workers therefore also work to ensure the wellbeing of society by reducing these public safety risks that offenders impose.

Chapter Summary

The need for social workers to balance public safety with ethical practice was established. Public safety is a priority within the criminal justice system. The NASW *Code of ethics*, particularly the obligation to challenge social injustice and engage in social action, can serve as a guide to achieve this aim.

In this chapter we examined formal and informal processes that occur in the criminal justice system, and established the four components that make up the system: (1) legislation, (2) law enforcement, (3) courts, and (4) corrections. Systems theory provides a useful framework for understanding the interdependence of these four components. We also examined the size and scope of the criminal justice system relative to incarceration and victimization rates, expenditures, and the number of employees within the system. Finally, we examined three types of crimes, common methods for measuring crime rates, and theoretical frameworks that explain crime and victimization, and traced the history of social work involvement in the criminal justice system. Restorative justice, rehabilitation, and therapeutic jurisprudence were introduced as criminal justice perspectives that are congruent with social work values, whereas crime control and retributive justice perspectives are not. Criminal justice perspectives that are relevant for social work practice will be discussed in greater detail in subsequent chapters.

Key Terms

Crime

Criminal justice perspectives

Criminal justice system

Ecosystems perspective

Felony

Misdemeanor

NASW *Code of ethics*

Public safety

Restorative justice

Social action

Social justice

Systems theory

Theory

Therapeutic justice

Questions for Review

1. What current issue in the criminal justice system interests you? Locate statistics that describe the size and scope of the issue similar to those provided in this chapter. What do the statistics reveal? Why are statistics important and how can they be useful?

2. Which statistics describing the size and scope of the criminal justice system were the most surprising? Why?

3. Describe the relationship between the four components of the criminal justice system. Why are these component considered a system. Which component interests you professionally? Why?

4. Summarize each of the seven criminal justice perspectives. Which perspective(s) do you disagree with most, and why? Do your views correspond to the criminal justice perspectives that are congruent with the values and mission of social work?

5. Define social justice. Summarize the ethical obligation of the social work profession to challenge social injustice based on the *NASW Code of ethics*. Identify how each component of the criminal justice system is both consistent and inconsistent with social justice.

Further Reading

Abadinsky, H. (1979). *Social service in criminal justice*. Englewood Cliffs, NJ: Prentice-Hall, Inc.

Roberts, A. R., & Brownell, P. (1999). A century of forensic social work: Bridging the past to the present. *Social Work, 44(4)*, 359–369.

Treger, H., & Allen, F. (2007). Social work in the justice system: An overview. In A. R. Roberts and D. W. Springer (eds.) *Social work in juvenile and criminal justice settings* (3rd ed.). Springfield, IL: Charles C. Thomas, Ltd.

2 Legislation and the Criminal Justice System

Chapter Overview

This chapter focuses on the legislative arena. Of the four components in the criminal justice system, legislation is the component where social workers are employed in fewest numbers. However, this does not mean that social workers are inactive in the legislative or crime legislative arena. Social workers engage in legislative advocacy and social and political action, and support legislation intended to enhance well-being. In fact, social workers have an ethical obligation to engage in political and social action. These efforts are achieved in numerous ways including participating in lobbying and testifying before legislators. In this chapter we examine legislation and crime legislation that is of most interest to the social work profession. Examples of current legislation and its relevance to the social work profession and the criminal justice system are reviewed. Some of the legislation discussed in this chapter has been enacted into law, whereas other examples have been proposed and are awaiting further legislative action.

The purpose of this section is not to introduce readers to an exhaustive list of crime legislation, but to illustrate legislation that has the potential to enhance social work practice in the criminal justice system. Several crime legislative acts include provisions for funding. This creates opportunities for social workers and affects services provided to individuals with criminal justice system involvement. Whereas legislative acts are passed at the federal, state and local levels of government, this chapter examines federal crime legislation that is most relevant for social work practice. This chapter also briefly reviews how a bill becomes federal law and the series of steps that lead to passage of a bill. Understanding the goals of crime legislation can help social workers to develop a plan for assessing whether the legislation is effective or has a harmful impact on individuals.

Social Work and Legislation

Many types of legislation are of interest to social workers. The Office of Government Relations and Political Action of NASW published the *NASW 2008 legislative agenda* which outlines several types of legislation supported by NASW. Various legislative acts that are the focus of the report include: the *Dorothy I. Height and Whitney M. Young, Jr. Social Work Reinvestment Act*; *The College Opportunity and Affordability Act* of 2007 *(H.R. 4137)*; the *Clinical Social Work Medicare Equity Act (S. 1212)*; the *Teri Zenner Social Worker Safety Act (H.R. 2165)*; Child welfare training through Title IV-B and Title IV-E; the *National Center for Social Work Research Act (S. 106)*; and the *Medicaid Foster Care Coverage Act (H.R. 1376)*, among others.

While the above examples are not crime legislation, they illustrate examples of legislation where individuals involved in the criminal justice system are likely to benefit from receiving services, and the wide range of legislation supported by NASW membership. Although crime legislation has an impact on individuals who become involved in the criminal justice, numerous other legislative acts also affect individuals with criminal justice involvement.

Following the 2008 legislative agenda, the NASW Office of Government Relations and Political Action issued the *Legislative agenda for the 11th Congress: January 2009–December 2010*. In this report NASW affirmed its commitment to ensuring that social work roles and social work research are recognized in federal legislation. Specifically, legislative advocacy efforts focused on health and mental issues, aging, children and families, education, economic security, military and veteran affairs, and the Social Work Reinvestment Initiative. Relative to criminal justice, NASW supported the *Local Law Enforcement Enhancement Act* for hate crimes.

NASW state chapters also develop their own legislative agendas specific to concerns within their state. For example, NASW Massachusetts published the *2009–2010 legislative agenda* (see NASW Massachusetts, n.d.). In its legislative session, Massachusetts NASW supported a legislative agenda that included issues pertinent to the profession and homeless issues, among others. Notably, the NASW Massachusetts Chapter members supported local criminal justice legislation. For example, *An Act to Reform CORI, Restore Economic Opportunity & Improve Public Safety HB 3523* is intended to reform the Massachusetts sentencing system and the criminal offender record information system (CORI). Members also supported *An Act Relative to Treatment versus Incarceration HB 1962* which provides diversion of low-level offenders into drug treatment instead of incarceration.

NASW chapters within each state develop and implement a Social Work Reinvestment Plan. The plans involve collaborations between schools of social work, social service agencies, and other community partners. The focus of these efforts is to address issues that impact the social work profession and clients, and plans may include legislative efforts (see Social Work Reinvestment Initiative, n.d.).

Fewer social workers are employed in State legislatures and Congress than other components of the criminal justice system. As of 2010, Pace (2010) counted nine social workers in Congress. The report titled *Social workers in Congress* published by NASW (2011) identified three congresswomen, two congressmen, and two senators who are social workers serving in the 112th Congress. The 112th Congress (January 2011 through January 2013) has a membership of 435 members of the House, and 100 members of the Senate for a total of 535 members. The seven social workers comprise 1.31% of congressional membership. These numbers do not include social workers who may hold state and local governmental legislative office.

Social and Political Action

As seen in Box 2.1, social workers have an ethical responsibility to participate in social and political action. Both efforts can be used by social workers to provide resources to criminal justice populations and ameliorate the social and other forms of injustice they experience.

Box 2.1 6.04 Social and Political Action

(a) Social workers should engage in social and political action that seeks to ensure that all people have equal access to the resources, employment, services, and opportunities they require to meet their basic human needs and to develop fully. Social workers should be aware of the impact of the political arena on practice and should advocate for changes in policy and legislation to improve social conditions in order to meet basic human needs and promote social justice.

Copyrighted material reprinted with permission from the National Association of Social Workers, Inc.

Barker (2003) defined *social action* as

A coordinated effort to achieve institutional change to meet a need, solve a social problem, correct an injustice, or enhance the quality of human life. This effort may occur at the initiative and direction of professionals in social welfare, economics, politics, religion, or the military, or it may occur through the efforts of the people who are directly affected by the problem or change.

(p. 401)

Moreover, *political action* is defined as

Coordinated efforts to influence legislation, election of candidates, and social causes. Social workers engage in political action by running for elected office, organizing campaigns in support of other candidates or issues, fundraising, and mobilizing voters and public opinion. Political action also includes lobbying, testifying before legislative committees, and monitoring the work of officeholders and government workers.

(p. 330)

Social action models (lobbying, mobilizing, and organizing) for achieving these aims are associated with 5 areas of change (goals, activists, targets, resources, and strategies). For example, change goals that are focused on passing legislation or electing legislators require the use of lobbying efforts. Long-term changes require the use of mobilizing tasks and small changes require organizing tasks. Change resources necessary for lobbying efforts include the amount of available finances, time, and staff who will conduct lobbying. Mobilizing models denote less financial resources, time, and staff, and organizing models require finances to support staff (Mondros, 2009). When engaging in social action it is important for social workers to understand these relationships so that social action models are matched with appropriate change efforts.

Social Justice

As shown in Box 2.2, social workers also have an ethical responsibility to challenge social injustice. The value of social justice is a core value of the social work profession. Social justice relative to social work practice requires that social workers become involved in social change to address social injustices. As discussed in Chapter 1, numerous social conditions contribute to criminal behavior that can be a basis for change.

Box 2.2 Value: Social Justice; Ethical Principle: Social Workers Challenge Social Injustice

Social workers pursue social change, particularly with and on behalf of vulnerable and oppressed individuals and groups of people. Social workers' social change efforts are focused primarily on issues of poverty, unemployment, discrimination, and other forms of social injustice. These activities seek to promote sensitivity to and knowledge about oppression and cultural and ethnic diversity. Social workers strive to ensure access to needed information, services, and resources; equality of opportunity; and meaningful participation in decision making for all people.

Copyrighted material reprinted with permission from the
National Association of Social Workers, Inc.

Hoefer (2006) observed that the NASW *Code of ethics* does not provide a definition for the concept of social justice. *Social justice* is defined as

> an ideal condition in which all members of a society have the same rights, protections, opportunities, obligations, and social benefits. Implicit in this concept is the notion that historical inequalities should be acknowledged and remedied through specific measures. A key social work value, social justice entails advocacy to confront discrimination, oppression, and institutional inequalities.
> (Barker, 2003, p. 405)

The fact that social workers strive to ensure access to information, services, and resources; equality of opportunity; and meaningful participation in decision making for all people is not inconsistent with social work practice in the criminal justice system. Social injustice can affect individuals with criminal justice system involvement in a number of ways. For example, the lack of finances to obtain adequate legal representation or lack of finances for bail is a direct result of insufficient resources.

Robinson (2010) suggested that perhaps the "greatest threat" (p. 91) to social justice practice in the criminal justice system pertains to legislative biases that negatively impact the other three components of the criminal justice system (law enforcement, courts, and corrections). These three systems enforce legislation. Robinson identified within each of the four components of the criminal justice system practices that are both consistent and inconsistent with social justice. Thus, Robinson also recognized four components of the criminal justice system and explained that the following areas support social justice: legislation (the Bill of Rights and due process); law enforcement (codes that define officers' conduct, the provision of services to community residents); courts (due process, the development of use of sentencing guidelines, and indigent defense services); and corrections (the use of an inmate classification system and the provision of rehabilitation services). Areas where the four components of the criminal justice system do not support social justice include: legislation (unequal access to the law, voting, and lobbying, and biased laws); law enforcement (police officers enforce biased laws, abuse police discretion, and practice racial profiling); courts (impose sentences and sanctions in response to biased laws, practice plea bargaining, and impose determinate and mandatory sentences); and corrections (also enforce biased laws and use disparate applications of sanctions and punishments).

The Federal Legislative Process

Legislation relative to criminal justice is defined as follows:

> Legislative decisions determining the number and types of crimes, authorized or mandatory penalties, and levels of funding for various agencies have a significant impact on the functioning of the criminal justice systems. These impacts are sometimes felt beyond a legislature's immediate jurisdiction (for example, when federal or state laws provide funding on condition that certain rules or procedures are adopted by the receiving state or local government).
>
> (Frase & Weidner, 2002, p. 380)

The legislative process occurs at federal, state, and local (county, city, and town) levels. The focus of this chapter is federal legislation. Readers are encouraged to use the exercises and skills acquired in this chapter to learn more about the legislative process that occurs at state and local levels of government.

Before proposed federal legislation becomes law, a bill must pass through several steps. A similar process is used in state and local governments. The federal legislative process involves the following steps. First, a bill may be introduced (proposed) in either the House of Representatives or the Senate. Second, the bill is then referred to a committee whose purpose is to hold a hearing on the bill and afterwards report the bill to the House or Senate. Third, the bill is scheduled for debates and/or amendments. Fourth, the House or Senate votes on the bill. The bill must be passed by votes in both the House and Senate. In other words the majority must vote in favor of the bill. Finally, if the bill passes both the House and Senate the bill is forwarded to the president who either signs the bill into law or vetoes the bill.

If the bill is signed by the president, it becomes law. In contrast, if the bill is vetoed by the president it does not become law. The president has the final authority to sign the bill into law.

Three Branches of Federal Government

The U.S. federal government is comprised of three branches. These are the legislative, judicial, and executive branches. Each branch has unique responsibilities and distinct members. The U.S. Government's Official Web Portal (found at usa.gov) summarizes these branches and their responsibilities. Each of the 50 states, the District of Columbia, and U.S. territories has established its own governmental structures which are described at usa.gov. This chapter will focus only on the federal legislative process.

The Legislative Branch

The legislative branch of the U.S. government functions to make laws. It is comprised of the Senate and House of Representatives. Numerous other agencies that assist congress are found in the legislative branch, such as the Congressional Budget Office (CBO), and the Library of Congress, among others.

The Judicial Branch

The function of the judicial branch is to interpret whether laws violate the U.S. Constitution. This is achieved by conducting judicial review of laws, and providing oversight to the legislative and executive branches. The judicial branch is comprised of the U.S. Supreme Court and several other courts such as the U.S. Tax Court (special courts), the U.S. Courts of Appeals and the U.S. District Courts (lower courts). Agencies such as the U.S. Sentencing Commission also make up the judicial branch.

The Executive Branch

The executive branch functions to enforce U.S. laws. This branch is comprised of the president, vice president, cabinet members, and other agencies such as the Department of Homeland Security (DHS), Department of Health and Human Services (HHS), and the Department of Justice (DOJ).

Locating Bills and Laws

GovTrack.us is a website operated by Civic Impulse, LLC. The website provides information describing the status of bills and laws, members of Congress and their voting records, and congressional district maps. Another useful tool for locating bills and laws is Thomas. Operated by the Library of Congress, the Thomas website provides information about the status of bills, congressional records and activities, government resources, treaties, and presidential nominations. Thomas can be accessed at http://thomas.loc.gov. Box 2.3 shows the basic steps for locating information about legislation using GovTrack.us.

Box 2.3 Using GovTrack.us to Locate Legislation

Step 1: Go to GovTrack.us.
Step 2: Locate the "Bill & Resolutions" link.
Step 3: Search for a current bill or use the advanced search feature to locate a prior bill or piece of legislation.
Step 4: If you know who sponsored or co-sponsored the bill, select the senator or representative from the drop down menu.
Step 5: If you know the status of the bill, select an option from the drop down menu

Note: as of this writing, bills can be sorted only by relevance.

While the U.S. Government's Official Web Portal contains information about state, local, and tribal governments (such as resources and websites relevant for each jurisdiction), searching local and state government official websites can also yield valuable information. These websites are invaluable for providing information about state policy makers and legislation. Box 2.4 describes the steps for locating information pertaining to a local government.

Box 2.4 Locating Local Governmental and Legislative Information

Step 1: Go to a local governmental website such as www.sfgov.org/. This is the official web site for the City and County of San Francisco, California.
Step 2: Locate and click the "Government" button.
Step 3: Search the content for relevant city and county governmental offices and legislative information.

Similarly, Box 2.5 describes the steps that can be used to locate state government legislative information.

Box 2.5 Locating State Governmental and Legislative Information

Step 1: Go to a state governmental website such as www.colorado.gov/. This is the official website for the state of Colorado.

Step 2: Locate and click the "Government" button.

Step 3: Search the content for relevant state governmental offices and legislative information. The Colorado Constitution can be found at this site. Clicking "eDemocracy" provides a link "Legislative information" where information about the legislative branch, bills, and the legislative calendar are posted.

Legislative Advocacy

It may be somewhat obvious that social workers engage in advocacy for individuals who are involved in the criminal justice system, whose civil or human rights have been violated, or who are in need of services to enhance their well-being and prevent criminal behavior. But what is advocacy? How do social workers practice advocacy? What do they do when they advocate? A form of advocacy relevant for criminal justice practice is legislative advocacy.

Prior to engaging in advocacy efforts social workers should have acquired information about the state executive branch of government, both elected and appointed officials. Moreover, when conducting outreach to elected officials, social workers should articulate the goals of changing the current policy, identify what the policy changes should be, and identify why changes to the current policy are needed (Squillace, 2010). Reisch (2009) defined *legislative advocacy* as

> Activities in the political arena that focus on the promotion of the common welfare or the securing and protection of rights and services of a specific population. By definition, it involves both partisanship and politics—roles that may produce discomfort among many social workers.

> (p. 893)

A preceding discussion provided information about locating bills and other legislative information from GovTrack.us and Thomas. NASW also provides resources in this regard.

Using the *Advocacy* link found at the NASW website, social workers can locate bills, view the number of sponsors for a particular bill, read the NASW position of support or opposition for the bill, obtain information about social workers who hold public office, and access a legislative glossary (NASW, 2011). Box 2.6 shows how to search the link.

Box 2.6 Searching the NASW Advocacy Link

Step 1: Go to http://socialworkers.org/.

Step 2: Click the "Advocacy" button.

Step 3: Scroll through the Advocacy site and click areas of interest. This site provides information about current legislation, important votes, a basic overview of Capital Hill, and contact information for senators and representatives as well as tips for addressing letters to senators and representatives. A legislative glossary can also be found at www.socialworkers.org/advocacy/resources/glossary.asp.

NASW also maintains a website that lists key bills in Congress by bill name, number of sponsors of the bill, and NASW's position on the bill. The bills are categorized in the areas of aging, civil rights, health, mental health, and military/veterans, among others. Some of the bills supported by NASW are related to criminal justice issues, for example, *S. 909 Hate Crimes Prevention Act*; *H.R. 1913 Hate Crimes*; and *H.R. 840 Military Domestic Violence and Sexual Assault Response Act* (NASW, 2007). Box 2.6 shows the steps for searching the NASW Advocacy site. The site also contains information about NASW-PACE (Political Action for Candidate Election). The purpose of the PACE committee is to publicly and financially support candidates for political office who support NASW policies.

Recent NASW Legislative Advocacy Efforts

Social workers assume advocacy roles, form coalitions, and engage in voting and letter writing campaigns. A recent example is NASW support for the *Second Chance Act* (Pace, 2011). The *Second Chance Act* is federal legislation that provides grants to state governments and nonprofit agencies. Grants fund employment assistance, substance abuse treatment, housing, and other services intended to reduce recidivism. The Act was first signed by former President Bush on April 9, 2008; on March 11, 2009, President Obama signed a bill for Second Chance Act programs (Reentry Policy Council, n.d.). NASW united with 250 organizations to support the *Second Chance Act* by mailing letters to lawmakers and encouraging them to support and fund the Act. It is anticipated that social workers will provide many of the services funded by the Second Chance Act (Pace, 2009). These services include substance abuse treatment, mental health treatment, mentoring, housing, education, and employment training, among other things.

A second example illustrating NASW legislative efforts is the recent virtual lobbying day. NASW held its first virtual lobby day on April 28, 2011. Social workers throughout the U.S. were invited to participate in support of the *Dorothy I. Height and Whitney M. Young, Jr. Social Work Reinvestment Act* by writing letters to representatives and other activities. While this Act is not directly related to crime legislation, it has implications for social work practice in the criminal justice system, as well as providing a model for social work participation in virtual lobbying.

Social Work Interest Groups

Teater (2009) identified five themes and three subthemes that form the basis of a framework useful for developing social work interest groups. The framework was developed on the basis of information provided by nine state legislators. First, *bubbled up from the bottom* refers to forming a local or grassroots interest group. Once formed, an interest group then joins with other interest groups which share a similar focus. In this way, the group's influence increases as the number of involved individuals increase. Second, *have a plan* means having a well defined mission, goals, and objectives, strategies and a plan for communicating with state legislators. Third, *keep your folks involved* denotes the methods used for informing interest group members about proposed legislation and how to communicate this information with legislators. Fourth, *raise the flag* refers to a social work interest group becoming known by state legislators. This process occurs through introductions and meetings. Finally, *relationship building* refers to developing a relationship with legislators. Teater described three subthemes associated with relationship building: *word's their bond* refers to the ability of the interest group to establish and maintain credibility. *Individualization—it's personal* suggests acquiring an understanding of how legislators prefer to receive information and acknowledging their preferences. *Presence* refers to the ability of the interest group to gain the attention of legislators and hold their attention through active participation and being present at the location where legislation is determined.

Case Example

The following example employs Teater's framework for developing a social work interest group. The group was formed by undergraduate students. The example illustrates the type of information needed to implement the group and the tasks students performed.

After learning about the proposed legislation in their social work practice in the criminal justice system class, a group of social work students became interested in supporting state legislation intended to eliminate mandatory minimum sentences imposed for drug offenses among individuals who experience a substance abuse problem. In class they participated in a thought-provoking discussion about the benefits and possible unintended consequences of the proposed legislation. They are interested in forming a social work interest group among the student body and include interested students attending other social work educational programs in the area. First, they form an interest group within their own social work program. They then contact students in other educational programs through contacts developed in their field placements. They discover that many students in the area are also interested in forming an interest group. Second, they utilize resources such as the NASW website, Thomas, and GovTrack.us, among others, to learn more about how to contact their state legislators. They also use the official state website to acquire information. Using content they learned in their human behavior and research classes, they are knowledgeable about the effects of substance abuse and how to conduct a literature review on the topic. They also conduct a search to gain knowledge about mandatory minimum sentences and court diversion options for substance abusers. They divide these tasks among themselves and agree on the mission for the group. Third, they utilize the social media Twitter and Facebook to communicate. They soon realize that many legislators also use Twitter to communicate with constituents. Fourth, instead of the entire group tweeting legislators they decide to assign one member who will be responsible for the tweets. The group first shares a draft of the communication among the group so that all members are informed before the tweet is sent. The group also engages in fundraising activities in each of their social work programs to raise funds intended to offset some of the costs associated with a day trip to legislative offices in support of the legislation. The face-to-face meetings contribute to the group establishing a relationship with legislators.

Examples of Federal Criminal Justice Legislation

Summaries of several examples of federal criminal justice legislation are provided below. A few of these examples have been enacted into law whereas others have not. Bills that are not enacted into law must be reintroduced in the House or Senate and identified with a new number. These pieces of legislative are of interest to social workers with an interest in criminal justice and are worth following.

National Criminal Justice Commission Act of 2011 (S. 306)

This bill is intended to establish the National Criminal Justice Commission. The Commission will be charged with several tasks that include the following: (1) The Commission will conduct a review of the policies and practices in the criminal justice system at all levels (federal, state, local and tribal), (2) The Commission will develop recommendations for criminal justice reform. These recommendations should emphasize methods to deter crime, reduce recidivism, and improve cost-effectiveness, (3) The committee will present these recommendations to the president, members of Congress, and state, local, and tribal governments. During the 111th Congress (2009–2010) the bill passed a vote in the House of Representatives. The bill did not become law during the 111th congressional session. The bill was reintroduced in the 112th Congress (2011–2012) on February 8, 2011. As of this writing the bill is awaiting a committee report, Senate and House votes and signature by the president if it is to become law (S. 306: *National Criminal Justice Commission Act* of 2011, n.d.).

The creation of a National Criminal Justice Commission is perhaps the most important piece of criminal justice legislation, and has implications for the social work profession. First, the Act will support rehabilitation through the provision of services such as substance abuse and mental health treatment. It will also increase services provided to inmates, thus creating new opportunities for social workers. Second, the Act is intended to reduce racial and class disparities within the criminal justice system, which is congruent with the social justice values of the social work profession (Wilson, 2010).

Fair Sentencing Act of 2010 (S .1789)

The *Fair Sentencing Act* of 2010 was signed into law by President Obama on August 3, 2010. The purpose of this law is to ensure that fair sentences are imposed for federal cocaine sentences. Sentencing for crack and powder cocaine has a history of unequal sentencing. This inequality has resulted in racial and economic disparities. The law also eliminates the mandatory minimum prison sentence of five years for first time for possessing crack cocaine. This law amends the *Controlled Substance Act* and the *Controlled Substances Import and Export Act* in the following ways: increasing the amount of crack cocaine an offender could possess for mandatory minimum sentences imposed for drug trafficking, increasing monetary fines, allowing for aggravating and mitigating factors to be considered during the sentencing phase, and increasing sentences for offenders who commit violent drug trafficking crime (S. 1789: *Fair Sentencing Act* of 2010, n.d.).

While the *Fair Sentencing Act* of 2010 is intended to reduce racial disparities, it does not address the sentencing disparities that have occurred in the past. Attorney General Eric Holder, Jr., supported a proposal that was under consideration by the U.S. Sentencing Commission. The proposal could affect approximately 12,000 federal prisoners. Attorney General Holder supports applying the newly revised sentencing guidelines to approximately 5,500 prisoners who did not use weapons in the commission of their crimes, and those who do not have extensive criminal histories. Most prison sentences would be reduced by an average of three years (Serrano, Savage, & Williams, 2011). Although the policy was approved by the U.S. Sentencing Commission on June 30, 2011, Congress may explore reversing the policy. Moreover, federal judges will make the final determination about whether to grant a prisoner an early release (Schwartz, 2011).

Criminal Justice Reinvestment Act of 2010 (S. 2772)

This bill was introduced to establish a criminal justice reinvestment grant program. If passed, the bill will allow federal grants to be distributed to local and state governments and tribal communities. The purpose of the program is to enable these jurisdictions to decrease spending for corrections services, address increases in prison and jail incarceration rates, and increase the use of public safety initiatives. This bill was last introduced on November 16, 2009. It was referred to committee and reported by committee. As of this writing the bill has not become law (S. 2772: *Criminal Justice Reinvestment Act* of 2010, n.d.). NASW supports passage of the *Criminal Justice Reinvestment Act* (Pace, 2011).

Honest Opportunity Probation with Enforcement (HOPE) Initiative Act of 2009 (H.R. 4055)

This bill will authorize a national Honest Opportunity Probation with Enforcement (HOPE) Program. It is anticipated that the program will consist of programs and services that reduce substance use, crime, and incarceration costs associated with these social problems. This bill was last introduced on November 6, 2009. It has been referred to committee, but as of this writing the bill has not become law (H.R. 4055: *Honest Opportunity Probation with Enforcement (HOPE) Initiative Act* of 2009, n.d.).

Youth Promise Act H.R. 1064—Youth Prison Reduction through Opportunities, Mentoring, Intervention, Support, and Education Act (The "Youth PROMISE" Act)

The purpose of this bill is to provide evidence-based interventions to youth. The interventions will prevent juvenile delinquency and gang involvement, and should be aimed at increasing individual, family, and community strength and resiliency. This bill was last introduced on February 13, 2009. The bill is also referred to as Mynisha's law. It was referred to committee but has not been enacted into law (H.R. 1064: *Youth Prison Reduction through Opportunities, Mentoring, Intervention, Support, and Education Act* 111th Congress: 2009–2010, n.d.).

Matthew Shepard Hate Crimes Prevention Act (S. 909)

The purpose of the bill is to provide assistance to states, local, and tribal jurisdictions. If enacted, this legislation will provide these jurisdictions with federal technical, forensic, and prosecutorial assistance. A statement in the bill acknowledges that jurisdictions lack the resources required to investigate and prosecute hate crimes. This bill was last introduced in a previous session of Congress but was not enacted into law. The bill was not passed during the 111th congressional session (2009–2010) (S. 909: *Matthew Shepard Hate Crimes Prevention Act*, n.d.).

Local Law Enforcement Hate Crimes Prevention Act of 2009 (H.R. 1913)

This bill was introduced to provide federal assistance to local and state governments and Indian tribes to prosecute hate crimes. This bill was last introduced on April 2, 2009. Although the bill was referred to committee, reported by committee and passed by a House vote, the bill was not enacted into law during the 111th congressional session (H.R. 1913: *Local Law Enforcement Hate Crimes Prevention Act* of 2009, n.d.).

Critical Issues in Crime Legislation

Numerous current issues and events influence crime legislation. These issues include repealing legislation that has unintended adverse effects or consequences on racial and ethnic minorities, and developing legislative proposals in the aftermath of a well publicized crime and public opinion.

As criminal justice reform efforts focus on ways to deal with crime, particularly violent crime, and balance punishment and rehabilitation perspectives, these perspectives have also influenced the passing of legislation and efforts to repeal legislation. Indeed, worries about crime and becoming a victim, and public outrage in the aftermath of a well publicized crime have driven crime legislation and other responses to crime. However, crime legislation should be determined and formulated on the basis of on scientific evidence, and not "ideology" (Barlow & Decker, 2010).

Funding Provided by Federal Legislation

The 103rd Congress (1993–1994) tied the receiving of federal funding to states to the enactment of federal legislation. This requirement has created some consistency in criminal justice policies across states. The *Violent Crime Control and Law Enforcement Act* of 1994 (H.R. 3355) provided Violent Offender Incarceration and Truth in Sentencing Incentive Grants. The Act stipulated that as a condition for states to receive federal funds, a state must demonstrate that offenders convicted of violent crimes serve actually not less than 85% of their imposed sentence (*H.R. 3355: Violent Crime Control and Law Enforcement Act* of 1994, n.d.). *Truth in Sentencing* refers to sentencing guidelines that require an offender to serve 85% of the imposed sentence prior to release. In 1998, 27 states and the District of Columbia received federal grants under the truth in sentencing program, and 13 states implemented truth in sentencing guidelines for specific offenses (Ditton & Wilson, 1999).

Tough on Crime Legislation

Tough on crime legislation characterizes the various attempts of state governments to deal with crime. As state laws, these laws are not uniform among the states. Federal legislation has also been enacted to deal with crime. Tough on crime legislation emphasizes deterrence and punishment rather than treatment or rehabilitation. Therefore perspectives such as retributive justice and crime control are emphasized, whereas the rehabilitation and restorative justice perspectives are not. Tough on crime legislation is not consistent with social work values because of the emphasis on punitive approaches to dealing with crime instead of treating the underlying causes of crime.

In general, tough on crime legislation targets drug crimes, violent crimes, and repeat criminal offenders. In some states these laws are in different stages of amendments. Two examples of tough on crime legislation are provided below.

The war on drugs was intended to reduce drug use and trafficking, although it has not reduced drug-related crime as intended (Albanese, 2008). The 1980s war on drugs consisted of legislation implemented at both state and federal levels. Overall, this legislation emphasized harsh deterrence and punishment strategies instead of treatment for drug offenders who used drugs. A shift is occurring as evidence shows that this legislation has not achieved the intended outcomes, and incarceration of drug offenders is very costly. Moreover, data demonstrating the efficacy of alternatives such as drug courts that emphasize treatment have been instrumental in promoting alternatives to tough on crime legislation.

Three Strikes Laws

Three strikes laws are supported by U.S. sentencing guidelines 18 USC § 3559(c) (1). These guidelines are applicable to offenders who are convicted of a serious violent felony (e.g., murder) who have also been convicted of two or more previous serious violent felonies or one or more serious violent felonies *and* one or more previous convictions for a serious drug crime (Families Against Mandatory Minimums, 2010).

As mentioned, three strikes laws have been implemented differently among states. In 1994, former California Governor Wilson signed Three Strikes and You're Out legislation representing "the most significant change in the state criminal justice system in more than a generation" (p. 1). This legislation was intended to ensure that offenders were incarcerated for committing serious and violent crimes. Some findings of a study conducted within one year after implementation showed that, for thousands of offenders who were charged with crimes under two or three strikes legislation, less plea bargaining was used, and bails were increased. As a result of the legislation more trials were held as offenders sought to avoid a third strike. Interestingly, the study findings report showed that during the first eight months of the law, the majority (70%) of offenders were convicted for nonviolent and nonserious crimes (Legislative Analysts' Office, 1995).

Differing viewpoints debate whether three strikes laws reduce crime through deterrence. For instance, Zimring, Hawkins, & Kamin (2001) asserted that three strikes laws do not deter crime, whereas Shepherd (2002) suggested that such laws do deter crime.

Examining the California three strikes legislation seven years after implementation, King & Mauer (2001) concluded that three strikes laws did not reduce serious and violent crime, but did increase racial disparities within the California prison system.

The Rockefeller Drug Laws

The Rockefeller Drug Laws are another example of state crime legislation. First enacted in New York State in 1973 by former Governor Nelson Rockefeller, the laws were intended to impose mandatory minimum sentences for drug possession or sales. The Rockefeller Drug Laws are among the harshest in the U.S. (Wilson, 2000).

Drop the Rock, a coalition formed among individuals and organizations from across New York State, is coordinated by the Correctional Association of New York. The focus of the coalition is to reduce the New York State prison population. In a 2009 report, Drop the Rock reported that, despite amendments made to the laws in 2004 and 2005, more than 42% of drug offenders who were sentenced and incarcerated under the law were incarcerated for drug possession, not selling drugs. Approximately 80% of the drug offenders were not convicted of violent felony drug offenses. African Americans represented 59.2% of the NYS prison population for drug offenses. Latinos were 30%, and Whites were 9.7% (Drop the Rock, 2009).

In April 2009, former Governor David Paterson signed legislation that once again reformed the Rockefeller Drug Laws. These reforms eliminated mandatory minimum sentences, reinstated judicial discretion for imposing sentences for certain drug offenses, provided for increased utilization of drug courts and alternatives to incarceration, reduced minimum sentencing lengths, and allows offenders convicted before 2005 to have their cases heard so that retroactive resentencing can be imposed for eligible cases (Drug Policy Alliance, 2009).

Crime Victims and Legislation

Popular movies depict victims' experiences. *Amber's Story*, a 2006 movie based on actual events, depicts the kidnapping and murder of 9-year-old Amber Hagerman. These events subsequently led to the implementation of the Amber Alert System, a system for tracking missing children. The system involves positing bulletins with participation from law enforcement, the media, transportation agencies, and wireless networks (United States Department of Justice, Office of Justice Programs, n.d.). *A Cry for Help: The Tracey Thurman Story*, a 1983 movie based on a true story, depicts the stabbing of Tracey Thurman by her estranged husband and led to the passage of The Thurman Law in Connecticut and other states.

The title of proposed legislation is frequently named after a crime victim. Many examples can be found throughout the country. For example, in October 2009 in New York City a family friend was driving under the influence and transporting eight children. Eleven-year-old Leandra Rosado was killed when the vehicle crashed. These events led to Leandra's Law. Among the provisions in the law is a requirement that any driver convicted of misdemeanor or felony drunk driving, regardless of whether a child under 16 was a passenger in the car at the time the offense was committed, install at the driver's expense an ignition interlock device in any car owned or used by the offender. New York State is among 36 states having child welfare laws that impose tougher penalties on offenders who drive under the influence of alcohol or drugs while transporting a child passenger. It is among ten states having a mandatory requirement that first-time offenders install an ignition interlock device (New York State Division of Criminal Justice Services, 2010).

Another example from California also involves the death of a child. Mynisha Crenshaw was 11 years old when she was killed inside her family's apartment in a gang-related shooting in San Bernardino, CA. Shortly after her death, community residents and community leaders became active in efforts to address community violence. Senator Barbara Boxer introduced Mynisha's Law to provide funding and address gang issues (Kennedy-Ross, 2006). The legislation was reintroduced in the 111th Congress but was not enacted into law (H.R. 2418: *Mynisha's Law*, n.d.).

Finally, Andrea Will was murdered by her ex-boyfriend. He was sentenced to 24 years in prison, but was released after serving 12 years. State Representative Dennis Reboletti, Andrea Wills's mother, and her college roommate proposed legislation (known as *Andrea's Law*) based on sex offender and child abuse registries. The proposed legislation would mandate former offenders convicted of first-degree murder to register with local jurisdictions for a ten-year period following release from prison. The legislation would also establish an online database to identify former offenders within communities. This legislation will allow victims' families and others to track the whereabouts of released murderers (Cox, 2011).

Racial Disparities

According to The Sentencing Project (2008) "racial disparity in the criminal justice system exists when the proportion of a racial or ethnic group within the control of the system is greater than the proportion of such groups in the general population" (p. 1). The report also identifies the occurrence of "illegitimate or unwarranted racial disparity in the criminal justice system [that] results from the dissimilar treatment of similarly situated people based on race" (p. 1). Racial disparities result from a combination of factors such as: different rates of criminal behavior among racial and ethnic groups, increased law enforcement patrol procedures in some racial and ethnic communities, legislative policies that have an adverse effect on some racial and ethnic groups, and intentional racial bias.

As an example of racial disparities, consider that African American youth comprise 17% of the youth population although they make up nearly half (46%) of juvenile arrests, 31% of the referrals made to juvenile courts, and 41% of juvenile cases transferred to adult courts (Snyder, as cited in The Sentencing Project). The Sentencing Project proposes four primary methods for reducing racial disparities in the criminal justice system:

1. Acknowledge the cumulative nature of racial disparities.
2. Encourage communication across players in all decision points in the system.
3. Know what works at one decision point may not work at others.
4. Work toward systematic change.

(p. 2)

To address racial disparities The Sentencing Project also recommends a five-step research process that can be used to assess whether racial disparities exist:

1. Determine whether the rate of minorities involved at any stage of the criminal justice system is disproportionate.
2. Assess the decision points where racial and ethnic disparities occur.
3. Identify a plausible reason for any disparity identified and the extent to which it is related to legitimate public safety objectives.
4. Design and implement strategies to reduce disparities.
5. Monitor the effectiveness of strategies to reduce disparities.

(p. 21)

Implications for Social Work Practice

Although fewer social workers hold public office or other employment in the legislative arena, numerous opportunities exist for social workers to become involved in social and political action. Social workers can perform these activities outside of their criminal justice or other employment provided that possible conflicts of interest are avoided.

Numerous resources are available that can be used to become knowledgeable about legislation. These resources include contact information for senators and representatives, templates for writing letters, and the position taken by NASW regarding specific legislation. In order to fully participate in social and political action specific to crime legislation, social workers require an understanding of the legislative process at federal, state and local levels of government. This understanding is essential to communicate with and engage key stakeholders.

Additional skills include advocacy, lobbying, testifying, research (monitoring and data collection), and organizing expertise. When these are coupled with data and factual information, social workers can provide persuasive arguments to legislators. These skills are shared with other fields and are not exclusive to the social work profession.

Chapter Summary

While this chapter was not meant to provide an exhaustive review of crime legislation, numerous examples of federal and state crime legislation that have been either enacted into law or proposed were reviewed. Many of the bills received the support of NASW. Whereas few social workers are employed in Congress or hold public office, social workers have an ethical responsibility to engage in social and political action. Social action and political action were defined, and the skills needed by social workers (lobbying, testifying, and monitoring) were presented. Social workers need not hold public office in order to engage in social and political action, or advocacy. A recent case example in which social workers participated in a virtual lobbying day demonstrates the professions' lobbying efforts on a national scale. Strategies were presented for utilizing resources to locate legislation. These resources included the NASW official website, GovTrack.us and Thomas. Social justice is sometimes not consistent with the goals and practices of the criminal justice system. These issues were explored. Finally, current critical issues impacting legislation were discussed. It is imperative that legislative outcomes be monitored owing to the potential to adversely affect vulnerable groups.

Key Terms

Advocacy	Judicial branch	Public law
Civil law	Legislation	Social action
Congress	Legislative branch	Substantive criminal law
Crime legislation	Political action	
Executive branch	Procedural criminal law	

Questions for Review

1. Define political action and social action. Summarize social workers' ethical responsibility to engage in social and political action on the basis of the NASW *Code of ethics*. How informed do you feel you are of the impact of the political and legislative arena on social work practice?
2. Briefly describe the process that occurs before a bill becomes federal law.
3. Write a plan to develop a social work interest group that will focus on a criminal justice issue. Be sure to include the steps you would take to gain the attention of legislators.
4. Use a strategy described in this chapter to locate an example of crime legislation (ether proposed or enacted). What are the aims of the legislation? State if the legislation has been proposed and is awaiting further legislative action or whether the legislation has been enacted.

Further Reading

Albert, R. (1986). *Law and social work practice*. New York: Springer Publishing Company, Inc.

American Civil Liberties Union (2008). *Breaking barriers to the ballot box: Felon enfranchisement toolkit*. Retrieved from www.sentencingproject.org/doc/publications/fd_aclutoolkit.pdf.

Wolff, T. (2001). A practitioner's guide to successful coalitions. *American Journal of Community Psychology, 29(2)*, 173–191.

3 Law Enforcement

Chapter Overview

Law enforcement is most often the entry point into the criminal justice system for offenders and victims. On the basis of media images of the police, social workers and others perhaps do not realize that crime-fighting tasks do not comprise the majority of police functions. The majority of police calls for service do not require a traditional law enforcement response (e.g., detain, arrest). Police officers spend most of their time responding to social problems. These situations require that police officers provide crisis intervention and mediation. In other instances individuals may require legal or counseling services that police officers can not provide. Consequently, officers refer these individuals to human service or other appropriate agencies. These events create unique opportunities for social workers to collaborate with law enforcement.

This chapter describes the various types of law enforcement agencies and identifies those that are most likely to employ and collaborate with social workers. A schema is presented for understanding law enforcement agencies (mission, basic organizational models, personnel characteristics, functions, and tasks). Police social work is presented as a unique practice area and the roles of police social workers are explored. In order to function within law enforcement agencies or provide adequate services to individuals involved with the police, social workers must understand police functions and roles. Law enforcement agencies are more likely to be accepting of those practices and interventions that are congruent with their mission, and fulfill organizational priorities. Community service is one such mission.

Law Enforcement Functions that Support Police Social Work

Cole & Smith (2004) described four major *law enforcement functions*:

1. peace keeping functions which involve protecting individuals and their rights from violence;

2. arresting perpetrators and crime fighting functions;
3. crime prevention;
4. providing social services.

Responding to homicides and robberies is an example of crime-fighting functions. Even this police response could have a service function since victims may require crisis intervention, emotional support, and referrals. Examples of social-service-related functions include responding to family disputes in which no crime has occurred and crisis intervention and mediation skills are required.

Webster (1970) asserts that, while the majority of police work comprises a social service response and assistance to citizens, media images often do not accurately reflect these facts. Webster explains this point in the following scenario:

> The cover of a major city's annual police report dramatically shows two policemen reaching for their guns as they burst through the doors of a massive black and white police car which is screeching to a halt . . . the flashing red lights and screaming siren complete the illustration. A less dramatic scene on an inside page of the report shows a policeman talking to a grateful mother whose lost child was returned. Which one of these illustrations most accurately describes the police role? How frequently do the events depicted by these illustrations occur? What percentage of police activity is violent and dangerous? What do policemen [sic] really do?
>
> (p. 94)

Peterson (1974) noted this relationship as well and went so far as to refer to police officers as social workers owing to the social-service-related functions they provide:

> The patrol officer is routinely involved in tasks that have little relation to police work in terms of controlling crime. His [sic] activities on the beat are often centered as much on assisting citizens as upon offenses; he [sic] is frequently called upon to perform a "supportive" function as well as an enforcement function. Existing research on the uniformed police officer in field situations indicates that more than half his [sic] time is spent as an amateur social worker assisting people in various ways. Moreover, several officers have suggested that the role of the uniformed patrol officer is not sharply defined and that the mixture of enforcement and service functions creates conflict and uncertainties.
>
> (p. 102)

Finally, Mastrofksi (1983) reports an early account of police:

> In those days that pestilence of Service which torments the American people today was just getting under way, and many of the multifarious duties now carried out by social workers, statisticians, truant officers, visiting nurses, psychologists and the vast rabble of inspectors, smellers, spies and bogus experts of a hundred different faculties either fell to the police or were not discharged at all.
>
> (Mencken, 1942, as cited in Mastrofksi, 1983, p. 33)

In a similar manner, police officers in the U.K. were described as having a social work role that could be used by police officers to improve community relationship through preventing juvenile crime by using social work principles (Jones, 1963).

Media images such as those shown in popular television shows and movies depict police officers involved in work that emphasizes the crime-fighting tasks involved in law enforcement. Rarely are police officers portrayed performing their service-related functions. The aforementioned scenario describing a police officer talking to a grateful mother whose lost child was returned suggests the variety of social-service-related skills that are needed by law enforcement officers. It is not difficult to imagine that the police officer would provide comfort and support, and perhaps child safety tips to prevent the situation that resulted in the child being lost from re-occurring. The provision of such services requires effective communication and crisis intervention skills. If the mother requests additional services such as counseling or a desire to learn more about child safety tips, this situation would require that an officer be knowledgeable about community resources and provide a referral.

Peterson (1974) recognized that not all of law enforcement tasks are related to crime, and stated that police officers spend more than 50% of their time "as an amateur social worker assisting people in various ways" (p. 102) as opposed to investigating and solving crimes. Treger (1987) also notes that 50% to 90% of calls that police receive require a social service response. In an early police time and task study, Webster (1970) found that officers spent more than 50% of their time performing administrative taks. More than 17% of the total police calls were "social services"-related and 13% of the total time spent by police officers on work-related tasks was service-related. Webster defined service-related police calls as family crisis situations, alcoholism, suicide, mental illness, ambulance service, and public nuisances, among others. These functions have been coined the service style of the police, which Wilson (1968) described as handling traffic, regulating juveniles, and providing other services.

In a discussion of crime-fighting tasks which concern violent crimes, nonviolent crimes, moral crimes, and suspicious circumstances and non-crime tasks which occur when officers' crime-fighting expectations are low, Mastrofski (1983) states that crime-fighting activities comprise the majority of training, career incentives, and performance evaluations, whereas non-crime services comprise the majority of police work. Non-crime services comprised 70.9% of law enforcement services, whereas crime incidents comprised 29.1%. Others (Scott, 1981; Morris & Heal, 1981; Trojanowicz & Dixon, 1974) have identified similar ratios. Little recent research has been conducted that quantifies the amount of social-service-related functions that police officers perform. However, it is doubtful that these ratios have changed much.

In sum, the social service function of law enforcement consumes the majority of police officers' time. The majority of tasks that police officers perform involve responding to citizens' calls for emergency services to deal with a wide variety of situations and social problems. These situations include runaway youth, domestic violence, homeless individuals, mentally ill individuals, landlord–tenant complaints, neighbor disputes, and custody issues, to mention but a few. Resolving these social problems can not be accomplished by law enforcement agencies alone and requires that police officers collaborate and form partnerships with human service agencies, other municipal agencies, hospitals, mediation centers, emergency shelters, and the court system, among others.

Owing to the economic recession, many states have reduced their mental health budgets. This has resulted in less availability of public mental health services. Individuals who relied on these public services are now calling upon law enforcement to meet their service needs. For instance, in Oklahoma police calls for mental health services increased 50% from 2009 through 2010. In Portland, ME, police calls for mental health needs increased from 1,424 in 2007 to 1,645 in 2009. As a result the Portland Police Department hired a full-time coordinator to assist the police department with managing mental health services. Law enforcement officials report that managing the increased calls for mental health issues has required that officers be reallocated from other police functions (Zezima, 2010).

Case Example

A local human service agency received a telephone call from a captain stating that police officers have noticed an increase in police calls responding to family disputes involving parents and children. These calls have not required a traditional police response because no violence or law violations have occurred. The captain requested a trainer to provide training to all new police recruits and veteran police officers. The law enforcement agency has a recruit class of 30, and employs 600 veteran police officers. All of the recruits will receive the training, and approximately 250 officers are anticipated to attend the in-service training. The training task was assigned to the social work administrator. The administrator was knowledgeable of family dynamics, developmental stages, and family services that were available within the community. The social worker requested to meet with the captain to discuss the details of the training. Questions were prepared in advance. During the meeting the social worker learned that the training would not involve police procedures but only information and referral resources for families. The training was scheduled for a two-hour block that would be offered eight times over a one-month period. A small training budget provides an honorarium. Training materials will be copied, and equipment will be provided by the police training academy.

In the above example the social work administrator lacked in-depth knowledge about law enforcement organizational culture, policies, and procedures. The knowledge the social worker had acquired was based on anecdotal information from friends, personal experiences with police officers, and media reports. However, the social worker was very knowledgeable about family issues and had several years of clinical practice and supervisory experience in this area.

Turning to the NASW *Code of ethics*, the social work administrator realized that accepting this assignment was ethical practice. The social worker is competent in family issues and is providing a service, in this instance training, after consulting with police officials and acquiring more information about the assignment. Moreover, the social worker is not training police officers about law enforcement policies and procedures in which obviously the social worker has no training. Accepting the assignment is consistent with the ethical value and principles of competence.

A Schema for Understanding Law Enforcement Agencies

Law enforcement agencies are governmental (public) agencies that protect life and property, preserve peace and public order, and prevent and suppress crime (Trojanowicz & Dixon, 1974). The characteristics and functions of law enforcement agencies warrant examination in order to understand the need for law enforcement agencies to collaborate with human service agencies. The following schema describes the mission and aims, basic organizational models including tribal, federal, state, county, and local levels of law enforcement, personnel characteristics, and the functions and tasks of law enforcement.

Mission and Aims

A *mission statement* is an agency's formal written description of its aims, values, goals, and services. Mission statements often include statements describing how the aims of the agency will be achieved and the population who are the recipients of the agency services.

The mission statements for law enforcement agencies are public information, and most law enforcement agencies have official websites that post the mission statement. Box 3.1 illustrates sample mission statements selected from several official law enforcement websites. These samples reveal common themes among agency missions such as: enhancing the quality of life, collaboration and partnership between law enforcement and the community, preserving peace, protecting the public and enforcing laws.

Similarly to most agency mission statements, law enforcement agencies generally identify how the agency mission aims and objectives will be achieved in their mission statements. For instance, reviewing the mission statement of the Chicago Police Department (CPD) suggests that their mission will be achieved by attaining "the highest degree of ethical behavior and professional conduct at all times" (City of Chicago, 2010).

A key common theme that appears among these mission statements is the concept of community partnerships. Law enforcement officials recognize that in order to successfully fulfill their mission they require community input.

Box 3.1 Samples of Law Enforcement Agency Mission Statements

Atlanta Police Department

The mission of the Atlanta Police Department is to reduce crime and promote the quality of life, in partnership with our community. Values—dedication, professionalism, integrity.

(www.atlantapd.org/)

Chicago Police Department

The Chicago Police Department, as part of, and empowered by the community, is committed to protect the lives, property and rights of all people, to maintain order, and to enforce the law impartially. We will provide quality police services in partnership with other members of the community. To fulfill our mission, we will strive to attain the highest degree of ethical behavior and professional conduct at all times.

(https://portal.chicagopolice.org/portal/page/portal/
ClearPath/About%20CPD/Our%20Mission)

Houston Police Department

The mission of the Houston Police Department is to enhance the quality of life in the City of Houston by working cooperatively with the public and within the framework of the U.S. Constitution to enforce the laws, preserve the peace, reduce fear and provide for a safe environment.

(www.houstontx.gov/police/mission.htm)

Portland Police Bureau

The mission of the Portland Police Bureau is to reduce crime and the fear of crime by working with all citizens to preserve life, maintain human rights, protect property, and promote individual responsibility and community commitment.

(www.portlandonline.com/police/index.cfm?a=28214&c=30541)

Community Policing

The Community Oriented Policing Services (COPS) website defines *community policing* as "a philosophy that promotes organizational strategies, which support the systematic use of partnerships and problem-solving techniques, to proactively address the immediate conditions that give rise to public safety issues such as crime, social disorder, and fear of crime." Community policing entails three basic concepts: (1) *community partnerships*, between the law enforcement agency, individuals, organizations, and communities that focus on problem solving and enhancing public trust in police officers; (2) *organizational transformation*, which emphasizes internal organizational management and personnel issues, as well as technology to enhance community partnerships and problem solving; and (3) *problem solving*, which centers on how crime and social problems are identified, prioritized and solved (United States Department of Justice, Community Oriented Policing, n.d.).

Basic Organizational Models

Numerous organizational models of law enforcement agencies exist; federal, state, local (city, county, towns), and tribal. In general, law enforcement officers are classified in four major areas: federal agents, state troopers, county sheriffs, and police officers. Although several types of law enforcement organizations will be briefly reviewed, emphasis will be placed on local law enforcement agencies and their unique role in responding to human need that requires a social service response. Local law enforcement agencies are more likely to collaborate with social workers, and their departments are more likely to hire police social workers.

The Bureau of Justice Statistics (BJS), a unit of the U.S. Department of Justice (DOJ), provides data describing federal, state, county, and local levels of law enforcement. These data were collected through a national survey, disseminated by the BJS, and are beneficial for understanding the operations, training and education, and personnel characteristics for the various levels of law enforcement.

Federal Law Enforcement Agencies

As of September 2004, there were 17 federal agencies that employed 500 or more full-time officers who were authorized to make arrests and carry a firearm. The seven largest agencies, in order of size, are; U.S. Customs and Border Protection, Federal Bureau of Prisons, which employs correctional officers, Federal Bureau of Investigation (FBI), U.S. Immigration and Customs Enforcement, U.S. Secret Service, Drug Enforcement Administration, and Administrative Office of the U.S. Courts which includes federal probation officers. The Bureau of Alcohol, Tobacco and Firearms' (ATF) law enforcement functions were transferred to the Department of Justice (DOJ), and in 2003 ATF became known as the Bureau of Alcohol, Tobacco, Firearms and Explosives representing the twelfth largest agency employing federal officers (Reaves, 2006).

Ten FBI priorities were identified in 2011 and include; protecting the U.S. from terrorist attack, foreign intelligence operations and espionage, cyber-based attacks and high-technology crimes. Additional priorities include addressing corruption, protecting civil rights, responding to transnational/national criminal organizations, white-collar and violent crime, and providing support to federal, state, local, and international law enforcement agencies (Federal Bureau of Investigation, n.d.a).

Although the social work profession shares a concern for some of these issues, particularly protecting civil rights, when compared to the tasks that local law enforcement agencies perform, social workers are more likely to be involved with local law enforcement agencies. However, the FBI does operate numerous specialized programs that provide services to victims. These programs include: the Terrorism Victim Assistance Unit, the Child Victim Identification Program (CVIP), the Forensic Child Interviewing Program, and the assignment of victim specialists who provide victim services to Native American victims of crime. Victim specialists provide resources and information to crime victims about local rape crisis centers, crime victims compensation programs, mental health and other services (Federal Bureau of Investigation, n.d.b). Additionally, the FBI implemented the Victim Assistance Rapid Deployment Team in 2004 to respond to the scene of mass disasters and violence (Federal Bureau of Investigation, n.d.c). Many of the victim specialists are primarily either licensed social workers or clinical social workers (Federal Bureau of Investigation, n.d.d).

Bureau of Indian Affairs and Tribal Law Enforcement Agencies

As of June 2000, the Bureau of Indian Affairs oversaw 37 law enforcement agencies, and American Indian tribes oversaw 171 law enforcement agencies. Tribal law enforcement agencies provide policing services similar to other agencies, such as school resource officers and community resource officers. In tribal communities, federal, state, and tribal law enforcement agencies all have jurisdiction over criminal offenses. Which agency has primary law enforcement jurisdiction is based upon where the crime was committed (inside or outside of a tribal community), the offender and victim (whether or not they are tribal community members), and the type of crime committed (Hickman, 2003).

State Law Enforcement Agencies

State law enforcement agencies are designated as either Highway Patrol or State Police offices. Hawaii maintains a State Public Safety office that employs sheriffs, and Alaska has a State Troopers office. Consequently states provide law enforcement functions in every state except Hawaii. These agencies provide highway safety patrols and traffic enforcement, general state patrol, criminal investigation, and training and crime laboratory services for local enforcement agencies. Additional functions and law enforcement authority are determined by each state. In some municipalities the state police are the only providers of law enforcement services. Among 49 state law enforcement agencies, fewer specialty units are operated than among local law enforcement agencies. For instance, in 1990 drug education was provided in schools by 69% of state law enforcement agencies. Sixty-five percent operated specialty units for drunk drivers, missing children 51%, child abuse 27%, community crime prevention 27%, gangs 20%, juvenile delinquency 14%, hate crimes 12%, domestic violence 10%, and victim assistance 6% (Reaves, 1992).

County Law Enforcement Agencies

County law enforcement agencies oversee the county jail system, the county court system, and provide highway and waterway safety and patrol. Each state constitution defines the authority of the county sheriff. County law enforcement agencies provide law enforcement services to counties and independent cities. Powers of jurisdiction in some counties may or may not extend to areas where local law enforcement agencies have jurisdiction, and some counties contract with county sheriffs' offices for law enforcement services (Hickman & Reaves, 2003b).

Local Law Enforcement Agencies

Local law enforcement agencies are municipal agencies that provide the majority of community oriented law enforcement services. Responses to citizens' calls for service are provided by local law enforcement agencies such as the Dallas Police Department and the Salt Lake City Police Department. As of 2000 there were approximately 13,000 local law enforcement agencies nationwide. These agencies employed about 565,915 full-time personnel (Hickman & Reaves, 2003a).

Large law enforcement agencies contain more specialty units than smaller agencies. Reaves and Hickman (2002) described the types of full-time or part-time specialty units that provide social-service-related resources to individuals residing in cities with a population of 250,000 or more between 1990 and 2000. For example, in 2000 local law enforcement agencies maintained full-time specialty units that dealt with child abuse (77%), domestic violence (81%), drug education in schools (73%), juvenile crime (68%), and missing children (66%). Many agencies also had specialty units for victim assistance (47%) and hate crimes services (26%). Additional specialty units provided by larger agencies include underwater rescue or scuba, mounted horse patrols, SWAT teams, community affairs, and canine (K-9) units.

Personnel

Police officers are referred to as *sworn personnel* and are civil servants who have taken an oath and are authorized to carry a firearm. Sworn personnel have the powers to make arrests (Hickman & Reaves, 2003a). Law enforcement agencies also hire civilian personnel who are also civil service employees and bound to civil service regulations. *Civilians* are non-sworn personnel employed in law enforcement supportive roles. They perform a variety of tasks such as technical support.

In 2000, 4.8% of law enforcement agencies required that police applicants possess a four-year degree, 9.7% required a two-year degree, and 22.6% required some college education, whereas 62.9% required a high-school diploma. Police recruit academy training consists of 880 median classroom training hours. The median number of field training hours for police recruits is 600. The amount of required annual in-service training time for veteran police officers was 40 hours (Reaves & Hickman, 2002). These figures amount to approximately 5½ months of classroom training within the academy, 3¾ months of field training, and 1 week of annual in-service training.

Functions and Tasks

Most contact with local police officers occurs through either patrol officers observing a situation or dispatched 911 calls. Local law enforcement agencies operate seven days a week, 24 hours a day with officers responding to a wide variety of social problems. These situations include alcohol and substance use and abuse, medical emergencies, the mentally ill, runaways, domestic violence and family disputes, child abuse and neglect, landlord–tenant disputes and neighbor conflicts, missing persons, and juvenile delinquency.

Owing to the volume of calls that were being received for non-emergencies, such as calls for information, many local law enforcement agencies have implemented a 311 call system. By dialing 311 individuals can obtain assistance with non-emergency situations such as information and referrals. In New York City 311 is on-line in addition to having a call-in center. Individuals can also text NYC311. The website provides services related to street parking, taxi, lost and found, landlord complaints, and bus and subway information, among other services.

A study found that 26% of the calls to the 911 dispatcher were for general advice and information, and 22% were related to victim needs. Interestingly, Briar (1985) concluded that these calls could be handled directly by social workers employed within communication centers. Indeed, most of patrol work is comprised of social-service-related functions, and consequently opportunities exist for collaboration between police officers, human service agencies, and social workers.

Police Social Work

Police social work is a small area of practice within the social work profession. As we have reviewed, police social work is possible because the majority of law enforcement functions involve a social service response. Yet, few law enforcement agencies hire social workers to perform police social work. A fairly extensive literature defines police social work, the types of social problems addressed, tasks performed, challenges that arise, and the benefits that can be derived from police social work practice.

Police social work practice has been recognized in numerous countries. Despite the various countries, numerous similarities between police social work functions, the challenges they face, and types of social problems they manage have been reported. Joint police and social work investigations of child abuse have been described in Great Britain (Garrett, 2004), and Scotland (Findlay, 1991; Waterhouse & Carnie, 1991). Fong & Cheung (1997) described child sexual abuse training with police officers, social workers, and clinical psychologists in Hong Kong. Conte, Berliner & Nolan (1980) described an innovative collaboration in which social workers, police officers, and prosecutors collaborated on cases involving child sexual abuse. Police social work collaboration has also been described in response to domestic violence in Australia (Cooper, Anaf, & Bowden, 2008), and the U.S. (Holmes, 1982).

The origin of police social work in the U.S. has been traced to female police officers from the 1920s through the 1960s. The first policewoman was a social worker (Odem & Schlossman, 1991; Roberts 2007a; Roberts, 2007b; Walker, 2006). An article titled "Coordinating police and social work" published in *The American City* (1952) described the first hiring of social workers (who were not female police officers) to work in the Rochester Police Department (RPD). Social workers intervened in marriage and family problems and youth and missing persons situations, and were considered effective. A primary expectation was that social work interventions would contribute to reduced crime rates. Nearly 60 years after this article appeared, the RPD continues to maintain a Family and Crisis Intervention Team (FACIT) comprised of counseling specialists who monitor police radios similarly to police officers and respond to social problems involving domestic violence, child and elder abuse, and neighbor disputes, among others (U.S. Conference of Mayors, 1999). During the team's history some counselors have been BSW and MSW social workers.

The Englewood Project was conducted in Chicago from August 1954 through August 1957. The goals of the project required that police officers refer juveniles and their families to a local social service agency for casework services. The project concluded that social service agencies were an important resource for police officers and should be expanded, and the juvenile unit should be expanded as well (Penner, 1959).

Later, social work students from the Jane Addams College of Social Work participated in two demonstration projects. One was implemented in 1970 in a police department located in Wheaton, IL, and the second in 1971 in Niles, IL. Each project included two social workers and four second-year MSW students. Their tasks included conducting assessments, crisis intervention, individual, marital, and family counseling, group work, and consultation (Michaels & Treger, 1973). These projects continue to operate in the Chicago area.

A more recent example is the Youth Service Providers Network (YSPN) program located in Boston, MA. The program was initially implemented with one police social worker in 1996 and increased to 13 as of 2000. The police social work program has been replicated in Albuquerque, NM (Calliantos, 2000). YSPN is a collaboration developed between the Boston Police Department and the Boys and Girls Club of Boston. Licensed Clinical Social Workers are placed in a police station and provide home visits each day in response to referrals provided by police officers or police reports for at-risk youth. In this way YSPN "gives the police officer the ability to get youth the social services they so desperately need, without the added burden of trying to actually perform the social work him/herself" (Robert Wood Johnson, 2001, p. 1).

Police Social Work Defined

Police social work has been defined differently among the entries found in influential social work reference works. Police social work first appeared as an entry in the

Encyclopedia of social work, 18th edition. At that time Treger (1987) identified police social work as a new area of social work practice in which social workers provide assessment and crisis intervention to persons experiencing delinquency, mental health issues, alcohol and substance use and abuse, family and neighbor conflicts. Additional tasks include providing services to crime victims, counseling police officers and their families, and providing training and consultation. Treger remarked that challenges arise when social workers and police officers collaborate owing to different roles, perceptions, and training. He suggested that despite these differences community residents and social workers can benefit from such collaborations. In the *Encyclopedia of social work*, 19th edition, Treger (1995) further articulated six characteristics that are essential for an effective police social work program. These characteristics include cooperation between social workers and police officers, appropriate salary and skills, staff who reflect community diversity, consultation opportunities, victim assistance services, and adequate training.

The following definitions also appeared in major social work reference works. Barker (2003) defined police social work as "professional social work practice" (p. 330) in police precincts, courts, and jails. Services provided include services to crime victims, individuals who have been accused of crimes, and family members. Barker observed that police social workers are both civilians *and* police officers who possess professional social work training.

Barton (2000) described the common objectives between police work and social work and the challenges that develop when police officers and social workers collaborate. Joint training related to social problems such as child welfare, domestic violence, and sex offenders is also described.

Knox & Roberts (2009) described the tasks performed by a police social worker during a single shift. A police social worker can intervene in varied situations which include a child protective case and family violence, among other things, within a single shift. Patterson (2008c) defined police social workers as professional social workers and individuals with related academic degrees due to civil service regulations that guide hiring practices. Police social workers provide services to clients referred by police officers; train police officers in stress management, mental illness, substance abuse, domestic violence, and child abuse; provide consultation to police officers; and counsel officers and their families.

Police Social Work Functions

Zimmerman (1998) sampled 21 police social work programs and found referrals to the programs were provided by police officers to all of the programs (n = 21), self-referral or referred by family or friends (16), schools (12), courts (11), human service agencies, churches (3), hospitals and probation department (2), and the fire department (1). Programs provided the following interventions: counseling (21); crisis interventions (13), referrals (8), assessment and consultation (7), community education and public speaking (4), advocacy, follow-up, and outreach (2), training student interns, transportation services, and victim services (1). The programs described the populations served, which also depicts the social problem situations: juveniles and any client referred to the team (9), a juvenile's family members (7), crime victims (3), adults, domestic violence cases, the elderly, rape victims, sexual abuse and neglect cases, and young males living with their family (1). Some programs excluded the following populations from receiving services: substance abusers (7), the mentally ill (3), adults without children (2), adults with pending criminal charges, children younger than 9 years old, chronic delinquents, developmental disabled, receiving public entitlement benefits, and transients (1).

In the same way, Patterson (2004) examined one police social work program and found that 85% of cases were referred to the program by police officers. In 1% of these cases officers made referrals either in person or by telephone. Individuals were self-referred through walk-in or called-in in 2% of the cases, and 12% were referred by courts or human service agencies. Interventions provided by the program included: crisis intervention (31%), referrals to human service and other agencies (25%) short-term counseling (19%), follow-up service (8%), law enforcement information (8%), mediation (5%), and case status information (4%). Case situations involving family matters comprised 65% of the cases and another 35% involved disputes and other problems. For example, criminal offenses (9%), mental health services (8%), transportation (8%), domestic violence (7%), and alcohol and substance abuse (5%), child protection cases (3%), and medical needs (1%). These situations were documented as the primary presenting problem.

Social Work Services for Police Officers and Their Families

Police social workers also provide services to police officers and their families, although social workers participate in these functions less frequently than providing clinical or direct services to individuals referred by police officers. Openshaw (2009) described the provision of group interventions for police officers and their spouses. Likewise, Patterson (2008b) described a cognitive-behavioral framework for conducting stress management groups with police officers. A social work perspective could have enhanced the debriefing services that were provided to police officers and avoided the problems that developed during the debriefing after the bombing of the Alfred P. Murrah Federal Building in Oklahoma City, OK (Callahan, 2000).

Training Police Officers

Training police officers is another area in which social workers collaborate with law enforcement agencies. Whether formalized through academy training or informal presentations provided at roll calls, social workers can provide an "outside perspective" and assist police officers with improving their service functions and their own psychological well-being.

However, social work educational programs have not provided educational opportunities for police social workers. Police academies and social work educational programs should collaborate to offer training for both police officers and police social workers (Roberts, 1978). Social workers can be involved in training police officers in mental health issues through incorporating social work courses into university officer training. Such collaboration resulted in improved relations between police officers and social workers and collaboration on programs (Slaght, 2002).

Social workers who provide training to either police recruits or veteran police officers should be familiar with the nature of police. In this way, they can help trainees to integrate training content into their work. O'Keefe (2004) noted that behavioral science training includes topics such as racism, sexism, and homophobia, culture and cultural conflict, and religious diversity. O'Keefe noted that these topics should not be taught in isolation but should be related and connected for police work. Second, they require different methods of instruction since these topics involve values and self-reflection. Third, newly hired police recruits possess less police experience and life experiences than veteran police officers. Training must consider these needs. Lastly, it should be recognized that recruits may feel uncomfortable discussing race and ethnicity and cultural diversity in an academy classroom.

Challenges in Police Social Work

Functioning within a law enforcement setting presents numerous challenges for social workers. Numerous challenges also arise when social workers collaborate with police officers. These include cooption, the loss of professional identity, negative views toward each occupational group, myths, mistrust, and perceptions that the other group is undependable (Treger, 1981).

Authors have identified a range of challenges inherent in police social work, some of which are common among the listings. For instance, Thomas (1988) reported the following challenges: the quasi-military structure of law enforcement agencies and consultative structure of social work agencies, differences in power, gender, education, and occupational culture. Stephens (1988) mentioned hostility, suspicion and mistrust between social workers and police officers. Richards (1976) asserted that police officers and social workers are more similar than they are different owing to their roles in children and youth cases, domestic violence, and the elderly and mental health cases. However, Richards did describe differences based on education, philosophy, age, gender, social class, societal demands, and professional responsibilities.

Parkinson (1980) suggested that the differences between police officers and social workers were formed based on sex role stereotypes, social structures of oppression, injustice and inequality and created a barrier to collaboration. Likewise, Bar-On (1995) suggested that police social work collaboration is impractical owing to the structure of the occupations and society, and because the differences in mission, objectives, social ideology, types of interventions, gender, and education are greater than the similarities between social workers and police officers. Others have noted the benefits derived from police social work practice and how these challenges are overcome. As a result of joint training and meetings between social workers and police officers, social workers gained a better understanding of law enforcement functions in response to child sexual abuse cases, and police officers gained an increased understanding of sexually abused children and their families. Consequently collaboration was enhanced as each group began to view each other's roles differently. In particular, police officers perceived that social workers gained an increased understanding of the criminal justice system (Conte, Berliner & Nolan (1980).

Police officers responded favorably and perceived a social work domestic violence team as effective especially because intervening with victims at the same time that police officers handled suspects was helpful for victims. The interventions included assisting domestic violence victims with orders of protection, providing information about the criminal justice system, referrals, and transporting victims to domestic violence shelters (Corcoran, Stephenson, Perryman, & Allen, 2001).

Some differences between social workers and police officers have been empirically supported in research studies. Home (1994) compared police and social workers' perceptions of responsibility and seriousness of domestic violence situations. In general, police officers attributed more responsibility for violence to women than men, whereas social workers attributed more to men than women. Police officers also attributed domestic violence to the family's socioeconomic status. These results were attributed to differences in gender and educational and professional values. Similarly, McMullan, Carlan, & Nored (2009) compared perceptions of domestic violence among law enforcement students, non-law enforcement criminal justice students and social work students. Results showed that the law enforcement students reported less sensitivity toward domestic violence than non-law enforcement criminal justice and social work students.

Similar studies were conducted that examined differences in attitudes toward child abuse. Cheung & Boutte-Queen (2000) investigated 37 emotional responses to child sexual abuse between police and social workers in Hong Kong and found that police officers and social workers differed in seven of the 37 responses. Social workers reported feeling uncomfortable helping children and were more empathetic. Police officers however reported more feelings of ambivalence in helping children and families and perpetrators, and more feelings of revenge against perpetrators.

Kelley (1990) examined attitude differences regarding responsibility for child sexual abuse and case management interventions between child protective workers, nurses, and police officers. Differences in attitudes were associated with the gender of the victim and occupation, among other things. Similarly, Trute, Adkins, & MacDonald (1992) conducted a study in rural Canada that compared attitudes regarding child sexual abuse between police, community mental health workers, and child welfare workers of whom the majority were social workers. Significant differences were found between child welfare workers and police officers.

Implications for Social Work Practice

Law enforcement agencies collaborate with practitioners from the fields of counseling, criminal justice, psychology, sociology, and social work, among others. Police social work has developed as a field in this regard. A primary principle for agency workers is to understand the agency context in which they work and how its structure and function are determined (Compton & Galaway, 1994). This chapter examined these principles relative to social work practice in law enforcement agencies. Because law enforcement agencies manage a wide variety of social problems that require a social service response, this creates clinical, training, and advocacy opportunities for social workers.

Police social workers require skills in crisis intervention, mediation, and referrals. The ability to resolve and work through the attitudinal and occupational differences between social workers and police officers identified in the literature is also an important skill. Social work collaboration with police officers is different from being employed within a police department as a police social work. Social workers employed in human service agencies form collaborations with police officers focused on specific social problems such as child welfare and mental health.

Police social workers who are employed in law enforcement agencies face numerous structural challenges that require consideration. These issues include: (1) obtaining funding and other resources to support police social work practice; (2) an awareness of civil service regulations as a requirement for employment that authorize a non-social-work academic degree; as a result some law enforcement agencies employ social workers and other disciplines, and in these instances "social worker" is not the official job title; (3) law enforcement officials may be concerned about the safety of unarmed civilians who respond to possibly dangerous situations; (4) police unions may not support police social work, sensing that social workers are performing police functions; (5) police social workers require training and social work supervision; (6) the type of law enforcement equipment (police radios or police departmental vehicles) that will be used by police social workers must be established; and (7) the unit within the law enforcement agency where police social workers will be stationed must be established. The unit functions should be compatible with social work values (Patterson, 2008a).

Finally, police social workers are not employed in law enforcement agencies to intervene in response to police misconduct situations. Unfortunately, testing, assessment and evaluation, and counseling provided to police officers and their families are typically the role of psychologists employed in law enforcement settings. Overall, the social work profession has not established itself as a service provider in these areas. Professional advocacy is needed to expand the responsibilities of police social workers into these areas.

Collaboration between social workers and police officers will remain an important area of social work practice in the future. Because police officers are first responders to traumatic incidents, disasters, and mass emergencies, they encounter individuals who require crisis services. These situations will also provide opportunities for collaboration.

Chapter Summary

This chapter reviewed the various types of law enforcement agencies and their functions. The majority of tasks performed by local law enforcement agencies consist of responding to calls for service that do not require a crime fighting response (i.e., detain, arrest). These calls require that police officers provide crisis intervention, mediation, and referrals. This sets the stage for police social work, which was presented as a unique area of social work practice. This chapter traced the emergence of police social work as an area of social work practice, as well as the fundamental challenges associated with police social work practice. Most of these challenges are associated with the differing demographic characteristics and roles between social workers and police officers. Domestic violence and child welfare are two areas that have received the most police social work practice and research consideration as evidenced through publications. Additional concerns connected to law enforcement such as racial profiling and police misconduct are examined in Chapter 7.

Key Terms

Community policing
Law enforcement functions
Local law enforcement agencies

Mission statement
Police social work

Questions for Review

1. Was it surprising to read that police officers spend the majority of their time responding to calls "as an amateur social worker"? Why might the general public perceive that police officers spend the majority of their time engaged in crime-fighting duties?
2. Why are local law enforcement agencies most likely to collaborate with social workers and employ them? Does your local law enforcement agency employ police social workers?
3. Trace the historical development of police social work.
4. Summarize the challenges of police social work practice. Do you feel the benefits that can be gained from employing police social workers outweigh the challenges? Why or why not?
5. Summarize the areas of collaboration between social workers and police officers.

Further Reading

Colbach, E. M., & Fosterling, C. D. (1976). *Police social work*. Springfield, IL: Charles C. Thomas.

Thomas, T. (1994). *The police and social workers* (2nd ed.). Aldershot, U.K.: Arena.

Treger, Harvey (1975). *The police–social work team: A new model interprofessional cooperation—A university demonstration project in manpower training and development*. Springfield, IL: Charles C. Thomas.

4 The Court System

Chapter Overview

This chapter briefly examines the structure of the U.S. dual court system, comprised of federal and state courts. The structure of state courts varies among states although a general pattern has been identified consisting of courts of original instance (lower courts) and appellate courts (higher courts). In addition to federal and state courts, tribal and local (which are part of a unified state court system) courts also exist. Courts hear cases that range from family and property matters, bankruptcy, and tax matters, to civil rights issues and cases that involve social problems such as substance abuse and mental illness. Social workers are involved with local courts more than other types of courts. Social workers are most often involved with local courts pertaining to matters involving juveniles, crime victims, domestic violence, and child welfare. Social workers also interact with specialty courts to provide substance abuse or mental health treatment, and conduct mediation within mediation centers for court referred cases.

Forensic social work and mitigation specialists are discussed as an area of social work practice which requires highly specialized skills and expertise. Similar to social work practice in other components of the criminal justice system, practice roles within the court system are wide-ranging.

Types of Laws

Laws affect many aspects of our daily lives. For example, traffic laws define speed limits and restrict certain behaviors such as texting while driving. Even social work licensure is governed by laws and regulated by legislation. Laws that regulate social work practice define who can and can not legally use the title "social worker." Licensure is regulated in each state although legislation varies among the states.

Laws regulate many types of personal and public interactions between individuals, and between individuals and government entities including family matters, the transfer of property, commerce, and conflict (Siegel, 2010). Siegel identified four categories of law. (1) *Substantive criminal law* defines criminal acts and punishment. (2) *Procedural criminal law* defines the procedures followed in the criminal justice system such as jury selection, arrest procedures, and the right to legal counsel. (3) *Civil law* defines interactions between individuals and businesses or corporations such as personal property cases. The type of civil law most common in the criminal justice system is torts. *Torts* are noncriminal acts that happen when legal obligations have been breached. Individuals can be sued for damages or sanctions can be imposed (Dressler, 2002). Siegel also identified three categories of torts. Intentional torts involve the injuries that an individual experiences because someone either knew or should have known that a situation would cause an injury. Negligent torts occur because an individual's behavior was careless or reckless. Strict liability torts occur when an injury occurs because an action causes an injury that is unlawful. (4) *Public law* defines how city, county, state, and federal government agencies are administered. Criminal laws are considered as crimes against society, whereas civil laws are not (Albanese, 2008).

Social Work and the Law

Social work practice and the law is an area of practice that involves interfacing with the law and legal matters (Braye & Preston-Shoot, 2006; Braye & Preston-Shoot, 1990; Phillips, 1979; Preston-Shoot, Roberts, & Vernon, 1998). Some individuals often seek solutions to their legal problems through contact with social workers in community centers as opposed to going to law offices. These persons seek to avoid using law offices because of expensive legal fees, and avoid legal aid offices because of long waiting lists. Because social workers can not resolve many legal problems, it is necessary for social workers to provide referrals to appropriate legal sources such as legal aid, pro bono, or private attorneys (Bertelli, 1998).

Early social work professionals were also lawyers. Each of the following individuals made significant contributions to the social work profession, and all were lawyers. Robert Weeks DeForest was the founder of the Charity Organization of Societies. This agency employed social workers and was responsible for assigning the title of social work to identify the profession. He also founded the first social work educational program, presently known as the Columbia University School of Social Work. Florence Kelley founded the National Consumer's League and the United States Children's Bureau. She is also portrayed as one of the founders of the social work profession. Sophonisba Breckinridge was at the forefront of introducing social work education into universities and advocated to develop courses focused on legal content into the curricula of social work education programs (Barker & Branson, 1993).

As discussed in Chapter 2, legislative positions through holding public office are an area where few social workers practice. Law is another area of practice with fewer social workers. Some social work educational programs offer joint degree programs granting a graduate social work degree and a law degree. Some attorneys also have MSW degrees. Coleman (2001) noted the challenges that arise among professionals with JD and MSW degrees. These challenges are primarily associated with differing ethical values and roles and tasks.

For most social workers, providing services to individuals experiencing a legal problem requires a referral to an agency that can provide legal services, or providing resources where individuals can obtain an attorney or legal advice. Others may provide services to clients experiencing a divorce, custody issues, or perhaps bankruptcy. During the course of providing services, these issues may arise but may not be the primary focus of services. As mentioned, social workers provide services to individuals outside the criminal justice system who have criminal justice system involvement. Social workers within these settings should possess skills to identify any legal problems for appropriate referrals or other actions.

Social work practice and the law involve addressing a variety of social issues and problems: for example, housing problems, neighbor disputes, accidents, death, property wills, matrimonial problems, mental illness, criminal offenders and crime victims, custody and adoption issues, unemployment, and social security (Phillips, 1979). Weil (1982) provided a similar list that included child dependence, custody and adoption, divorce, and juvenile offenders (p. 393). Joslin & Fleming (2001) described the use of social workers as case managers in a law office. Cases involved guardianship or conservatorship issues. Case management issues required telephone or e-mail contact and home visits.

Madden (2000) suggested that social workers should possess collaboration, advocacy, and the following legal policy skills relative to social work and the law:

• the ability to assess legal rights;
• the ability to conduct research pertaining to law;
• the ability to influence social policy through the use of litigation procedures and administrative law;
• the ability to engage in lobbying efforts;
• the ability to testify as an expert witness, write reports and conduct evaluations for the court;
• the ability to provide education and information to lawyers and judges about family and mental health issues;
• the ability to form collaborations with attorneys and legal organizations;
• the ability to retrieve, synthesize, and evaluate case evidence.

Although extensive arguments have been made that link social work practice and the law, social work training and education do not adequately prepare social workers for practice in the courts system, or the interface between law and social work practice. Suggestions have been provided regarding how to improve social work curricula in educational programs. One method for increasing social workers' knowledge of the law and ability to practice is education (Braye & Preston-Shoot, 1990; Kopels & Gustavsson, 1996; Madden, 2000; Preston-Shoot, Roberts, & Vernon, 1998; Weil, 1982). Most social work educational programs do not provide classes in law, or field work opportunities for social workers to practice in legal or court settings.

Social work and the law require that the provision of social work services should be grounded in ethical and legal standards (Braye & Preston-Shoot, 2006). Many situations may arise in practice which involve legal issues for both social workers and individuals who seek social work services. Social workers should possess knowledge of the law that is applicable to practice; this helps social workers to resolve ethical conflicts that arise in practice, and understand the legal grounds for intervening in a particular case situation (Braye & Preston-Shoot, 1990). Similarly, Madden (2000) suggested that, in addition to knowledge about law and legal systems, social workers should possess the skills to identity social justice issues that arise in the legal system.

Although Roche (2001) identified several commonalities between social work values and legal values, such as respect for the individual and individual rights, a commitment to equality, and eradicating discrimination, as is the case in other areas of the criminal justice system, conflicts between social workers, attorneys, and other legal professionals are certain to arise. Weil (1982) suggested that social workers can benefit from education and training that focuses on interdisciplinary collaboration, the court system, and personnel and legal issues. Likewise attorneys can benefit from an increased understanding of the social work role, and the services social workers provide. These strategies can help to reduce conflict that arises from interdisciplinary collaboration.

Some problems may impede lawyers and social workers from collaborating. Phillips (1979) suggested that social workers may hold views of distrust toward attorneys. Ignorance and hostility may impede working relationships. Madden (2003) noted that, when social workers and attorneys collaborate, attorneys provide services based on the law. Conversely, social workers use the values of the profession as a basis for providing services. These professional differences are often a source of "distrust" and "miscommunication" between the two professions.

NASW Legal Resources

In 1972 the NASW Board of Directors approved the creation of the NASW Legal Defense Fund (LDF). The purpose of the LDF is to support social workers facing lawsuits and promote social work values in legal cases. The LDF also files court briefs known as *amicus curie* (friend of the court). Recent court briefs related to criminal justice issues have included the strip searches of minor children in schools and charges filed against pregnant women with substance abuse problems (NASW, 2010).

NASW publishes nearly 100 Legal Issues of the Month reports intended to educate social workers about legal issues. These publications are regularly updated and available on-line. Examples include *Social Workers and the Supreme Court* (2010) and *Responding to a subpoena* (2009). These publications are not intended to provide legal advice to social workers. For legal advice, social workers should contact appropriate legal counsel. The NASW LDF also publishes law notes relevant to social work and the law. Examples include *Client confidentiality and privileged communications* and *Social workers as expert witnesses*. These law notes are available for a fee from the LDF.

The NASW LDF publication titled *Social workers as death penalty mitigation specialists* (2003) describes the submission of a NASW *amicus curie* brief in *Wiggins v. Smith*. This court case was filed regarding Kevin Wiggins who was convicted of murder. During the sentencing phase of his trial his attorneys planned to present mitigating evidence during a second hearing that was never held. In the absence of mitigating evidence, Wiggins received the death penalty. After the death penalty was imposed, another hearing was held in which a licensed social worker presented mitigating evidence based on Wiggins's social history. The U.S. Supreme Court vacated the death sentence on the basis that Wiggins's defense attorney failed to obtain the social history earlier, thereby not appropriately representing Wiggins. The NASW *amicus curie* brief also noted that clinical social workers provide expert testimony and conduct social histories which have the potential to significantly impact the sentencing decisions for offenders facing the death penalty.

Overview of the Court System

An overview of the court system begins with a court case that was heard in the U.S. Supreme Court. The case involved a social worker who provided mental health services to a police officer, which is at the forefront of protected communication statutes (*Jaffee v. Redmond*, 518, U.S. 1, 1996). A police officer, Mary Lu Redmond, responded to a call for service at which she shot and killed Ricky Allen. Karen Beyer, a licensed clinical social worker in Illinois, provided psychotherapy to the officer following the shooting (see Colledge, Zeigler, Hemmens, & Hodge, 2000; *Jaffee v. Redmond*, 518, U.S. 1, 1996).

Jaffee v. Redmond resulted in the creation of the psychotherapist–patient privilege. The psychotherapeutic privilege articulated in the U.S. Supreme Court is applicable to federal courts, and social workers have been granted the privilege. Because this is a federal law, state laws may vary (Colledge, Zeigler, Hemmens, & Hodge, 2000). The website *the federal psychotherapist–patient privilege (Jaffee v. Redmond, 518, U.S. 1)— History, documents, and opinions* provides information regarding recent developments on psychotherapist–patient privilege (see http://jaffe-redmond.org).

As this case illustrates, courts hear and resolve much more than the types of crimes presented in this book. Courts also hear and resolve matters that impact a wide range of personal and professional matters. Courts function at local (city and county), state, tribal, and federal government levels. Each court has a distinct function. Social workers employed in the court system provide services in pre-trial diversion programs and victim and witness assistance programs (Young, 2008).

Tribal Courts

Three hundred and fourteen federally recognized American Indian tribes exist in the lower 48 states. Among these tribes, 175 have developed a tribal court. Among the 175, 91 tribes reported having an appellate court, 80 a juvenile court, and 51 a family court. Tribal courts provide victim services, child support enforcement, paternity, and child support among other services (Perry, 2005).

Federal Courts

As mentioned in Chapter 1, the U.S. criminal justice system has a dual court system. Each system is responsible for hearing a specific type of case. The U.S. court system is comprised of two separate court systems: (1) the federal court system which has jurisdiction over matters involving federal laws, and (2) the state court system which has jurisdiction over matters involving state laws. In a typical year approximately 7,000 cases are presented to the U.S. Supreme Court. The court decides which cases it will hear, and usually hears between 100 and 150 cases (Administrative Office of the United States Courts, n.d.a). The federal court and state court systems could be involved in the same case depending upon the type of case. Federal courts hear cases that involve bankruptcy, disputes between states, and the constitutionality of laws, for example. In contrast, state courts hear cases involving family law, criminal offenses, and personal injury cases. The U.S. Constitution establishes the basis for state and federal courts. Some judicial powers are given to the federal government, whereas other powers are given to state governments (Administrative Office of the United States Courts, n.d.b). Box 4.1 shows that basic structure of the federal court system. The U.S. Supreme Court is the highest federal court followed by intermediate appellate courts, and lastly courts of original instance. Federal court cases begin in courts of original instance. Appeals are heard in intermediate appellate courts.

Box 4.1 Federal Court Structure

Federal Court

U.S. Supreme Court

United States Courts of Appeals United States Courts of Appeals for the Federal Circuit United States Courts of Military Appeals	Intermediate Appellate Courts
District Courts United States Tax Court United States Court of International Trade United States Court of Federal Claims	Courts of Original Instance

Adapted from: Administrative Office of the U.S. Courts. Retrieved from www.uscourts.gov/EducationalResources/FederalCourtBasics/CourtStructure/UnderstandingFederalAndStateCourts.aspx.

Cole & Smith (2004) observed that the dual court system contributes to variations in how laws are interpreted among states. Social and political regional differences influence how states interpret laws. For example, while Americans regardless of geographic region share similar American values, views regarding gun ownership are different in the Northeastern U.S. when compared to the South or West.

State Courts

The adult court system is comprised of criminal, family, and civil courts. Although each of these courts also hears a different type of case, in some jurisdictions a case may be heard in more than one court. For example, in some jurisdictions domestic violence cases may be heard in either criminal or family court.

State court systems are not alike because each state can structure its own court system. A typical model of state court structures includes courts of limited jurisdiction (courts that hear civil, criminal, juvenile, and traffic cases); courts of general jurisdiction (hear the same types of cases); intermediate appellate courts (courts with mandatory and discretionary jurisdiction over cases); and courts of last resort (these courts also have mandatory and discretionary jurisdiction over cases). State courts also adhere to a hierarchical structure from the lowest state courts (courts of limited jurisdiction) to the highest state courts (courts of last resort) (Rottman & Strickland, 2004).

Most state courts are combined into a unified court system. The New York State Unified Court System is an example. The system is structured and authorized according to Article VI of the New York State Constitution. The court of appeals is the highest court in New York State. In general, appeals courts do not hear new evidence but review the existing case as it applies to procedural law. Box 4.2 illustrates the basic structure of the New York State Court.

Box 4.2 New York State Criminal Court Structure

Criminal Court

Court of Appeals

Appellate Divisions of the Supreme Court Appellate Terms of the Supreme Court County Courts	Intermediate Appellate Courts
Appellate Terms of the Supreme Court *Supreme Courts County Courts District Courts* *NYC Criminal Courts City Courts Town Courts* *Village Courts*	Courts of Original Instance

Source: New York State Unified Courts (2004). Retrieved from www.courts.state.ny.us/courts/structure.shtml.

Relevant for social workers, professional malpractice claims are heard in state courts. Felony crimes are defined in state statutes, consequently the majority of criminal cases appear in state courts (Albanese, 2008). Social workers work in the largest numbers with families, youth, and domestic violence cases in local courts. These social workers may not be directly employed within the courts.

Civil Courts

Civil courts hear cases involving personal injury in which compensation is sought. Civil courts place monetary limits on the claims that may be brought before the court. In general, the limit is several thousand dollars. Cases that exceed the civil court monetary limit are heard in higher courts. In civil courts, persons filing claims do not require legal representation. Examples of civil court cases include landlord–tenant disputes and cases that involve damaged or stolen property. Box 4.3 shows the New York State civil court structure.

Box 4.3 New York State Civil Court Structure

Civil Court

Court of Appeals Appellate Divisions of the Supreme Court	
Appellate Terms of the Supreme Court County Courts	Intermediate Appellate Courts
Appellate Terms of the Supreme Court *Supreme Courts County Courts Surrogate's Courts* *Family Courts Court of Claims District Courts* *NYC Civil Courts City Courts Town Courts* *Village Courts*	Courts of Original Instance

Source: New York State Unified Courts (2004). Retrieved from www.courts.state.ny.us/courts/structure.shtml.

Family and Juvenile Courts

Box 4.3 shows that in New York State family courts are part of the civil court structure. Some states use the term juvenile court instead of family court. Chapter 1 mentioned that social work played a prominent role in the establishment of the first juvenile court which had the goal of rehabilitating instead of punishing juvenile offenders. Today, a wide variety of family matters are heard in family or juvenile courts.

Unlike the proceedings in an adult criminal court, which are open for the public to attend, the proceedings in a family court are private and confidential. Consequently the court is closed to the public. Students can appear in court and observe a criminal trial, or write papers about the proceedings, or family members or the media can appear unless the court is closed to the media or cameras. This is not the case in a family court. Also, in family courts a juvenile's court records are "sealed." In other words, the records are confidential, unlike the public records of adults. The juvenile court also utilizes different language from adult criminal courts. Table 4.1 summarizes some of these differences emphasizing that juveniles are not offenders but youth who require rehabilitation.

Table 4.1 Differences between Terms Used in Criminal and Juvenile Courts

Criminal court terms	Family or juvenile court terms
Crime	Delinquent act
Arrested	Taken into custody
Arraignment	Initial appearance
Trial	Fact-finding hearing
Represented by defense attorney	Represented by a law guardian
Sentencing phase	Dispositional hearing
Incarceration	Commitment

Case Example

A family seeks services from a social worker employed in a nonprofit human service agency. The parents state that their 14-year-old son is running away, skipping school, not following the rules at home, talking back to them, and hanging out with the wrong crowd. His grades have recently dropped as well. The parents state that as far they know their son is not involved in gang activity or committing crimes. They also do not think that he is using drugs or alcohol, although the father did find a pack of cigarettes in his back pocket while doing laundry. The parents further state they are worried that this behavior will influence their 11-year-old son who is doing very well both at school and home. Mom insinuates that she has thought about asking her 14-year-old son to leave their home. The social worker explains that parents are legally responsible because he is a minor and that an appropriate plan must be developed. This infuriates mom who feels that she has no control, and that laws favor her 14-year-old son. The social worker explores with the parents their interest in family counseling. Over the next several months the family sporadically attends family counseling sessions. After some exploration, the parents mention they have a family friend who obtained a PINS (Person in Need of Supervision; this is known by other names such as CHINS—Children in Need of Supervision— in some jurisdictions) for their son who was exhibiting similar behaviors. They express interest in obtaining a PINS petition. The social worker is aware that status offenses are handled by the juvenile probation department and that the family must attend a probation intake appointment for screening and assessment. The social worker is also aware that PINS diversion will occur first. The social worker informs the family of these details and that PINS is a criminal justice intervention. The family is asked to consider whether they want criminal justice involvement for this situation. Their immediate response is yes, that he might learn something from this process. Several months later the family contacted the social worker stating they received a PINS petition and will wait to see how the PINS petition helps their son. They will no longer attend family counseling, but would like the option to attend sessions in the future if they feel it is needed.

In this case, the family decided to pursue a PINS petition and chose this option instead of family counseling. Although the parents selected an option that involved the criminal justice system instead of the mental health system, an option which the social worker felt might have been amenable to family counseling, the parents exercised their right to self-determination.

Criminal Courts

Criminal courts are adult state courts. These courts hear cases that involve crimes defined in state statutes. As previously mentioned, states vary in how they define criminal offenses. As seen in Box 4.2, criminal cases are initially heard in town, city, and village courts. As with other courts, appeals are heard in the intermediate appellate courts, and the court of appeals is the highest court in the state.

Specialty Courts or Problem-solving Courts

Specialty courts or problem-solving courts are unique courts that hear only cases related to a specific social problem. Social problems include drug use, domestic violence, mental health issues, neighborhood and community problems, and reentry of former offenders into communities. The primary goal of problem-solving courts is to provide treatment and services to offenders who experience these social problems.

The courts are operated by judges with expertise in these problems. Instead of imposing sentences that emphasize incarceration and punishment, offenders receive substance abuse treatment and services to achieve sobriety and prevent future criminal behavior, for example. Non-compliance with the court order, to either attend treatment or keep scheduled court appearances, can result in sanctions such as incarceration.

Specialty courts were founded on the principle of therapeutic jurisprudence which was introduced in Chapter 1. The goal is to apply the law in such as way that it has positive therapeutic benefits for individuals in terms of their mental health outcomes and other functioning. This perspective is consistent with social work values. It provides social workers with opportunities to become involved in the law, and with courts, in such a way that individuals receive a therapeutic benefit as a result of their involvement. Birgeden (2004) suggested that therapeutic jurisprudence is a legal theory associated with "responsivity in offender rehabilitation" (p. 283).

The increase in problem-solving courts has resulted in increased opportunities for social workers (Roberts & Brownell, 1999). Social workers are involved with mental health and drug courts using advocacy skills; social workers can apply these skills to advocate for specialty courts within their local court jurisdictions as task force members who are responsible for developing and implementing courts, or administrative or direct service practitioners (Tyuse & Linhorst, 2005). Social work practice in the court system and in legal settings involves interdisciplinary practice.

Community Courts

As the name implies, community courts involve members of the community working together with the local court system to identify issues affecting their community. Community courts began in 1993 with the development of the New York City Midtown Community Court. They are presently found in jurisdictions throughout the country and address neighborhood-specific problems such as crime, abandoned property, and public disorder (Lee, 2000). Social workers with training and expertise in community organizing can facilitate community court goals.

Community organizing is practice that brings together key community stakeholders such as business leaders, community residents, criminal justice agencies, colleges and universities, policymakers, and others to work together on issues impacting the community. In addition, community practice emphasizes improving the quality of life within communities, advocacy, human and social economic development, service, assessment and planning, political and social action, and social justice (Weil & Gamble, 2009). To complement community organizing skills, social workers should also have an understanding of the criminal justice system, particularly the role of courts and the relationship between the court and community problems. Community courts combine traditional sentences with alternative forms of sentencing. These courts are actually collaborations formed with community residents, local government, social service and criminal justice agencies, and community civic organizations. These groups work together to solve neighborhood or community crime problems (New York State Problem Solving Courts Brochure, n.d.).

Drug Courts

The first drug court was established in Florida at the Dade County Circuit Court in 1989. The goals of the court were to provide community-based treatment, rehabilitation, and community supervision to felony drug offenders, and reduce recidivism. As of 2009, there were more than 2,140 drug courts operating throughout the country with an additional 284 that were in various stages of development (Office of National Drug Control Policy, n.d.).

Drug courts provide an alternative to incarceration for individuals with substance abuse problems. These courts offer treatment and services focused on recovery and rehabilitation. While these courts offer alternatives to offenders, the majority of courts do not actually provide the services. The courts lack the expertise and facilities to offer treatment. Social workers and other practitioners skilled in substance abuse assessment and treatment provide these services. This includes social workers who receive referrals from the courts and who are employed in either private for-profit or nonprofit human service agencies.

Mental Health Courts

The Bureau of Justice Assistance (n.d.) describes a mental health court as a problem-solving court which has

> a specialized docket for defendants with mental illnesses that provides:
> - The opportunity to participate in court-supervised treatment
> - A court team composed of a judge, court personnel, and treatment providers, which defines terms of participation
> - Continued status assessments with individualized sanctions and incentives, and
> - Resolution of case upon successful completion of mandated treatment plan.
>
> (p. 1)

The BJS report also notes that, among the courts participating in the mental health court grant program, the number of participants enrolled in each court ranged from 15 to 800. Some mental health courts required that offenders plead guilty as a condition of their participation, whereas others deferred prosecution until treatment was completed or used a combination of these approaches.

Similarly to their involvement with other problem-solving courts, social workers are likely to be involved with mental health courts. Social workers employed in for-profit and nonprofit human service agencies are likely to receive referrals to provide services. This requires expertise in assessment and treatment of mental illness and skills necessary for interdisciplinary collaboration. Individuals with mental illness are likely to be involved with other mental health professionals such as psychiatrists.

Domestic Violence Courts

The goals, policies, and practices of domestic violence courts are less defined than for mental health and drug courts. In their survey of 208 domestic violence courts, Labriola, Bradley, O'Sullivan, & Moore (2009) found agreement among the courts in relation to why the courts were established, the goals of the court, and common characteristics among them. These included increasing safety for victims of violence, holding offenders accountable for their behavior, and reducing future violent behaviors. Agreement was not found among the courts concerning the most effective policies for achieving these goals. The courts also described different practices for addressing domestic violence. In sum, no uniform model was found among the 208 courts. In general, services provided by the courts were victim advocacy, orders of protection, and courtroom safety.

Juvenile Drug Courts

A juvenile drug court is "a drug court that focuses on juvenile delinquency (e.g., criminal) matters and status offenses (e.g., truancy) that involve substance-abusing juveniles" (Office of Justice Programs Drug Court Clearinghouse and Technical Assistance Project, n.d., p. 3). Juvenile drug courts emerged in the mid-1990s as an approach to address substance abuse and alcohol problems among juveniles (Bureau of Justice Assistance, 2003).

Reentry Courts

Reentry courts were established in 2000 when the Office of Justice Programs initiated the Reentry Court Initiative (RCI) with the goal of creating support services for offenders as they reenter communities. The purpose of reentry courts is to provide appropriate assessment and planning prior to release, improve community supervision of former offenders, provide appropriate community-based services, and reward former offenders for successfully completing reentry court programs and services (Delaware Judicial Information Center, 2008).

An evaluation of the Harlem Parole Reentry Court found that court participants who graduated, as well as those who did not, reported fewer arrests and reconvictions after one to three years following release. Among participants who completed the reentry court program, parole revocation was lower than a comparison group. Finally, among participants who completed the reentry program they were more likely to have had a prior parole sentence, to be married or living with a partner, to have obtained a high school diploma and to have been previously enrolled in a drug treatment program (Hamilton, 2010). Reentry is discussed in greater detail in Chapter 5.

Restorative Justice

Restorative justice is an approach to justice in which victims' and offenders' concerns are addressed in a non-adversarial manner (van Wormer, 2008). Several limitations associated with the restorative justice approach have been reported. Noting that the most common restorative justice approach involves offenders paying financial restitution to their victim(s), Albanese (2008) considered several limitations of this approach. First, most offenders do not have the financial means to provide restitution. Second, the benefits derived from the crime have been lost by the time the restitution process begins. Consequently property often can not be returned to the victim. Third, offenders frequently lack education and employment skills to earn money for restitution. Fourth, victims may have experienced psychological or physical injuries during the crime which have a lasting impact. Finally, secondary victims include family members and others who were affected by the crime. Secondary victims are impacted because the victim's injuries or lost property also affect their livelihood and well-being.

Furthermore, several studies have identified the limitations of the restorative justice approach. Restorative justice did not result in statistical significance as an approach to developing empathy among sex offenders towards their victim (Roseman, Ritchie, & Laux, 2009). Also, Latimer, Dowden, & Muise (2005) conducted a meta-analysis of 22 published studies comparing the effectiveness of restorative justice programs with a control group of nonrestorative justice programs. Using the outcome measures of victim satisfaction, offender satisfaction, compliance with restitution arrangements, and recidivism, they found higher levels of victim satisfaction and offender satisfaction, and more offender compliance with restitution arrangements was associated with less recidivism. Importantly, the authors urge that these results be interpreted with caution because restorative justice programs are voluntary: both victims and offenders must voluntarily agree to participate. While offenders who did volunteer had lower recidivism rates, little is known about those who do not volunteer in restorative justice approaches.

These issues require a realistic examination of the benefits of restorative justice on the part of social workers in terms of what the restorative justice approach can actually achieve and with whom. Chapter 1 presented statistics that show when offenders recidivate they primarily commit new crimes which provide an economic gain such as motor vehicle theft, having or selling stolen property, larceny, burglary, and robbery.

Mitigation Specialists

The Encarta MSN Dictionary defines a mitigation specialist as "a member of a criminal defense team who gathers detailed information about a defendant in order to persuade a jury not to impose the death penalty" (MSN Encarta Dictionary, 2009). Of course, mitigation specialist tasks are applicable only in those states which impose the death penalty.

Among the states that impose the death penalty, mitigating factors are defined differently on the basis of state law. According to the State of Arizona Supreme Court *Capital sentencing guide* (2010):

Pursuant to A.R.S. § 13–751, each death sentence must rest on two findings: proof beyond a reasonable doubt of at least one aggravating circumstance set forth in A.R.S. § 13–751(F), and a finding "that there are no mitigating circumstances sufficiently substantial to call for leniency." A.R.S. § 13–751(E). Mitigation is defined by our statute as evidence relevant to "any aspect of the defendant's character, propensities or record and any of the circumstances of the offense."

Personality, social, health, family, education, employment, and criminal history are factors used to assess mitigation and aggravating issues. Mitigation factors are those that explain why an individual facing the death penalty should be given a life sentence instead of death. Aggravating factors are those that suggest why convicted offenders should be given the death penalty (Guin, Nobel, & Merrill (2003). During the sentencing phase of a capital trial, aggravating and mitigating factors that contributed to the crime can be presented and considered in the imposed sentence. This is achieved by presenting a competent social history and expert testimony based on theory and research (Andrews, 1991). Whereas social workers are skilled in conducting social histories, mitigation specialists represent a variety of disciplines including social work, law, and psychology, among others.

Social work has been identified as playing a key role in capital trials. In many trials jurors make decisions about imposing life in prison or the death penalty on the basis of their emotional reactions to the defendant, the defendant's demeanor, and lack of clarity about the law and their roles. To reduce the effects of these events, Schroeder, Guin, Pogue, & Bordelon (2006) proposed that social workers engage in proactive interventions with the defendant, defense team, and jury. Such an approach acknowledges evidence demonstrating how jurors make decisions in capital trials.

Forensic Social Work

Rome (2008) defined forensic social work as an area of social work practice in which social workers have direct involvement with the court system. Rome observed that forensic social workers provide recommendations to courts regarding individuals' competency to stand trial or risk of violence, or contribute to the court's decision to impose alternative sentencing options through conducting forensic interviews, psychosocial assessments, and expert witness testimony. Forensic social workers also provide treatment to court-ordered offenders. Examples of the types of social problems handled by forensic social workers include: domestic violence, child maltreatment, custody, mental health, immigration, elder abuse, divorce, visitation, foster care, adoption, criminal and juvenile justice, and substance abuse. As this list shows, social workers are much more directly involved in the court system than in the legislative arena. Social workers will not be skilled in all of these areas.

The NASW LDF recognized the need for social workers to posses accurate information regarding expert testimony and published the report *Are licensed clinical social workers authorized to provide expert witness testimony concerning the diagnosis and treatment of emotional and mental disorders?* (2002). The report describes a case in which the Maryland Court of Appeals determined that the expert testimony of social workers should be evaluated and considered on the same criteria used for other expert witness. However, the report cautions that, while in the majority of states licensed clinical social workers are recognized as mental health providers, state statutes vary regarding whether social workers can act as expert witnesses. Siegel (2008) also reported that not all states admit the expert testimony of social workers and added that some states still require that the mental health professional be a psychiatrist or psychologist.

At first it was thought that this was due to lack of social work licensure. However, as social workers gained licensure in states, recognition as expert witnesses did not keep pace. Social workers are not disqualified from conducting forensic mental health evaluations although criminal statutes identify psychiatrists and psychologists as competent forensic experts (Ashford, 2009). Undeniably social workers have had a difficult time gaining recognition as forensic social workers and expert witnesses. Forensic efforts when performed by those in the social work profession have not shared the same status as other professions such as forensic psychiatry, forensic psychology, or forensic odontology. Perhaps because so few social workers practice forensic social work relative to their numbers within the profession, advocacy efforts have yielded slow progress.

Nonetheless providing expert testimony can be financially and personally rewarding for social workers. Social workers should have a contract outlining the scope of services, be knowledgeable about the case, rehearse the preparation, distinguish between facts, personal, and professional opinion, and be aware of the tactics of opposing attorneys (Barker & Branson, 1993).

Critical Issues in the Court System

The U.S. court system is presently facing many critical issues. These include racial disparities, wrongful convictions, and the death penalty to mention but a few. Each of the issues has implications for social justice and social work involvement.

Racial Disparities

Racial disparities occur within each of the four components of the criminal justice system. As we saw in Chapter 2, mandatory sentencing laws were intended to remove judicial discretion and ensure that sentences would be imposed in a fair manner that would not consider individual circumstances. These policies have had adverse affects on African Americans. Racial disparities are evident in sentencing but also throughout the other criminal justice components. Some states have developed initiatives to address these disparities. For example, observing that African American males were incarcerated at rates approximately 20% higher than White males, on March 22, 2007, former Governor Doyle signed an Executive Order to establish the Commission on Reducing Racial Disparity in Wisconsin's Criminal Justice System. The commission's charge was to assess discrimination at each stage of the Wisconsin criminal justice system and to develop strategies for reducing racial disparities (Racial Disparity Commission, 2007).

Wrongful Convictions

Wrongful convictions raise numerous social justice issues. *Wrongful convictions* refer to situations in which an innocent person has been convicted of a crime. Recently, this has referred to capital offenses such as homicide in which an offender faces the death penalty.

According to the Innocence Project (n.d.), wrongful convictions occur as a result of eyewitness testimony that misidentifies individuals, inept lawyers, informants who provide inaccurate information, false confessions made by accused defendants, poor-quality forensic scientific evidence, and government misconduct. Among the first 225 exonerated cases handled by the Innocence Project, 173 were exonerated because of misidentification through eyewitness testimony, 116 for poor-quality forensic scientific evidence, 51 for false confessions made by accused defendants, and 36 for informants who provided inaccurate information. As these figures show, cases can have multiple causes. Although wrongful convictions often resulted from a combination of these factors, eyewitness testimony misidentifying an accused individual occurred in more cases.

On September 21, 2011 Troy Davis was executed in Georgia for killing a police officer. Troy Davis maintained his innocence until his execution which raised numerous issues concerning eyewitness testimony in death penalty cases. Several eyewitnesses recanted their testimony and although some eyewitnesses did not recant their testimony his execution highlights the problems associated with imposing the death penalty on the basis only of eyewitness testimony and underscores the need for DNA and other evidence to corroborate eyewitness testimony before imposing the death penalty. States are not consistent in the role that eyewitness testimony plays in death penalty sentencing (Bynum, 2011).

The Death Penalty

No federal law mandates the death penalty. Consequently, each state can determine its own legislation regarding the death penalty. According to the Death Penalty Information Center (2010), 34 of the 50 states have enacted the death penalty. States that have the death penalty as of 2010 include: Alabama, Arizona, Arkansas, California, Colorado, Connecticut, Delaware, Florida, Georgia, Idaho, Indiana, Kansas, Kentucky, Louisiana, Maryland, Mississippi, Missouri, Montana, Nebraska, Nevada, New Hampshire, North Carolina, Ohio, Oklahoma, Oregon, Pennsylvania, South Carolina, South Dakota, Tennessee, Texas, Utah, Virginia, Washington, Wyoming. (The U.S. government and U.S. military also have death penalty statutes.)

The 16 states without death penalty legislation are: Alaska, Hawaii, Illinois (recently abolished in 2011), Iowa, Maine, Massachusetts, Michigan, Minnesota, New Jersey, New Mexico, New York, North Dakota, Rhode Island, Vermont, West Virginia, Wisconsin (also the District of Columbia does not have death penalty statutes). Michigan abolished the death penalty in 1846 and Illinois most recently abolished the death penalty in 2011.

Most states define a *capital offense* (a crime eligible for the death penalty) as first-degree murder, or murder with aggravating circumstances. A few states consider crimes such as kidnapping, robbery, drug crimes, or sexual assault of a minor as capital offenses (Snell, 2010).

Owing to religious, cultural, or other values and beliefs, individuals may or may not support death penalty legislation. NASW opposes the death penalty. In the policy statement titled *Capital punishment and the death penalty* put forth by the 2008 NASW Delegate Assembly, NASW reported that the death penalty is in opposition to the values of the social work profession. NASW further articulated that the death penalty is a human rights violation, even for individuals who have committed serious criminal offenses. Six positions have been articulated in the policy statement:

1. State governments that have death penalty legislation should abolish the death penalty.
2. Until the death penalty is abolished, state governments should institute a moratorium on all executions.
3. States with legislation that allows the death penalty for individuals aged less than 18 years old should immediately raise the age to 18 until a moratorium is instituted or the death penalty is abolished.
4. States having legislation that imposes the death penalty on individuals with mental illness should reverse this legislation to prevent mentally ill persons from receiving the death penalty.
5. Until the death penalty is abolished, states should ensure that individuals have access to appropriate legal representation. Attorneys should have appropriate training and experience in representing death penalty cases.
6. NASW supports life sentences in lieu of the death penalty.

(NASW, 2009)

Although death penalty legislation has been overturned in many states, including New York in 2007, it was overturned because the death penalty was found to be unconstitutional. It was not the result of empirical evidence demonstrating that the death penalty as deterrence strategy is ineffective. In the case of *People v. Taylor, 9 N.Y.3d 129 (2007)* it was found that some parts of the death penalty legislation in New York State were unconstitutional. Consequently it has been overturned (Snell, 2010).

Another factor that has states reconsidering death penalty legislation is the huge costs associated with the death penalty. Since 1978 when the death penalty was reinstated in California, the state has spent approximately $308 million for each of 13 executions for a total of more than $4 billion. In a *Los Angeles Times* article, Williams (2011) summarized these figures from a study that concluded more funding should be allocated to maintain death penalty legislation, the types of capital offenses should be reduced, or death penalty legislation should be abolished. The later two options will result in cost savings to taxpayers.

Implications for Social Work Practice

Social workers occupy a variety of roles and perform numerous tasks in the court system. Social work practice in the court system encompasses a wide range of social problems. These problems include substance abuse, mental illness, juvenile delinquency, and domestic violence, among others. Whereas the social work profession has made significant progress regarding involvement and recognition in the court system, the profession continues to lack full recognition in the area of forensic social work, primarily related to expert witness testimony. Although the efforts of NASW have established the credibility of social work expert testimony, in some states more professional advocacy is needed to obtain recognition.

Social work practice as described in this chapter requires highly specialized skills relevant for court settings. It requires training and experience beyond that provided in most social work educational programs. For example, few if any social work educational programs provide opportunities for social work student interns to receive training as a mitigation specialist. In addition advanced certification and credentialing may be necessary. Several organizations provide social workers with the training and expertise needed to practice this work. Membership in professional organizations such as the National Organization of Forensic Social Work (NOFSW) may be beneficial for increasing skill development.

On July 1, 2010, NASW established a specialty practice section titled *Social work and the courts*. The author is an inaugural member of the section. This is a much-needed addition to the other 10 NASW specialty practice sections. The other specialty practice sections are: health, mental health, private practice, school social work, aging, social and economic justice and peace, child welfare, children, adolescents and young adults, and administration and supervision. Although the title might imply that only court social workers are involved in the section, it includes members who are not only court-involved but also involved with law enforcement correctional institutions, probation, and parole. Members provide forensic evaluations, expert testimony and offender assessments (NASW, n.d.)

Finally, forensic cases such as death penalty cases require highly specialized skills. Other types of cases exist where social workers may experience difficulty providing services on the basis of the nature of the crime. Social workers uncomfortable with certain types of cases should not accept such assignments. Consider the options to transfer the case whenever possible, or decline the assignment although sometimes this is not possible.

Chapter Summary

This chapter reviewed the U.S. dual court system and social work roles within the court system. Numerous types of courts, including specialty or problem-solving courts, were reviewed. The interface between social work and the law was presented as an essential element in social work practice. Critical issues facing the court system such as wrongful convictions and racial disparities were also presented, as were issues related to the death penalty, mitigation specialists, and social work expert testimony. The argument was presented that forensic social work has not yet fully shared the recognition and status afforded to other disciplines that provide forensic services.

Key Terms

Capital offense

Civil court

Expert testimony

Family or juvenile court

Federal court

Forensic social work

Mitigation specialists

Specialty courts or
  problem-solving courts

State court

Wrongful convictions

Questions for Review

1. Summarize the differences between criminal and family (or juvenile) courts. What types of cases are heard in each court? How and why would you provide a referral to each court?
2. What are specialty or problem-solving courts? Why were they developed?
3. What is forensic social work? Why do you think that forensic social work has not shared the status or prestige of other occupations that provide forensic services?
4. Describe the role of a mitigation specialist. What information should be included in a social history prepared by a mitigation specialist?
5. Do you personally oppose or favor the death penalty? What are your thoughts about entering a profession that is opposed to the death penalty? How might you resolve potential conflicts between your personal beliefs and the position of your professional organization?

Further Reading

Bernstein, B. (2005). *The portable guide to testifying in court for mental health professionals: An A–Z guide to being an effective witness.* Hoboken, NJ: John Wiley & Sons, Inc.

Melton, G. B., Petrila, J., Poythress, N. G., & Slobogin, C. (2008). *Psychological evaluations for the courts: A handbook for mental health professionals and lawyers.* Hoboken, NJ: John Wiley & Sons, Inc.

Pollack, D. (2003). *Social work and the courts: A casebook.* New York: Brunner-Routledge.

Saltzman, A., & Furman, D. M. (1999). *Law in social work practice* (2nd ed.). Chicago, IL: Nelson-Hall Inc.

Stein, T. J. (2004). *The role of law in social work practice and administration.* New York: Columbia University Press.

Umbriet, M. S. (1994). *Victim meets offender: The impact of restorative justice and mediation.* Monsey, NJ: Willow Tree Press, Inc.

Vogelsand, J. (2001). *The witness stand: A guide for clinical social workers.* New York: Haworth Social Work Practice Press.

5 Corrections

Chapter Overview

The purpose of this chapter is to describe the correctional system and its various components, and the role of social work within corrections. The correctional system is comprised of institutional settings (detention centers, jails, and prisons including private prisons) and community supervision settings (probation, parole, home confinement, and monitoring). Correctional facilities are operated by federal, state, and local governments, private corporations, and tribal communities. The goal of the institutional corrections system is to incapacitate offenders convicted of committing crimes. Correctional facilities focus on control of inmates. Managing a large number of inmates safely is a primary concern within correctional institutions. Rehabilitation, while a priority among social workers, may not be a priority among correctional administrators. Importantly, inmates should receive services that prepare them for reentry because the majority will be released at some point. The goals of community-based corrections are to punish offenders or restrict their behaviors. Community-based services should be offered to offenders regardless of whether they are transitioning to communities or only received supervision and monitoring orders under the jurisdiction of community-based corrections.

Overview of Correctional Facilities

In Chapter 1, the correctional system was identified as a subsystem within the criminal justice system. Although the correctional system is a subsystem, for purposes of conceptualizing the various corrections components it may be useful to think of corrections as a system itself comprised of numerous systems. This is because both institutional and community-based settings make up the correctional system. For example, the District of Columbia Department of Corrections (n.d.) has contracts with community correctional centers and half-way houses that, as alternatives to incarceration, provide rehabilitation services to offenders awaiting trial and those convicted of misdemeanor offenses.

It is also important to keep in mind that separate juvenile and adult correctional facilities and community-based supervision agencies exist. These include separate institutional facilities for juveniles and adults as well as separate adult and juvenile probation systems. Rowland (2009) described a juvenile parole system for juveniles who reenter communities after confinement in residential institutions.

The demographic characteristics of jail and prison inmates are similar to those of individuals who are arrested. Inmates tend to be male and poor, and to represent racial and ethic minorities. These characteristics are similar throughout all components of the criminal justice system, and are reflected in arrests, inability to post bail, inadequate legal representation, and racial and ethic bias within the criminal justice system (Siegel, 2010).

Local Correctional Facilities

The first American prison was established in Connecticut in 1773. Later, the Walnut Street Jail was established in Pennsylvania in 1790 and with it American corrections institutions were started (Sullivan, as cited in Alexander, Young, & McNeece, 2008). As previously mentioned, the goal of correctional institutions is to incapacitate offenders convicted of committing crimes. *Incapacitation* refers to the ability of the correctional system to prevent offenders from committing future crimes through incarceration. In this way, offenders are no longer considered a threat to public safety because they have been removed from communities.

A *jail* is a local correctional facility operated by local police departments or country sheriff departments. In general, jails incarcerate inmates for a period of one year or less for misdemeanor offenses, or while individuals are awaiting trial. Thus inmates are incarcerated for offenses such as petit larceny and assault. Minton (2011) provides a definition of jails that was used in the nationwide annual survey of jails (ASJ):

> Jails in the ASJ include confinement facilities—usually administered by a local law enforcement agency—that are intended for adults but may hold juveniles before or after adjudication. Facilities include jails and city or county correctional centers; special jail facilities, such as medical or treatment release centers, halfway houses, and work farms; and temporary holding or lockup facilities that are part of the jail's combined function. Inmates sentenced to jail facilities usually are sentenced to serve a year or less.
>
> (p. 3)

Minton went on to describe the functions performed in the jails that were included in the survey. These were: to incarcerate individuals awaiting arraignment, trial, conviction, or sentencing, and those who violate probation, parole and bail bond; to temporarily detain juveniles awaiting transfer to a juvenile facility; to temporarily detain mentally ill individuals until they are transferred to a mental health facility; and to incarcerate inmates transferred from federal or state facilities owing to overcrowding in these facilities.

In jails, social workers and correctional counselors provide a variety of services. Inmates are transitioning to incarceration even if they have been incarcerated before. A social worker in this relatively short-term facility ensures that inmates have access to legal resources and other support systems as well as needed health and mental services. Social workers also provide counseling focused on the anxiety associated with incarceration and family matters. The following case example illustrates how a social worker conducts a mental health assessment and referral within a jail setting.

Case Example

A correctional officer (CO) refers a jail inmate to a social worker for evaluation. The recently incarcerated inmate has displayed what the CO reported as inappropriate behavior during meals and while in his cell. The CO stated the inmate was banging on the cell bars, yelling, not eating, and engaging in self-mutilation behaviors. During the assessment interview the inmate explained that prior to incarceration he was taking anti-psychotic medication and has a psychiatric history. Using DSM-IV-TR the social worker diagnosed the inmate. The jail employs a part-time psychiatrist whereas the social worker is employed full-time. The social worker referred the inmate for psychiatric consultation, and as per jail procedures the CO and warden were notified of self-endangerment.

State and Federal Corrections Facilities

State corrections facilities are operated by state governments and federal corrections facilities are operated by the federal government. Inmates are incarcerated in these facilities for longer sentences than those in jails, and are incarcerated for felony offenses (i.e., homicide and robbery). The term *prison* is used to refer to state and federal corrections facilities instead of the term *jail* which is used only to refer to local facilities. Inmates incarcerated in state and federal facilities are referred to as prisoners. Their sentences range from one year to life in prison. Levels of security range from supermax prisons, the highest level of security, to maximum security, medium security, and minimum security. In 2004 the average prison sentence for a violent felony was 90 months, although prisoners actually served an average of 60 months (Durose & Langan, 2007). On the basis of the differences in the length of incarceration, social workers employed in state and federal facilities provide longer-term services than those in jails. West (2010) summarized the differences between jails and prisons:

Compared to jail facilities, prisons are longer-term facilities run by a state or the federal government and typically hold prisoners with sentences of more than 1 year. However, sentence length may vary by state. Connecticut, Rhode Island, Vermont, Delaware, Alaska, and Hawaii operate integrated systems which combine prisons and jails.

(p. 4)

Private Corrections Facilities

Private prisons are facilities that are not operated by states or the federal government but run by private agencies. The privatization of prisons began in the 1980s as a result of ineffective deterrence strategies, and the need for states or the federal government to operate these facilities at a lower cost thereby reducing correction expenditures (Albanese, 2008).

As of midyear 2005, Texas, Oklahoma, and Florida reported having a higher number of prisoners incarcerated in private facilities than other states. Combined, private facilities that incarcerated state prisoners had 74,684 prisoners, and those that held federal prisoners incarcerated 26,533 prisoners representing 6.7% of all state and federal prisoners. These numbers have been increasing since 2000 (Harrison & Beck, 2006).

Some evidence shows that private prisons may actually cost states more to operate than if the prisons were state-run. Moreover, some cost-saving approaches used in private prisons involve transferring prisoners who require costly health or mental health treatment out of private prisons. In effect, this reduces the costs incurred by private prisons and passes these costs on to state prisons that are required to pay for this care (Oppel, 2011). In this way it appears that private prisons are operated at lower costs.

Cost savings are not the primary goal for contracting with private prisons, and when costs are compared such comparisons are not easy to make. Prisons vary in terms of how long they have been operating, structural design, level of security and other services provided, and different cost accounting procedures. Few studies have been conducted that assess the cost savings of private prisons although the few available studies do not show any savings (McDonald, Fournier, Russell-Einhourn, & Crawford, 1998).

Corrections Services

Corrections facilities, regardless of type, struggle to balance supervising and controlling inmates with competing of rehabilitation, incapacitation, and retribution perspectives. In corrections facilities the main aims of COs are to supervise inmates. This includes transporting them safely to different locations in the facility. Rehabilitation is not the focus of their efforts. Rehabilitation services, such as counseling or vocational training, are provided not by COs, who form the largest group or corrections employees, but by a small number of civilian employees. These employees include educators, social workers, and other mental health professionals, faith workers, and medical and health care workers, among others.

Indeed, inmates are in need of varied health and mental health care, dental care, and rehabilitation services such as counseling, employment and educational services, and alcohol and substance abuse treatment while incarcerated. As we saw in Chapter 1, one of the primary reasons that former inmates recidivated was associated with committing new crimes which provided economic gains. Social workers provide a variety of services in jails and prisons that are helpful in this regard. These services can help inmates adjust upon reentering communities. It is essential that services continue upon release.

Communities with large numbers of people of color experience higher rates of poor health and illnesses. Willmott and van Olphen (2005) observed that these communities also have disproportionate incarceration rates, incarceration in turn increases existing health disparities, and inmates receive substandard medical care. These disparities further negatively affect communities and families. Indeed, helping inmates to qualify for health insurance pre-release or upon release, especially those diagnosed with health and mental health problems while incarcerated, can contribute to successful reentry (Visher & Courtney, 2007).

Mental Health Services

Ideally, inmates who receive mental health treatment prior to incarceration will continue to receive treatment while incarcerated. Conversely, inmates who receive mental health treatment while incarcerated will receive treatment without disruption upon release. Young (2002, 2007) reported the following 16 types of non-psychiatric mental health services provided by social workers in a county jail: crisis intervention, individual counseling, group work, assessment, follow-up, psychiatric referrals, referrals to nurses, social workers, and other providers, evaluation for jail housing units, consultation, discharge planning, responding to inmate self-referral to be seen by social worker, conducting of court-ordered evaluation, contact with the legal system, contact with a psychiatrist within the community, contact with inmates family and other support systems, and any other social work service not included in the previous 15 categories.

Health Care

Inmates experience higher rates of medical and mental health problems than the general population as a result of living as transients in crowded conditions, poverty, and high rates of intravenous drug use (Petersilia, 2000). Health problems such as mobility, hearing, speech, and vision impairments, as well as chronic illnesses, mental illness, and terminal illness require unique housing units within prisons and jails that take into account these problems (Anno, Graham, Lawrence, Shansky, Bisbee, & Blackmore, 2004).

More linkages are needed between corrections and community-based health services, and case management services are necessary to meet prisoners' health care needs within communities (Freudenberg, 2004). Upon reentry, inmates with infectious and chronic diseases, substance abuse, and mental health problems return to low-income communities where these problems are exacerbated owing to lack of access to health care and the effects of ineffective reentry policies (Freudenberg, Daniels, Crum, Perkins, & Richie, 2005).

In a report to Congress, the National Commission on Correctional Health Care (2002) identified numerous barriers to preventing, screening, and treating diseases among inmates. The list included:

- unwillingness of public health agencies to advocate for improving correctional health or collaborating to promote health improvement;
- failure to recognize the need for improved health care services;
- short periods of incarceration;
- security-conscious administration procedures for distributing medication;
- poor discharge planning;
- inadequate funds to meet health care service needs including medication costs, and
- delays caused by the need to escort inmates by correctional personnel.

(p. xiv)

Dental Care

Owing to substance abuse, tobacco use, and poor dental hygiene, offenders require dental care to address a variety of dental needs. Morse and Kerr (2006) conducted a study to examine oral and pharyngeal cancer, mortality, and survival rates among Black and White Americans. They found that rates of oral and pharyngeal cancer were highest among Black males, who also experienced a mortality rate 82% higher than White males and the lowest survival rates over a six-year period.

Morse and Kerr conclude that dentists can reduce these disparities by adding to their course of dental therapy prevention and cessation assistance for smoking and alcohol abuse. Because of the disproportionate numbers of Black males who are incarcerated it is imperative that these dental needs be addressed in corrections facilities.

Substance Abuse Treatment

As Table 5.1 shows, the majority of state prisoners reported using drugs in the month prior to committing a crime, and about half of federal prisoners used drugs in the month prior to committing a crime. More than half of state prisoners, and 45% of federal prisoners, met the DSM-IV criteria for either drug dependence or drug abuse. These numbers remained nearly unchanged from 2004 to 2007 (Mumola & Karberg, 2006). These statistics underscore the need for substance abuse treatment in prisons.

Therapeutic Community (TC) treatment is well suited for adaptation and implementation in prisoners and jails. In these settings inmates are immersed in a total treatment environment where they are separated from prison violence, drugs, and other prison factors that can negatively impact treatment success (Inciardi, Martin, & Butzin, 2004). Key components of the TC model involve the prisoner beginning treatment while

Table 5.1 State and Federal Prisoner Drug Use Before and During a Crime (%)

	2004	2007
Drug use in the month prior to committing a crime		
State prisoners	56	57
Federal prisoners	50	45
Substance use at the time of committing a crime		
State prisoners	32	33
Federal prisoners	26	22

Adapted from Mumola, C. J., & Karberg, J. C. (2006). *Drug use and dependence, State and Federal prisons.* Washington, DC: U.S. Department of Justice, Office of Justice Programs, Bureau of Justice Statistics.

incarcerated then transitioning to community care after release. TC is the most effective treatment for substance abuse, and cost benefits can be derived from utilizing TC when the level of TC is matched to the level of offending (Lipton, 1998).

Several studies sampled more than 65,000 participants who received services in publicly funded treatment settings, including TC programs and short-term inpatient and detoxification programs. Data collected at admission and 12 months or more after completing treatment indicate that those who participated in TC reported less substance use, criminal behavior, unemployment, and depression (National Institute on Drug Abuse, 2002). De Leon (1998) summarized the effects of prison-based TC programs: (1) TC is effective with criminal justice populations for reducing drug use and criminal behavior, (2) modified in-prison and in-jail TC programs reduce recidivism and drug use relapse, (3) modified in-prison TC programs show the greatest and most consistent reductions in recidivism and substance abuse relapse when combined with community-based treatment, and (4) community-based programs that are linked with in-prison treatments are effective.

Educational Programs

Educational programs as a component of rehabilitation are intended to provide inmates with educational credentials that will qualify them for employment or to pursue higher education upon release. Little is known about the effects of correctional educational programs on recidivism. Some studies show that educational programs reduce recidivism whereas others do not (MacKenzie, 2006).

More opportunities are needed for offenders to pursue higher education while incarcerated, as well as for former offenders. Pell Grants provide financial assistance for pursuing higher education although a ban has been instituted on prisoners receiving federal Pell Grants. Numerous groups are advocating that the ban be lifted (Abdul-Alim, 2010). Barriers to higher education may be a contributing factor to recidivism.

Employment Training Programs

Numerous forms of corrections-based employment programs exist. Some programs employ inmates in positions such as cooking meals, whereas others train inmates for work or trades upon release. Wilson, Gallagher, & MacKenzie (2000) conducted a meta-analysis to examine the effects of education, vocation, and in-prison work programs on post-release employment and recidivism rates. Because of the quasi-experimental nature of the study designs, the analysis did not support a reduction in recidivism rates. However, the authors concluded that although the results were inconclusive such programs can be beneficial for increasing psychological well-being, earning ability, and participation in non-criminal behavior.

Family Programs

Family programs assist mothers and fathers and their children with maintaining bonding and family ties during incarceration. These programs have the potential to enhance the reunification process upon release because visitations occurred during incarceration at which time parents and their children were not estranged. Hairston (2001) noted that caretakers who have care for the children during incarceration, corrections officials, and social service workers oppose corrections visitations for children. Opposition centers on beliefs that children should not have contact with certain offenders, a prison setting is not a place for children, and children who visit prisons may normalize prisons as part of their experiences. Despite these oppositions, Hairston also notes that no empirical evidence supports these views although evidence does support maintaining parent–child relationships.

Correctional Social Work

Correctional social work is an area of practice in which the social worker provides services in juvenile justice, works in military prison settings, or provides services to individuals on probation and parole supervision. Correctional social workers also provide a wide variety of rehabilitation services related to alcohol and substance abuse, and conduct mental health assessments in correctional facilities (Stoesen, 2004). These functions are also provided by workers who do not hold social work degrees but hold degrees in counseling, sociology, psychology, or criminal justice. As mentioned elsewhere in this book, "social worker" may not be included in the job title for these reasons.

Correctional social workers must adhere to the same ethical values as social workers employed in other settings, but correctional settings present unique ethical issues. One challenge is to provide advocacy in a correctional environment for inmates who have been convicted of serious crimes. Second, social workers must fulfill the mandates of the correctional institution while simultaneously providing services to inmates (Severson, 1994). Severson summed up correctional social work practice quite well in stating

"Social workers who believe that prison administrators and correctional officers are uncaring and philosophically opposed to social work values will have considerable difficulty working in a jail or prison system" (p. 543).

Anti-oppressive Practice with Incarcerated Individuals

Social workers experience difficulty functioning in correctional settings not only because of differences in values between social work and corrections officials but also because correctional settings (including community-based corrections) are viewed as oppressive settings. Dominelli (2002) took an interesting perspective on oppression, asserting that all individuals are oppressed, including the wealthy. The clients whom social workers help may oppress others while at the same time experiencing their own oppression; social workers themselves may be oppressed while at the same time oppressing their clients while simultaneously providing empowerment services.

The aforementioned framework requires that social workers rethink the concept of oppression and what it means to avoid practicing in settings they may view as oppressive. It also requires creative solutions to practice in settings characterized by oppression. For example, Pollack (2004) suggested that peer support be used as a method to integrate anti-oppressive practice for women in prison settings.

Community-based Corrections

Former offenders under the jurisdiction of community-based corrections must comply with sanctions intended as punishment that place conditions on their behavior. As such, community-based corrections take on two forms:

1. Sanctions that are *alternatives to incarceration* in jail or prison, such as monetary penalties, probation, intensive supervision, and home confinement with electronic monitoring.
2. Supervision in the community *after a sentence of incarceration* has been served. Here the goal is to promote a smooth transition from confinement to freedom. Parole, work release, furloughs, and halfway houses fall into this category.

(Albanese, 2008, p. 392)

Prisoner Reentry

Reentry is a component of community-based corrections. Some former offenders may receive community supervision (parole) after release from prison, whereas others will no longer be under the jurisdiction of the correctional system and will not be mandated to comply with conditions for release. Thus, reentry is associated with community-based supervision or having no mandated conditions after release from a corrections facility, usually a prison. The majority of jail and prison inmates are eventually released.

Consequently they will return to most often the communities where they lived prior to incarceration. Reentry has become such an important issue that former President Bush proposed in his 2004 State of the Union Address to allocate $300 million over a four-year period to provide reentry services (Office of Justice Programs, n.d.).

Reentry has been defined in several ways. Most definitions emphasize the programs and services provided to incarcerated individuals to enhance their functioning upon release. The primary aims of reentry are to reduce recidivism, improve employability, or increase community support depending upon the specific program goals (Solomon, Palmer, Atkinson, Davidson, & Harvey, 2006). Hughes & Wilson (2002) defined reentry as the process of transitioning prisoners to community-based supervision. Seiter & Kadela (2003) defined prisoner reentry as "correctional programs (U.S. and Canada) that focus on the transition from prison to community (prerelease, work release, halfway houses, or specific reentry programs) and programs that have initiated treatment (substance abuse, life skills, education, cognitive/behavioral, sex/violent offender) in a prison setting and have linked with a community program to provide continuity of care" (p. 368). Petersilia (2003) suggested that reentry is "all activities and programming conducted to prepare exconvicts to return safely to the community and to live as law abiding citizens" (p. 3). Finally, Solomon, Palmer, Atkinson, Davidson, & Harvey (2006) described reentry in terms of programs that provide services in specific areas such as employment or housing services, and are both prison-based and community-based.

Case Example

A 34-year-old female was recently released on parole from prison for a drug offense. She is the mother of three children ages 5, 7, and 17. She is in need of substance abuse treatment and housing. A social worker made calls to emergency shelters with available room for Samantha and her children. Many emergency shelters would not admit Samantha because she was not a victim of domestic violence. Samantha wanted to be reunited with her children who were being cared for by her mother. Her mother was finding it difficult to get the children ready for school and assisting them with homework and other needs. The mother experiences health problems but agreed to take care of the children during Samantha's incarceration because she wanted the children to be together and be cared for by a family member. The only possible housing option was an emergency facility that would not accept children older than 12, thereby not accepting teenagers in order to create a comfortable and safe environment for women and young children. Moreover, the facility could accommodate only two children per parent.

This example illustrates some of the issues faced by mothers after release from prison. Reentry is difficult not only for offenders but also for children and other family members. Housing is a need that many women have. Although family members provide support during incarceration, in many situations family support can not be sustained long-term including upon reentry. Naser and La Vigne (2006) found that former male prisoners relied exclusively upon their family members for housing, financial assistance, and emotional support during reentry.

Assessing Reentry Rates

The number of former offenders reentering communities is estimated by counting the number of state and federal prisoners who are released within a one-year period. Using this approach, the number of released prisoners increased during the period from 1980 to 2000. Releases increased from approximately 170,000 offenders in 1980 to 585,000 in 2000. A second approach counts the number of former offenders who are on parole at any given time point (Lynch & Sabol, 2001). This approach indicates that the number of former offenders receiving post-release supervision more than tripled between 1980 and 1999, from 222,000 to 713,000. The two approaches yield two entirely different reentry estimates. Despite the discrepancy in reentry estimates obtained from the two approaches, clearly the reentry rate has steadily increased since 1980.

Mapping Reentry Rates

Neighborhoods with high rates of reentry can be identified using zip code data. In 2002, the Urban Institute established the Reentry Mapping Network (RMN) (La Vigne & Cowan, 2006). RMN is a partnership between the Urban Institute and community-based organizations that utilizes neighborhood-level mapping and data analysis to identify reentry and community well-being patterns that become the focus for interventions (Urban Institute, 2008).

Using this approach in Maryland the data showed that among 59% of released prisoners who returned to the City of Baltimore in 2001, 30% were released into six neighborhoods (Harrison & Beck, 2006). Another example found that during 2002, among 95% of the prisoners who were released from Georgia prisons, 43% were released to eight counties and 9% were released in Atlanta. Released prisoners primarily returned to five Atlanta neighborhoods. Demographic data show that these neighborhoods also experienced a higher percentage of families living in poverty, unemployment, and female-headed households when compared to other Atlanta neighborhoods (La Vigne & Mamalian, 2004). These demographic data are typical of the neighborhoods where large numbers of prisoners are released, although some neighborhoods in Cleveland were located in or near working-class neighborhoods (Lynch & Sabol, 2001).

Former prisoners are released into communities that are the least able to provide services and support (La Vigne & Kachnowski, 2003). Within these communities former prisoners are more likely to receive parole supervision and monitoring instead of services (Seiter & Kadela, 2003). On the basis of most recent data, California, Florida, Illinois, New York, and Texas accounted for approximately half of the releases from state prisons in 2001. Prisoners from these five states were released to 50 counties that accounted for 38% of these releases; 18 counties were located in California, five in Florida, and four each in New Jersey, New York, and Texas (Hughes & Wilson, 2002).

Unquestionably the majority of these communities are characterized by large numbers of residents who are people of color living in poverty. Marbley & Ferguson (2005) observed that African American and Latino families and communities have been disproportionately impacted by prisoner incarceration, reentry, and recidivism. Iguchi, London, Gorge, Hickman, Fain, & Riehman (2002) reported that reentry disproportionately impacted minority communities where drug offenders experienced higher rates of recidivism. As a result of incarceration these communities experienced poorer child–family relationships, inaccessibility to health care, housing benefits, and higher education assistance, deportation of immigrants convicted of drug felonies, lack of employment opportunities, voting restrictions due to felony convictions, and recidivism resulting from substance use.

A great deal of information can be gleaned from the RMN approach that has implications for social work practice at micro, meso, and macro levels. For instance, at the micro practice level services that address poverty and unemployment may be needed in communities. Implications for meso-level practice include agencies and programs that provide reentry services, and macro-level interventions suggest legislative strategies.

Reentry Barriers

The lack of sufficient services and programs for the large numbers of former offenders who require them is a major barrier to successful reentry. Whether prison-based or community-based, the majority of offenders do not receive or participate in needed programs. Insufficient funding restricts the provision of services to large numbers of released prisoners and confines services to specific areas (Travis, Keegan, Cadora, Solomon, & Swartz, 2003), and former prisoners need for services is often greater than the capacity of a program to provide services (Solomon, Palmer, Atkinson, Davidson, & Harvey, 2006).

A barrier to reentry that is worthy of note is high-security segregation requiring prisoners to be housed in units separate from other prisoners and sometimes locked alone in cells for as much as 23 hours a day. Isolation provides no or few opportunities for prisoners to receive reentry services and upon release they return directly to communities. Between 1995 and 2000, the growth rate in the number of prisoners who were placed in segregated housing was 40% which outpaced the 28% growth rate in the prison population (Gibbons & Katzenbach, 2006). Although these practices may aid correctional authorities, they offer little to prepare prisoners for successful reentry.

Numerous barriers present challenges to successful reentry (Lynch & Sabol, 2001; Petersilia, 2003). The National Governors Association (NGA) (2005) also noted that reentry has an adverse effect on former prisoners, social service systems, and communities. NGA identified five crucial barriers to successful reentry: (1) the risk factors associated with release (substance abuse, mental illness, chronic disease, HIV/AIDS, lack of education, high unemployment, homelessness); (2) legal barriers to receiving public services such as bans on receiving public assistance, public housing restrictions and limited transitional housing options, and difficulty obtaining state-issued identification; (3) poor coordination between social service systems which may negatively affect parole conditions; (4) high parole officer caseloads and an inadequate response to parole violations; and (5) the lack of alternative sentencing options and sanctions such as half-way houses for those who reoffend or violate parole conditions. Without alternative options many offenders are likely to be reincarcerated.

NGA also proposed a total of 29 strategies for governors and other state policy-makers to implement that have the potential to increase the chances of successful reentry and improve the reentry process. A sample of these strategies includes addressing reentry as a public safety concern instead of only a concern for corrections, developing state-wide interdisciplinary reentry policy committees, identifying and involving key constituents in the reentry process, and enhancing how prisoners are prepared in prison for release.

Public Health Issues

Former prisoners during reentry have been described as a *public safety* risk and a *public health* risk to communities (Lynch & Sabol, 2001; Petersilia, 2000, 2001; Stoesen, 2004; Travis, 2005; Travis , Keegan, Cadora, Solomon, & Swartz, 2003). This is due in large part to their poor health status and potential to reoffend.

For instance, a study of all prisoners released from the Washington State Department of Corrections from July 1999 through December 2003 found that, of the 30,237 released prisoners, 443 died during their first 1.9 years of release. The overall mortality rate was 777 deaths per 100,000 person-years. The leading causes of death were drug overdose, cardiovascular disease, homicide, and suicide. The risk of death among former prisoners was 3.5 times that among other state residents, during their first two weeks after release. The risk of death among former prisoners was 12.7 times that of other state residents, with a higher risk of death from drug overdose (Binswanger, Stern, Deyo, Heagerty, Cheadle, Elmore, & Koepsell, 2007).

Parole

Some parole officers are also social workers. Practitioners employed in these roles face some of the same challenges as social workers employed in other corrections settings. Providing services to individuals under parole supervision raises numerous ethical and practical issues. These issues are often associated with the purpose of parole.

Parole is "a period of conditional supervised release following a prison term. Prisoners may be released to parole either by a parole board decision (discretionary parole) or according to provisions of a statute (mandatory parole)" (Hughes, Wilson, & Beck, 2001, p. 2). In 1995, the total population on parole in federal, state, and local jurisdictions combined was 679,421. By 2006, the population had increased to 798,202 (Glaze & Bonczar, 2007). Prior to the 1980s, most state prisoners received parole after serving a portion of their original sentences (discretionary release to parole). During the 1980s, a shift occurred as states began to implement determinate sentences and mandatory parole. By 1989, eight states had ended the use of discretionary release to parole. During the 1990s, discretionary releases to parole accounted for 39% of state prison releases. By 2000, the number of prisoners receiving discretionary release decreased to 24% of state prisoners, 16 states abolished the use of discretionary release, and four eliminated parole for certain crimes. In 20 states the majority of prison releases were mandatory parole release and the use of mandatory parole among jurisdictions increased from 29% of all state prison releases to 41% in 1999. Consequently mandatory parole has become the most common type of release from state prisons (Hughes, Wilson & Beck, 2001).

Prisoners are released in one of two ways: conditional release, or unconditional release. *Conditional releases* are granted when prisoners are released to parole supervision and required to comply with specific parole conditions. If any of the conditions of release are violated the former offender can be reincarcerated. The majority of prisoners (80%) are released from prison with a conditional release to parole supervision (Hughes & Wilson, 2002).

Two types of conditional release can be granted. The first, a *discretionary release*, is granted when a prisoner is conditionally released after review by a parole board or similar authorized entity. The second type of release, a *mandatory release*, is granted when a prisoner is conditionally released after serving some part of the original sentence. Jurisdictions that grant mandatory releases also tend to grant determinate sentences, and presently 40% of former offenders receive a mandatory release. Determinate sentences are predetermined sentences that are reduced only by applying good time served or other credit that reduces the sentence (Solomon, Kachnowski, & Bhati, 2005).

Unconditional release is granted to prisoners who serve their entire prison sentence. Prisoners are released only at the end of their original sentence. After completing a sentence, a prisoner is released. No conditions are imposed on the release (i.e., parole or monitoring). Moreover, the release can not be rescinded since no conditions were imposed upon release (Solomon, Kachnowski, & Bhati, 2005).

Three primary agencies are responsible for prisoners' release: corrections (e.g., jails and prisons); agencies that are responsible for release and oversees release and parole revocation decisions (i.e., a parole board); and supervision agencies within the community (e.g., parole department). Generally the transition process from prison to the community consists of seven components: assessment and classification, plans that involve transitional accountability, release decisions, community-based supervision and services, mechanisms to respond to release violations, mechanisms to terminate the terms of supervision and jurisdiction, and aftercare and community-based services (National Institute of Corrections, 2002).

Some research has provided information about parole success rates. Among state parole releases in 2000, 41% successfully completed their term of parole supervision, whereas 42% were returned to prison or jail, and 9% absconded from parole. The parole nonsuccess rate was 51%. Half of the ex-prisoners reentering the community under state parole supervision are not successfully completing parole supervision (Langan & Levin, 2002). In a study investigating recidivism rates among 108,580 released prisoners who were tracked in 11 states in 1983, results show that 62.5% were rearrested within three years (Beck & Shipley, 1989). A later study followed 272,111 released prisoners in 15 states in 1994 and found that 67.5% were rearrested within three years, and that the rearrest rate increased during the period 1983 to 1994 from 50.4% to 66.7% for drug offenders (Langan & Levin, 2002).

Probation

Similarly to the situation with parole, some probation officers are also social workers. These social workers are both adult and juvenile probation officers. Chapter 8 reviews a job announcement intended for social workers describing a probation officer position with the U.S. Probation Department. Offenders are also required to comply with conditions of probation. A sample of such conditions is also reviewed in Chapter 8.

Probation is an imposed sanction of community-based supervision, often combined with other sanctions such as community service, used as an alternative to incarceration. The first probation officer, John Augustus, was a shoemaker in Boston, MA, who petitioned courts to sentence homeless individuals and those with alcohol problems to his custody and care. He provided a range of rehabilitative services. As a result of his activities, in 1878 Massachusetts was the first state to implement probation legislation and provide salaries for probation officers (Cromwell and Killinger, as cited in Butts, 2008). Since that time the use of probation has dramatically increased nationwide. In 1995 the total population on probation in federal, state, and local jurisdictions combined was 3,077,861. By 2006, the population had increased to 4,237,023 (Glaze & Bonczar, 2007).

Some of the duties of probation officers as articulated in a job announcement include carrying a gun, conducting investigations and enforcement, conducting field visits in dangerous neighborhoods, executing warrants, and taking probationers into custody who are wanted by law enforcement officials. Social workers holding both undergraduate and graduate degrees qualify for this position and are specifically referenced in the announcement, among individuals holding degrees in education, law, sociology, psychology, criminology, counseling, and other related degrees (New York City Department of Citywide Administrative Services, 2005). A probation officer position does not appeal to large numbers of social workers, particularly those who have an interest in providing clinical services to treat mental health issues.

Implications for Social Work Practice

Social workers practice in corrections settings that range from institutional to community-based settings. Similarly to the issues raised in Chapter 3 regarding collaboration between police social workers and police officers, when social workers collaborate with corrections officers or other corrections practitioners, similar challenges can arise. Some challenges are associated with social work practice in host settings, whereas others are associated with practice in authoritarian settings. Challenges can be heightened according to the priorities of each occupation. For instance, differences in criminal justice perspectives are likely to result in conflict as correctional offices emphasize safety and control of inmates whereas social workers emphasize rehabilitation services.

Also, similarly to the issues presented in Chapter 1 regarding law enforcement stress, correctional officers experience stress stemming from the correctional organizational environment (i.e., shift work) and aspects of their work (i.e., managing inmate violence) (Finn, 2000). Reducing officer work and life stress through the provision of effective stress management interventions can improve their functioning within correctional facilities and at home.

Whereas some literature describes stress management for law enforcement provided by social workers, providing stress management training to correctional officers is a relatively unexplored area of social work practice. A similar need is noted for probation and parole officers.

Social workers must be cautious not to become coopted and guard against cynicism. This conduct can have an adverse affect on inmates, parolees, or probationers. Self-awareness, use of consultation and supervision, and continuing education can be useful in this regard.

Correctional social workers must be skilled at balancing social control with social change, and coercion efforts used to manage inmates with treatment and punishment perspectives (Chaiklin, 2008). Moreover, upon release former prisoners are considered a public safety risk and a public health risk to communities (Stoesen, 2004). Social workers must also be comfortable using an inmate classification and offender management systems that assign housing units and treatment on the basis of classification level and risk-need classification schemas that assign community-based treatments according to the level of risk for reoffending.

Finally, the NASW *Code of ethics* states that social workers can limit individuals' right to self-determination when their behaviors or future behaviors create a threat to themselves or others. It can be argued that offenders and former offenders who commit chronic and serious violent offenses, and those classified as high risk for reoffending pose threats to public safety. This limiting of their right to self-determination can reduce the potential for further criminal behavior. Whereas social workers can use their professional judgment to make such determinations, in correctional settings these decisions are frequently made by other practitioners.

Chapter Summary

In this chapter, we examined institutional and community-based components of the correctional system. Among formerly incarcerated offenders, a seamless transition from institutional services to community-based services is necessary to enhance post-release functioning and well-being. This is not always the case since some incarcerated offenders do not receive necessary services, and upon release some communities lack adequate services. Post-release community-based services are important to provide regardless of whether former offenders are granted conditional or unconditional releases. Community-based corrections, as an alternative to incarceration, also require that offenders participate in programs or services. Without programs and services such as education and job opportunities, offenders face a higher risk of reoffending.

Key Terms

Anti-oppressive practice	Jail	Probation
Community-based supervision	Parole	Prison
Correctional social work	Private corrections facilities	Reentry
Inmate		

Questions for Review

1. Describe the corrections system. Be sure to include institutional and community-based corrections settings and provide examples of each type of setting. What are the goals of institutional and community-based corrections?
2. Why is it important for inmates to receive a range of correctional services within prisons and jails? What are the potential consequences of not providing correctional services?
3. In this chapter, reentry was discussed. What do you think about the circumstances of former offenders who return to communities where few employment opportunities, inadequate housing, and high crime rates exist?
4. Which area of corrections interests you the most and why? Identify a criminal justice perspective(s) from Chapter 1 that you feel is relevant to the corrections setting you chose.
5. How would you balance the goals of corrections with social work values?

Further Reading

Blakely, C. R. (2005). *America's prisons: The movement toward profit and privatization.* Boca Raton, FL: BrownWalker Press.

Clear, T. R., Cole, G. F., & Reisig, M. D. (2009). *American corrections.* Belmont, CA: Thomson Wadsworth.

Cree, V. E. (2010). *Sociology for social workers and probation officers* (2nd ed.). London: Taylor & Francis, Inc.

Scott, D. (2010). *Controversial issues in prisons.* Berkshire, U.K.: McGraw-Hill, Open University Press.

6 | Alternative Criminal Justice Reforms and Programs

Chapter Overview

In this chapter alternative criminal justice reforms and programs are reviewed. The purpose of this chapter is not to provide an exhaustive review of reforms and programs, but instead to introduce readers to such efforts. The reforms and programs described in this chapter were selected on the basis of documented sources. These efforts are consistent with the mission and values of the social work profession. As such, they strive to ensure justice, protect public safety, and improve the efficiency of the criminal justice system. The efficacy of some reforms and programs is presently unknown, and many more are presently being evaluated. It is essential that social workers be knowledgeable about alternative reform and program efforts. Indeed, they have the potential to transform the criminal justice system.

The Need for Alternative Criminal Justice Reforms and Programs

Alterative criminal justice reforms and programs are necessary for several reasons. First, all four components of the criminal justice system require reform to ensure fairness and justice, increase the efficiency and effectiveness of the criminal justice system, and protect public safety. The system should not be static and, on the basis of available data, changes should be made to address problematic issues. Second, the criminal justice system should address the underlying causes of crime. Unless underlying causes are addressed, some offenders are likely to continue patterns of criminal behavior. Accordingly, alternative programs and services for individuals who require specialized interventions are being offered to enhance criminal justice outcomes, improve efficiency, and in some situations as a cost-saving measure. Finally, as a consequence of violent crime, high recidivism rates, relapse to substance and alcohol abuse, extensive criminal records and histories of reoffending, as well as racial disparities in the criminal justice system, policymakers and practitioners seek alternative programs that have the goals of addressing these problem areas and improving the effectiveness and efficiency of the criminal justice system.

Among the numerous benefits derived from penal reform is the potential to humanize prisons, increase efficiency, and increase public safety (Blakely, 2007). As a result of jail and prison overcrowding, and the failure of the correctional system to rehabilitate offenders, judges impose alternative sentencing options. Judges can use their discretion to consider a range of alternative sentencing options such as imposing fines, house confinement, or community-based treatment (Phelps, 2002). Police officers can also consider alternatives to arrest. Most alternatives provided by law enforcement are offered to juveniles. By considering alternatives and not taking juveniles into custody, police officers can divert them away from the criminal justice system. Advantages include saving the costs of processing minor offenses and leaving resources available to process more serious juvenile offenses (Gottfredson & Gottfredson, 1988). In Connecticut, police officers are authorized to use five documented options in their response to juveniles: issue a warning only, release the juvenile to the custody of his or her parents, provide a referral to a community-based agency, provide a referral to a formalized youth diversion program, or take the juvenile into custody (Office of Policy and Management, 2011).

To avoid abuses of police discretion, it is important to monitor which groups of juveniles are diverted away from the juvenile justice system as compared with those who are formally processed and do not receive diversion options. *Discretion* refers to the ability to make choices and decisions. While the study did not examine race, social class, neighborhood characteristics, or police departmental policies regarding mandates to take youth into custody, Allen (2005) found five factors that shaped police officers' decisions to take youth into custody. These five factors were: (1) whether youth showed disrespect toward the officer, (2) whether youth were socializing on the streets late at night, (3) whether youth were behaving in a suspicious manner, (4) the youth's gender, and (5) the police officer's age. Allen found that youth who showed disrespect toward an officer were four times more likely than those who did not to be taken into custody, suspicious-appearing youth were two times more likely to be taken into custody, suspicious-appearing youth who were out late at night were three times more likely to be taken into custody, and officers who took youth into custody were less than 34 years old. Police officers who were older and had acquired more police experience were less likely to take youth into custody on the basis of these criteria.

Clearly, the potential exists for abuse of discretion. In other words, discretion may not be applied equitably among all juveniles. Moreover, the use of discretion can be highly subjective as officers consider youths' deportment. Without general orders that mandate police officers to respond in a consistent manner abuses of discretion can occur.

Some alternative criminal justice programs intended to provide services to individuals involved in the criminal justice system are mandated through legislation. Legislation provides funding and establishes the goals and purpose of a program or services. Whereas legislation and programs or services are linked, a distinction is made between criminal justice reforms and programs. As used throughout this chapter, the term *criminal justice reforms* refers to changes or modifications to policies or practices through legislative efforts. For instance, the American Civil Liberties Union (ACLU) is very involved in criminal justice reform efforts and advocacy for the civil rights of individuals involved in the criminal justice system, often through legislative efforts (ACLU, n.d.). The term *alternative criminal justice programs* refers to those programs and services specific to criminal justice populations and their problem situations. For example, the Phoenix House website points out that the agency has a long record of providing innovative criminal justice services and programs for individuals involved with the system. These services are offered in a variety of criminal justice settings to both juvenile and adult criminal justice populations, as well as individuals who are mandated to community-based treatment as an alternative to incarceration. Of special note are the agency's services for persons with co-occurring mental health problems and gender-specific services. Their website further suggests that community-based treatments are less expensive than incarceration in correctional facilities

Implementing reform efforts in the criminal justice system is a difficult task. The difficulties result from managing large caseloads that practitioners in the criminal justice system are required to handle, utilizing outdated technology, working in poor facilities, and managing the multiple and varied social problems that criminal justice populations experience such as mental illness, homelessness, and substance abuse. Developing and implementing criminal justice reforms requires time which criminal justice practitioners such as judges, probation officers, and prosecutors do not have since they are active managing these issues which allows little time to explore innovative approaches to reform (Fox & Gold, 2010). In addition criminal justice practitioners can not resolve these complex social problems without the input of other disciplines.

The reforms and programs reviewed in this chapter are not intended to be an exhaustive list. Throughout the country innovative reform efforts and programs have been implemented that could fill an entire book, not just a chapter. Moreover, some of the topics previously discussed in this book represent alternative programs. Specialty or problem-solving courts are an example.

Criminal Justice Reforms

The Fair Sentencing Act

The Fair Sentencing Act was signed into law by President Obama on August 3, 2010. Sentencing for crack cocaine and powder cocaine has a history of unequal sentencing that has resulted in racial (and economic) disparities. The purpose of this legislation is to ensure that fair sentences are imposed for offenders. The legislation increases the amount of crack cocaine needed in one's possession in order to impose the mandatory minimum sentences, and eliminates the five-year mandatory minimum sentences imposed for first-time offenders convicted for crack cocaine possession (GovTrack.us, n.d.). The mandatory five-year minimum federal sentencing legislation has resulted in racial disparities in which people of color have received harsher sentences for crack cocaine convictions than Whites for powder cocaine sentences. These disparities should have been anticipated prior to enactment of mandatory minimum legislation (The Sentencing Project, 2008).

A proposal submitted to the U.S. Sentencing Commission seeks to retroactively apply the sentencing guidelines outlined in the Fair Sentencing Act to prisoners who have not used weapons during crimes and those without extensive criminal histories. If this is approved, many prison sentences will be reduced by an average of three years (Serrano, Savage, & Williams, 2011).

Racial Disparity Reform at the State Level

Observing the racial disparities throughout Wisconsin's criminal justice system, on March 22, 2007, former Wisconsin Governor Doyle signed an Executive Order to create the Commission on Reducing Racial Disparities in Wisconsin's Criminal Justice System. Members were appointed from faith-based organizations, community businesses, and various components of the criminal justice system. The Wisconsin criminal justice system ranks among one of the highest state criminal justice systems in the country with a disproportionate number of people of color having criminal justice system involvement, and African American youth are incarcerated at rates almost 20 times that of White youth. The charge of the Commission is to assess whether these events are the result of discrimination in each of the components of the Wisconsin criminal justice system and to develop approaches to eliminate racial disparities (Wisconsin Department of Corrections, 2007).

Health Care Reform

Many offenders experience health, mental health, and substance abuse problems that are inadequately treated in part because of lack of health insurance. Most incarcerated offenders will be ineligible for health care coverage under the *Patient Protection and Affordable Care Act* (ACA) (H.R. 3590) (also known as the health care reform bill) signed into law by President Obama on March 23, 2010. However, pre-trial detainees and released offenders will be eligible for health care coverage in QHPs and SHPs (qualified health plans and standard health plans). It is anticipated that the ACA will provide offenders with much-needed health care coverage (Blair, Greifinger, Stone, & Somers, 2011). These provisions are dependent upon a Supreme Court decision expected in 2012 that will determine the constitutionality of the ACA.

Impact Legislation

Calling attention to the relationship between school-to-prison and school dropout rates among youth in Texas, Fowler, Lightsey, Monger, Terrazas, & White (2007) reported that the dropout rate among students attending alternative educational programs that provide discipline is five times that of mainstream schools, over one-third of the youth in the Texas public school system dropped out of school in 2005–2006, and one in every three youth who were referred to the Texas Youth Commission and over 80% of the inmates in Texas prisons are school dropouts. They also reported that African American youth were referred more than any other group to alternative educational programs that provide discipline and were more likely to be suspended. In some school districts these rates were 21% to 65%, representing more than twice the proportion of African American students enrolled in the Texas public school system. It seems that the school district a student attended was more associated with these racial disparities than the type of the offense that resulted in disciplinary action or juvenile justice system referrals.

Kim, Losen, & Hewitt (2010) described the school-to-prison pipeline as a situation in which the K-12 public educational system and juvenile justice system fail to serve at-risk youth. This phenomenon occurs as a result of the treatment that youth receive in public schools and inadequate educational resources. Overcrowded classrooms, racially segregated communities, insufficient school counselors, inadequate alternative schools, discrimination, inadequate services for special needs students, and harsh discipline policies including zero tolerance policies all contribute to youth being referred to the criminal justice system. In sum, educational policies, lack of educational recourses, and the juvenile justice system's emphasis on punishment as opposed to educational and mental health services result in youth having criminal justice system involvement.

Whereas Fowler, Lightsey, Monger, Terrazas, & White (2007) presented examples of best-practice models from research studies that emphasize interventions for the entire student body, the use of evidence-based interventions, training, and collaboration between teachers, parents, school, and community service providers, Kim, Losen, & Hewitt (2010) proposed reform efforts to address the school-to-prison phenomenon that places emphasis on impact litigation combined with grassroots organizing, legislative lobbying, and policy advocacy. Kim, Losen, & Hewitt support legislative amendments to states' definitions of what is meant by an "adequate education" and school resource litigation asserting that inadequate school resources are contributing factors to youths' involvement in the criminal justice system. These later approaches are congruent with the ecosystems perspective. Merely diverting youth away from the criminal justice system or providing interventions to youth and their families does little to change the environmental factors that contributed to criminal justice involvement. The school environment, including the lack of resources, should also be a focus for change. While changing environmental conditions is not an easy task, litigation provides a method for achieving change.

As mentioned, the juvenile justice system has been increasingly moving away from its original emphasis on rehabilitation towards punishment of juvenile offenders. This change developed as a result of increased juvenile violent crime and arrest rates, desires to hold youth accountable for their offenses, and deterrence as a method for reducing the juvenile crime rate (Bureau of Justice Assistance, 1998). In contrast, reform efforts are under way to restore the juvenile justice system to its original mission of rehabilitation, mainly to keep juveniles out of the adult criminal justice system, thereby remaining under the jurisdiction of the juvenile justice system.

Thus, reforms are under way that seek to keep youth under the jurisdiction of the juvenile justice system. In a review of legislative reforms enacted between 2005 and 2010, Arya (2011) stated that during this period approximately half of the states either enacted reform legislation or considered such legislation to remove juveniles from the jurisdiction of the adult criminal justice system. These innovative reforms have focused on four areas: (1) the removal of juveniles from adult and local and state jails and prisons, (2) raising the age for keeping juveniles within the jurisdiction of the juvenile court system, (3) reforming transfer laws so that juveniles remain under the jurisdiction of the juvenile court system, and (4) reevaluating juvenile sentencing laws. Similarly to these reforms, Arya urged policymakers to reform the juvenile justice system by: removing every juvenile from local and state jails and prisons, raising to age 18 the jurisdiction within the juvenile court system, reforming juvenile transfer legislation so that youth remain in the jurisdiction of the juvenile justice system, and eliminating mandatory minimum sentences for youth who have been tried and convicted in the adult criminal justice system.

Alternative Programs and Services

The majority of social workers practice in programs where they provide clinical and other services to individuals involved in the criminal justice system. Fewer social workers are directly involved in the abovementioned criminal justice reform efforts. Standard approaches to services when made available to criminal justice populations may not meet their needs. This occurs for a variety of reasons. First, the services may not be provided within a framework that acknowledges criminal behaviors. Second, court-imposed sanctions, while valuable as innovative alternatives to criminal justice involvement, may hinder individuals' ability to form an essential relationship for treatment. Finally, in addition to criminal justice considerations, demographic factors are also an important component to services.

Some organizations provide global services aimed at improving criminal justice outcomes. For example, the United Nations Office on Drugs and Crime (UNODC) maintains a Justice Section located within its Division of Operations. The purpose of the Justice Section is to provide assistance to countries throughout the world to address crime, drugs, and terrorism. The UNODC provides services that include: assessment of crime prevention activities and criminal justice systems, training, technical assistance, capacity building and development, and support for penal and judicial reforms among other services (United Nations Office on Drugs and Crime, 2010).

Law Enforcement

Problem-oriented policing is an innovative approach for police officers and law enforcement agencies to address social problems and aimed at improving policing (Goldstein, 1990). Problem-oriented policing is an approach that focuses on prevention, and relies more upon community members and public and private agencies instead of the criminal justice system to address community problems. It includes implementation and evaluation and dissemination aimed at making best problem-oriented policing available for adoption and review by law enforcement agencies. Awards are given to police officers and law enforcement agencies in the U.S. and U.K. that demonstrate effective application of innovative problem-oriented policing strategies (Center for Problem-Oriented Policing, 2011).

Courts

Alternative court programs have several aims. These include providing alternatives to adversarial litigation, reducing overcrowded court dockets, and reducing court costs. In essence, alternative court programs provide services to individuals who meet eligibility criteria and oftentimes are motivated to participate in alternative court programs.

The use of mediation and family group conferencing to resolve disputes has increased in the areas of child welfare and aging. This is particularly relevant for social work professionals who use these tools to better serve these populations. However, despite increased use of these conflict resolution techniques, few social work educational programs offer field placement opportunities or coursework in conflict resolution, and professional associations have not identified conflict resolution as an area of social work practice. It is anticipated that conflict resolution techniques will become an integral part of social work practice in the future (Mayer, 2008).

Mediation

Mediation is an alternative to the adversarial court system. It provides opportunities for individuals, groups, and communities to resolve their differences in a cooperative manner. Cases are referred for mediation by courts and other sources including law enforcement. A wide range of legal matters are referred and resolved through mediation. These include neighbor disputes, parent–child conflicts, and divorce cases, among others. It might be thought that because mediation is connected with the legal system, and because decisions made during the process are legally binding, only attorneys can perform mediation. In fact, this is not the case. Social workers as well as others can become certified mediators and practice mediation.

Numerous mediation centers have been established across the country. According to its website, the Center for Dispute Settlement (CDS) located in Rochester, NY, provides mediation services through the use of trained volunteers and consultants in the areas of divorce, child custody issues, and disputes with schools, businesses, police, and the criminal justice system. It also offers alternatives to violence. CDS was founded in 1973 by the American Arbitration Association as a nonprofit organization. CDS provides training and certification in mediation and arbitration, and offers several comprehensive community mediation programs (i.e., community mediation, arbitration, small claims mediation, and arbitration) and police programs (i.e., police complaint intake, law enforcement civilian oversight review, sheriff's review panel, police/community relations program, Kops n Kids). Its goals are to provide alternatives to dispute resolution for individuals, communities, and organizations without the adversarial litigation usually associated with court involvement although case findings are legally binding (Center for Dispute Settlement, 2011).

As mentioned above, CDS provides several alternatives to disputes with law enforcement officers. These alternative options include civilian oversight and review of misconduct by police and sheriff's officers, a conciliation program in which individuals who file a complaint against police officers can engage in the process of conciliation, and a police complaint intake process in which individuals can file a formal complaint against police officers. In the instance of oversight and review, complaints against officers have previously been investigated by the law enforcement agency and the civilian mediators subsequently review the complaints and departmental outcomes. Mediator recommendations are then forwarded to the police chief. This process provides opportunities for community members to offer input into these complaints and point out how the officer's actions affected the individual(s) and the community (Center for Dispute Settlement, 2011).

Divorce Mediation

Divorce mediation is a special type of mediation specifically focused on divorce issues, providing an alternative to court involvement. In this type of mediation the emphasis is kept on divorce matters such as property issues, child custody, and visitation issues, and expressing feelings for example. Social workers can also receive training to perform as certified divorce mediators. One of the primary benefits for couples who participate in divorce mediation is practicing the right to self-determination (Elkin, 1987). Therefore, the practice of divorce mediation is consistent with the ethical standards of social work practice relative to self-determination. Social workers help individuals to identify and fulfill their own objectives, and in the process of divorce mediation assisting couples with this process not only involves social workers in alternatives to the court system but does so in a way that is in agreement with the ethical standards of professional social work.

Arbitration

Unlike mediation, which is applied to a variety of disputes and legal matters, *arbitration* has a much narrower focus. Arbitration is also a process used to resolve legal disputes, and case findings are legally binding and determined by a trained arbitrator. Arbitration is most often used for employee–employer disputes and disputes with businesses. Social workers can also receive training and become certified to conduct arbitration. For example, a complainant whose car was damaged by an automotive repair shop could participate in arbitration together with the business were the case to be referred for arbitration. The amount of monetary damages or other settlements are determined by the arbitrator. Once a finding is determined both the complainant and respondent are bound to the settlement.

Community Arbitration

Similarly to mediation, arbitration can occur at a mediation center or other locations and takes on a variety of forms such as *community arbitration*. In Seminole County, Florida, the Seminole County government operates a community arbitration program for repeat nonviolent juvenile offenders. The program utilizes trained volunteer arbitrators who impose sanctions on juvenile offenders. If offenders comply with the sanctions and complete the program, charges are not formally filed. A similar program is managed by the State Attorney's Office in Brevard County, Florida. The benefits of both programs include reduced court costs as a result of diverting these cases to community arbitration, freeing up the juvenile courts to deal with serious juvenile offenders, acknowledging the needs of victims, and holding juvenile offenders accountable for their behaviors (Office of the State Attorney 18th Judicial Circuit of Florida, 2000).

Alternatives to Incarceration

Numerous alternatives to incarceration programs have been described. The term *alternative to incarceration programs* (ATI) refers to those programs that focus on diversion away from the correctional system and the provision of community-based supervision and human services instead of incarceration.

A recent example in which alternatives to incarceration programs have not been fully utilized despite evidence demonstrating the effectiveness of the programs is found in Pennsylvania. Taylor (2011) reported that alternative sentencing programs were effective for reducing the number of incarcerated state inmates and the costs associated with incarceration, but the programs were not being widely implemented. The Recidivism Risk Reduction Incentive program was enacted into law in 2008. This program enables a reduction in the length of minimum sentences imposed for nonviolent crimes based on good behavior and participation in programs designed to reduce criminal behavior while incarcerated. The State Intermediate Punishment program was enacted into law in 2005. This program enables an individual convicted for a drug offense to serve a two-year sentence. Seven months of the sentence are served in prison and the remaining 17 months are served in a community-based therapeutic community for at least two months, and at least six months of the sentence are served in an outpatient treatment program.

Both programs have resulted in savings of $43 million since they were enacted into law. Offenders with prior convictions for sex offenses and violent crimes are ineligible to participate in the programs. However, whereas 9,676 offenders met the eligibility criteria to participate in the State Intermediate Punishment program, fewer than 2,500 were referred by the courts. Low referral and participation in the programs is attributed to refusal from judges, district attorneys, and offenders. Although the legislation requires that eligible offenders be referred to the Recidivism Risk Reduction Incentive program, district attorneys can override the legislation. New legislation has been introduced that would end this practice.

Reentry and Community-based Programs

Alternative programs and demonstration projects have also been developed to provide a variety of community-based services to former offenders and to address crime within communities. Examples include the Transition from Prison to Community Initiatives (TPCI), Prisoner Reentry Initiative (PRI), Weed and Seed, Second Chance Act programs, and the Serious and Violent Offender Reentry Initiative (SVORI).

Transition from Prison to Community Initiatives (TPCI)

Between December 2000 and October 2001 TPCI was developed by an advisory board, five working groups and the National Institute of Corrections (NIC). TPCI is a public safety initiative developed to improve the reentry process, reduce recidivism, prevent new victimization by former offenders, improve the use of limited resources in correctional facilities and communities, and increase public safety. The goals of TPCI are focused on providing community-based services to help former prisoners remain arrest-free and become self-sufficient members of the community. TPCI consists of two initiatives; Transition from Prison to Community (TPC) and Transition from Jail to Community (TJC). In 2002, TPCI was tested at eight sites in Georgia, Indiana, Michigan, Missouri, New York, North Dakota, Oregon, and Rhode Island (NIC, 2002).

The Indiana Department of Corrections describes TPCI as a national reentry model that supports state correctional facilities through the use of evidence-based practices. These practices are relative to inmate assessment and classification, release planning, and community-based supervision and services (Indiana Department of Corrections, n.d.). Little empirical evidence is available that supports the efficacy of the TPCI model.

Prisoner Reentry Initiative (PRI)

Former President Bush in his 2004 State of the Union address proposed a four-year demonstration grant program to allocate $300 million for PRI (White House, 2004). The goals of PRI were to strengthen urban communities and reduce recidivism through the provision of faith-based and community-based services. Services include job training, housing, mentoring, and other transitional services for former offenders (U.S. Department of Labor, 2007a).

Within the first year that PRI was implemented, 30 grantee organizations provided 43,495 services to 6,442 former offenders, 3,378 of whom obtained employment (U.S. Department of Labor, 2007b). Initial data on PRI recidivism rates showed that recidivism rates were 20%, less than one-half the national figures of 44% reported by the Bureau of Justice Statistics (White House, n.d.).

Weed and Seed

Weed and Seed is a community-based initiative funded by the U.S. Department of Justice (DOJ). It is a collaborative effort between criminal justice, crime prevention, and community revitalization agencies. More than 250 Weed and Seed sites have been established throughout the U.S. in communities with populations ranging from 3,000 to 50,000 residents. Weed and Seed is a two-step process aimed at reducing crime and the fear of crime, and improving community revitalization. First, violent offenders and substance abusers are removed from communities (weed); and, second, community-based private organizations collaborate to provide social services, prevention, intervention, treatment, and neighborhood restoration programs (seed). Weed and Seed has four basic components: (1) law enforcement, (2) community policing, (3) prevention, intervention, and treatment provided by human service agencies, and (4) community/

neighborhood restoration projects. It is based on the following principles: collaboration, coordination, community participation, and sharing scarce resources (Community Capacity Development Office, n.d.). The Weed and Seed Data Center website maintained by Community Capacity Development Office contains numerous evaluation studies of local weed and seed initiatives.

Weed and Seed was implemented in 1991 as a demonstration project in which approximately $1.1 million was awarded to 19 project sites for an 18-month period. The funds were most often used for weeding initiatives rather than seeding initiatives. The weeding initiatives were focused on drug and violent offenses. The projects did increase collaboration between community residents, the criminal justice system, and human service agencies. When seeding initiatives were implemented, their emphasis was on children and youth services (Roehl, Huitt, Wycoff, Pate, Rebovich, & Coyle, 1996).

The Akron Ohio Weed and Seed program operated from 1995 through 2004. The objectives of the program were to address violent, drug, and juvenile crimes. Program outcomes demonstrated reductions in crimes reported to the police and arrests in the Weed and Seed neighborhoods. Fewer arrests were made that involved guns although juvenile arrests, predominantly for drug offenses, increased. Community residents were generally satisfied with law enforcement although they were less satisfied with community-based human services (Shoaf, 2005).

Although Weed and Seed initiatives have demonstrated numerous benefits, several barriers to implementing reentry programs as part of Weed and Seed have also been reported. These barriers include former prisoners' lack of participation in services, lack of housing, employers' unwillingness to hire former prisoners, poor coordination between human service and other agencies, and inadequate access to mental health and substance abuse services (Solomon, Palmer, Atkinson, Davidson, & Harvey, 2006).

The Serious and Violent Offender Reentry Initiative (SVORI)

Serious and violent offenders have different reentry needs owing to their histories of chronic, serious, and violent crimes. The SVORI federal program provided 3-year grants to states ranging from $500,000 to $2 million to develop or expand reentry programs for adults and juveniles (Lattimore & Visher, 2009). Reentry programs were provided during incarceration, parole, and post-parole supervision. SVORI was established in 2003 to address these needs. One study among 274 former prisoners who received reentry services from a social worker between July 2003 and September 2005 found that those who were unemployed, did not live with family members, and were assessed as higher risk for reoffending were less successful in the SVORI program (Listwan, 2009). Another impact study that included a sample of 2,391 juveniles and adults from 14 states who were released from detention centers and prisons between July 2004 and November 2005 shows that adult SVORI programs increased service utilization (i.e., employment, education, and substance abuse treatment) provided during incarceration and post-release. Although SVORI programs offered approximately 50% more reentry services during incarceration and post-release periods prior to implementation of SVORI programs, only a small number of prisoners actually received services. Lattimore & Visher suggested that the lack of long-term implementation of SVORI programs may explain the small number of prisoners who received services. Another significant finding revealed that SVORI programs were unable to provide support services for former prisoners during the crucial release phase when adults were most in need of such services (Lattimore & Visher, 2009). The Serious and Violent Offender Reentry Initiative Multi-site Evaluation website (www.svori-evaluation.org) provides further information about evaluations of the SVORI program.

Women's Advocacy Project

Some reform efforts are intended for a specific demographic population and their unique experiences with the criminal justice system, and combine reform efforts, advocacy, and the provision of services such as housing, employment, and health care. The Women's Advocacy Project was developed by the Women's Prison Association in 2003. The purpose of the project is to actively involve previously incarcerated women in advocacy efforts to reform prisons and jails, eliminate discrimination in housing, employment, and sentencing policies, and address issues related to being mothers. Women who are full-time advocates as well as unpaid volunteers staff the project.

Several advocacy efforts of women who have been previously incarcerated have been established. These efforts are national in scope and represent many states such as:

- Alabama Women's Resource Network / Long-Timers located in Alabama;
- The Women's Reentry Network located in Arizona;
- The Center for Young Women's Development and A New Way of Life Reentry Project both located in California;
- Visible Voices located in Illinois;
- Power Inside located in Maryland;
- ReConnect, Women of Substance, Women On The Rise Telling HerStory, and the Women's Advocacy Project all located in New York;
- Women Evolving located in Vermont.

(Women's Prison Association, 2009)

The Innocence Project

Another example in which reforms and services are provided together within the same agency is the Innocence Project. Most individuals may have become familiar with deoxyribonucleic acid (DNA) evidence in trials during the O. J. Simpson trial. The Innocence Project makes extensive use of DNA evidence.

The founders of the Innocence Project are Barry Scheck and Peter Neufeld, who established the organization in 1992 at the Benjamin N. Cardoza School of Law at Yeshiva University. The primary mission of the organization, which is now an independent organization although it maintains ties with the Benjamin N. Cardoza School of Law, is to provide legal representation and/or assistance to prisoners using DNA testing and evidence to exonerate innocent prisoners (Innocence Project, n.d.a).

Because few states provide post-release services for exonerated individuals the Innocence Project operates a social work program that provides financial, employment, and other assistance to help individuals transition to community living (Innocence Project, n.d.b). The team of social workers help exonerees adjust to community living while the Innocence Project works toward implementing fair compensation laws for exonerees in all states (Innocence Project, n.d.c).

Looking Forward

The U.S. has recently experienced several long-term wars. Veterans from all branches of military service may experience criminal justice system involvement upon their return home. Within their military branches military police and courts exist, but returning veterans are likely to become involved with local criminal justice systems. This situation occurs because of cases that involve domestic violence, child abuse and neglect, assaults, and driving under the influence, for example. Some returning veterans experience PTSD, substance abuse, health problems, and injuries that result in disabilities and other problems as they readjust to civilian life.

Whereas some military branches hire military social workers who practice military social work, a highly specialized area of practice, these social workers are not employed in local criminal justice systems. Social work practice with veterans having criminal justice system involvement requires an understanding of their situation as well as effective criminal justice practice. The remaining chapters of this book will examine special populations with criminal justice involvement, social work practice concepts, and evidence-based criminal justice practice.

Implications for Social Work Practice

Social workers providing services to individuals with criminal justice system involvement should be aware of criminal justice reforms as well as alternative programs and services in their communities. Many of these reforms and alternative programs help individuals with specialized needs. Social workers should also know that the efficacy of some reforms and programs may not yet be determined because these efforts are either recently implemented or because no rigorous outcome studies have been conducted.

The social work profession's ethical mandate to evaluate policies, programs, and interventions can be useful as judicial reform efforts move to restore judicial discretion and eliminate mandatory minimum sentences. Because mandatory minimum sentences have been ineffective and resulted in racial disparities, ongoing monitoring and evaluations of these policies is consistent with social justice.

Important questions that need to be asked are: what policies and practices in the criminal justice system should be the focus of reform? How will progress be measured and evaluated in reform efforts? How will success or failure be measured? What if reform and programs have unintended negative consequences for individuals? Moreover, social workers can and do actively participate in alternative programs in the criminal justice system. Participation includes the provision of clinical and administrative services, as well as advocacy and program evaluation activities. Certified mediators and arbitrators with specialized training can resolve matters diverted by courts and referred by police officers and others. Restorative justice has been suggested as an alternative to the retributive and rehabilitative approaches to criminal justice (Walgrave, 1999) and has applications within prisons (Swanson, 2009).

It is imperative that social workers should not just provide and participate in these alternatives in the hopes that they will improve individuals' lives, but be actively involved in evaluation and monitoring efforts. For example, outcomes should be clearly articulated beforehand. If these outcomes include reduced recidivism, then social workers should monitor programs to investigate whether reduced recidivism has occurred. If an outcome is increased services, then services should be monitored not only to assess whether they have increased but also to determine whether they were effective. These activities present another area of practice for social workers as program evaluators.

What then is the role of the social work profession in alternative reform and programmatic efforts? In terms of reform efforts, joining with organizations, lending expertise and knowledge, and political action are needed. In terms of programs and services, clinical and evaluation practice is needed. Because of the social justice mission of the profession, social workers should engage in these reform efforts since they may have an adverse effect on vulnerable populations.

Chapter Summary

Although this review of alternative criminal justice reforms and programs was not meant to be an exhaustive list of current reforms and programs, those presented here are illustrative of documented efforts. This chapter has reviewed but a handful of those in existence. Social workers can be involved in these efforts in several ways. One area of involvement concerns monitoring and evaluating current legislative reforms and programs. As we shall see in Chapter 9, social workers have an ethical responsibility to evaluate whether programs, policies, and interventions have achieved their intended outcomes. While rigorous evaluation methods may not always be feasible, other types of evaluation methods can be beneficial. These are also addressed in Chapter 9.

Key Terms

Alternative criminal justice programs	Criminal justice reform	Impact legislation
Arbitration	Discretion	Mediation
Community arbitration	Divorce mediation	Restorative justice

Questions for Review

1. Identify some of the reasons that alternative reforms and programs are being developed and implemented in the criminal justice system.
2. What is mediation and what are its goals? Is there a mediation center or centers located in your community? What types of cases does the center deal with?
3. Select a reform or program effort presented in this chapter. Search the internet to locate and retrieve further information regarding the reform or program. Summarize your results.
4. Violent and chronic offenders are a population with unique challenges. Write a proposal to address some of the issues that violent and chronic offenders experience. Use resources such as websites, textbooks, and articles to support your proposal.
5. Define the term *impact legislation*. Write a proposal to form an interdisciplinary collaboration that will utilize impact legislation to address a social problem that comes to the attention of the criminal justice system.

Further Reading

Bureau of Justice Assistance (1998). *1996 national survey of state sentencing structures*. Washington, DC: U.S. Department of Justice, Office of Justice Programs, Bureau of Justice Assistance.

Constitution Project (2010). *Core issues*. Retrieved from www.constitutionproject.org/coreissues.php.

Constitution Project (2011). *Smart on crime recommendations for the administration and congress*. Washington, DC: Author.

Lengyel, T. E. (2003). *Emerging issues for incarcerated parents and their children: Hawai'i in a national perspective*. Milwaukee, WI: Alliance for Children and Families. Retrieved from www.alliance1.org/Research/articlearchive/EmergingIssuesNov2003.pdf.

New York State Commission on Sentencing Reform (2009). *The future of sentencing in New York State: Recommendations for reform*. Retrieved from http://criminaljustice.state.ny.us/pio/csr_report2-2009.pdf.

Taxman, F. S., & Byrne, J. M. (2005). Racial disparity and the legitimacy of the criminal justice system: Exploring consequences of deterrence. *Journal of Health Care for the Poor and Underserved, 16*, 57–77.

Umbreit, M. (1994). *Victim meets offender: The impact of restorative justice and mediation*. Monsey, NY: Willow Tree Press, Inc.

7 | Special Populations and Emerging Issues within the Criminal Justice System

Chapter Overview

This chapter considers populations having criminal justice involvement who because of their status require special attention. These groups include juveniles, women, felons, crime victims, the disabled, persons with HIV and AIDS, sex offenders, immigrants, the chronically mentally ill, and older inmates. Individuals have differential experiences in the criminal justice system on the basis of their gender, race, parental status, level of ability, age, and social class position, among other characteristics. Victimization and crime rates also vary on the basis of demographic characteristics.

Additionally, this chapter examines emerging issues within the criminal justice system. In the context used here, "emerging issues" implies that these problems are current issues within the justice system, not that they are necessarily up-and-coming issues. The emerging issues examined include racial profiling, racial disparities, police misconduct, suicide-by-cop, bullying, school, campus and workplace violence, chronic and violent offenders, juvenile sex offenders, teen dating violence, the release of low-level offenders, and gerrymandering. The demographic characteristics, statuses, and emerging issues presented in this chapter are significant since these groups experience injustices throughout the criminal justice system.

Special Populations

In the numerous editions of the book titled *Social work: A profession of many faces* each edition has focused on vulnerable populations and the implications for social work practice. For instance in the eleventh edition, Morales, Sheafor, & Scott (2007) note that "social workers need to pay careful attention to existing national and state benefits and welfare policies and to laws and regulations affecting vulnerable client groups, such as children, the homeless, welfare families, and institutionalized psychiatric and corrections populations, to ensure that they receive services and benefits to which they are entitled" (p. 203).

Each of the populations examined in this chapter experiences unique issues prior to becoming involved in the criminal justice system which oftentimes interact with their treatment in the system. In each of the four components of the criminal justice system their unique statuses requires recognition of these statuses and skills for intervention. Owing to their demographic characteristics and statuses, some populations experience social exclusion, particularly in the criminal justice system. Barker (2003) defined *social exclusion* as

> Marginalization of people or areas and the imposition of barriers that restrict them from access to opportunities to fully integrate with the larger society. Those who are most vulnerable to social exclusion are people who are poor, inadequately educated or trained, physically handicapped, or ex-offenders and people of various racial and ethnic groups.
>
> (p. 403)

Native Americans

A theme mentioned throughout the discussion in this book regarding federal criminal justice funding and services is the inclusion of tribal communities located in Indian Country. Tribal criminal justice systems include: tribal detention facilities, tribal victim services, tribal court judge selection and tribal courts, and tribal law enforcement and corrections (Perry, 2005). Native Americans have been suspicious of federal, state, and local criminal justice systems because of the negative ways in which the system has been used against them. Native American tribes are seeking to explore way to integrate indigenous practices into their current criminal justice practices. With sufficient funding to support this process and given the ability to establish their own criteria for assessing effectiveness, Native American criminal justice systems have the potential to succeed (Gould & Ross, 2006).

Juveniles

By definition, a *juvenile* is a person between the ages of 10 and 17. As Table 7.1 shows, in 2007 delinquency rates among juveniles increased as their age increased. Among 10-year-olds the rate was 3.4 delinquency cases per 1,000 juveniles. Among 17-year-olds the rate was 116.0 delinquency cases per 1,000 juveniles. A *juvenile delinquent* is a person aged 10 to 17 who has committed one or more of the following offenses. Among the 1,666,100 juvenile delinquency cases that occurred in 2007, 409,200 were person offense cases (i.e., assault); 594,500 were property offenses; 190,100 were drug offenses,

Table 7.1 Delinquency Rates per 1,000 Juveniles

Age of juvenile	Delinquency rate per 1,000 juveniles
10	3.4
11	7.2
12	17.3
13	36.3
14	61.1
15	85.4
16	107.5
17	116.0

Source: Adapted from Puzzanchera, Adams, and Sickmund (2010). *Juvenile court statistics 200–2007.*

and 472,300 were public order offenses (i.e., disorderly conduct, weapons offenses, and violations of liquor laws).

Also in 2007, more than 31 million juveniles were involved in the juvenile court system representing the following age ranges: 79% were between 10 and 15; 12% were 16; and 9% were 17. During 2007, only three states processed youth aged 16 in the juvenile court system, and ten states processed youth aged 17 (Puzzanchera, Adams, & Sickmund, 2010). These procedures are responsible for the lower percentage of youth involved in the juvenile court system as their age increases. Clearly as juveniles grow older they are more likely to become involved in the criminal justice system, but as these statistics illustrate they are more involved in the adult criminal justice system.

Generally juveniles are labeled with two types of classifications: status offender and juvenile delinquent. The *Michigan guide to compliance with laws governing the placement of juveniles in secure facilities* (n.d.) defines a status offender, provides several examples, and outlines why these behaviors are regarded as an offense:

> A status offender is different from a "delinquent" or criminal-type offender. A status offender is a person whose behavior is against the law because of his or her status as a minor. Common examples of status offenses are truancy, incorrigibility, curfew violations, and being a runaway. None of these behaviors are against the law for adults because adults have no obligation to stay at home, attend school, or obey parents.
>
> (p. 9)

The guide also summarizes four requirements outlined in the federal *Juvenile Justice and Delinquency Prevention Act* (JJDPA) signed into law on September 7, 1974, and reauthorized in 2002, which must be met in order for states to receive federal grants under the JJDPA. These requirements include the following: (1) a status offender must be deinstitutionalized (not institutionalized in secure juvenile correctional facilities or adult correctional facilities); (2) juvenile delinquents and status offenders can not be institutionalized in correctional facilities with adult inmates; (3) whereas juveniles can not be institutionalized in adult facilities, some exceptions apply: for example, juveniles transferred to adult court or charged with a felony offense can be confined in adult facilities; and (4) the JJDPA contains a disproportionate minority contact (DMC) clause which requires that states that have identified a disproportionate number of minority youth who are involved in the juvenile justice system must develop and implement an assessment and interventions strategy designed to address DMC.

In 2007 among juveniles classified as status offenders who were petitioned in courts, cases were adjudicated (convicted or determined to be a delinquent or status offender) in the following order from most to least: curfew violation, violations of liquor laws, ungovernable behavior, truancy, and runaways. Thus, whereas curfew and liquor law violations were most likely to be adjudicated, truancy and runaway cases were least likely to be adjudicated in courts (Puzzanchera, Adams, & Sickmund, 2010).

Although the juvenile justice system was founded on values associated with treatment and rehabilitation, and juveniles were removed from the adult criminal justice system, over time the death penalty was applied to youth. In fact, the U.S. more than any other country applied death penalty legislation to persons under the age of 18. This was attributed to high juvenile violent crime rates, society's interest in retribution, and the waiver or transfer of juveniles into the adult criminal justice system (Child Welfare League of America, 2002). In March 2005, the U.S. became the last country in the world to abolish the death penalty for persons under the age of 18 when the Supreme Court ruled the juvenile death penalty was unconstitutional based on the eighth amendment. Prior to March 2005, 15 states allowed the juvenile death penalty for youth aged 16, and four states imposed a minimum age of 17 (Borger, 2005).

Social workers provide services to both status offenders and juvenile delinquents. It is important to keep in mind that these are two distinct and separate categories and to be aware of these issues as services are provided to youth and their families. Particularly in regard to status offenders, family counseling and other interventions are needed to address the underlying behavior such as mental health issues. This is why assessment is crucial prior to intervention. In either situation a behavior which has its origin in mental health issues has the possibility of being managed by the criminal justice system instead of the mental health system.

Social justice practice issues with juveniles require that attention be given to the disproportionate numbers of minority youth involved in the juvenile justice system, the prosecution and incarceration of juveniles in the adult criminal justice system, the provision of services to children who are victims of abuse and neglect while simultaneously serving status offenders and juvenile delinquents, the treatment of juveniles with mental health issues, and reentry and human rights for juveniles (Sarri, 2008).

Women

At midyear 2007, approximately 809,800 of the 1,518,535 individuals incarcerated in prison were the parents of children under 18 years old (Glaze & Maruschak, 2008). Nationally, as of midyear 2007, 65,600 mothers were incarcerated in state and federal prisons (58,200 were incarcerated in state prisons and 7,400 in federal prisons). These mothers reported a total of 147,400 children under the age of 18 (131,000 among state prisoners, and 16,400 among federal prisoners). They also reported more homelessness, prior physical or sexual abuse, and current medical and mental health problems than men who were fathers. Moreover, a higher percentage of women were incarcerated in state prisons for drug offenses (Glaze & Maruschak, 2008).

As seen in Table 7.2, females with children under the age of 18 represent a higher percentage of incarcerated parents than males. Their offenses include public disorder, property offenses, drug offenses, and violent offenses in that order.

Female drug offenders are often minimally involved in drug sales and use, although their treatment in the criminal justice system is not reflective of this fact. Women convicted of drug offenses are wives, girlfriends, sisters, mothers, and so forth. They become involved in drug-related crimes as a result of their relationships with male drug offenders, which may include a romantic relationship. They may also be financially dependent upon a male drug offender or fear a male drug offender. Gaskins (2004) referred to these women as "women of circumstance" because of their unique situations, and suggested that mandatory minimum sentencing laws have an adverse impact on these women.

Female felons face multiple challenges owing to the obstacles associated with being a felon, although Wilbanks (1986) found that, among 181,197 felony cases processed in California courts in 1980, female felons were treated more leniently than men, though such treatment was not similar across all components of the criminal justice system and was dependent upon the type of offense committed. Women involved in the criminal justice system also experience unique situations and require services that are gender-specific and consider their parental status of minor children. These services include family reunification and parenting skills. It is important to note that parental rights are not necessarily lost because of the above crimes or incarceration. Several studies have found that either children were placed in foster care or custody rights were lost prior to a mother's incarceration (Moses, 2006) and some children were not living in their mother's care prior to incarceration (Hairston, 1991). Therefore incarceration is not the primary reason for foster care placement or losing custody of minor children.

When incarcerated mothers were asked "What is the most difficult thing about being in jail?" (p. 17), 70% stated that being separated from their children was most difficult (Hairston, 1991). Family programs have been developed and implemented in state

Table 7.2 State Prison Inmates with Children under 18 in 2004 (%)

Criminal offense	Male	Female
Violent offenses	47.1	57.3
Property offenses	48.2	64.7
Drug-related offenses	59.3	62.5
Public disorder offenses	59.6	65.0

Source: Adapted from Glaze & Maruschak (2008). *Parents in prison and their minor children.*

prisons for female inmates to help them maintain family relationships. These include visitation programs, parenting programs, support groups, and individual counseling and information services (Hairston, 2007).

In Canada, according to Blanchette, the *Corrections and Conditional Release Act* (CCRA, 1992) mandates that federal correctional facilities provide gender-specific services for female offenders, and consult with individuals who possess expertise in the area of female offending (Blanchette, 2002). Whereas the U.S. does not have such legislation mandating gender-specific services for female offenders, Blanchette asserts that female-specific criminogenic needs are personal and emotional attributes such as low self-esteem, a history of victimization as a child and adult, self-injurious behavior, and suicide attempts. Addressing criminogenic needs in treatment reduces recidivism and reoffending.

Felons

In 75 of the largest U.S. counties in May 2006, 58,100 felony charges were documented. In order of occurrence these felonies involved drug offenses (36.5%), property offenses (29.2%), violent offenses (22.9%), and public order offenses (11.4%) (Cohen & Kyckelhahn, 2010). The term *felon* is used to describe a person who has been convicted of a felony offense. A felony is an offense for which a sentence of one year or more is imposed, and state statutes vary regarding which offenses are felonies.

Upon reentry, a felon status affects individuals in numerous ways such as employment, disenfranchisement, and purchasing or carrying a firearm, among other exclusions. Professional licensing restrictions can also affect felons. For example, professional licensing requirements in fields such as social work require that individuals report felony (and often misdemeanor) convictions. The effects of these convictions are determined by state licensing boards.

Siegel (2011) reported that 48 states do not allow felons to vote while incarcerated in correctional facilities, and 35 states do not allow parolees to vote. For instance, in Washington State felons can not vote until after they have fulfilled the conditions of their parole supervision and are no longer under community-based supervision. This has resulted in voting disparities in which large numbers of Black, Latino, and Native Americans are denied the right to vote in Washington State. Evidence shows that racial disparities in the criminal justice system translate into racial bias in voting. Throughout the country more than 5 million individuals are barred from voting owing to convictions, of whom 1.4 are African American. The National Association for the Advancement of Colored People (NAACP) has challenged these practices in Washington State (Abudu, 2010). Observing that the social work profession as whole has not challenged felony disenfranchisement, Siegel noted that some social workers do participate in voter registration campaigns, advocacy, and research to address this social problem.

The *Democracy Restoration Act* of 2011 was introduced in the House of Representatives (112th Congress—2011–2012) on June 16, 2011. Because states vary in their disenfranchisement practices—for example some states practice lifetime disenfranchisement of offenders—the Act would establish the right to vote in a federal election for individuals released from correctional facilities (GovTrack.us, 2011).

The Reentry Council (2011) has issued *Reentry mythbusters* which are a series of one-page myths and facts publications providing factual information regarding the impact of federal legislation on formerly incarcerated offenders and their families. For example, it is a myth that a parent having a felony conviction is banned from Temporary Assistance for Needy Families (TANF). In reality only 11 states have implemented this ban and most states have eliminated the ban.

Crime Victims

In 2009, about 20 million crimes were committed against victims who were 12 years old or older. Of these offenses, the largest category, 5.6 million (78%), comprised property crimes such as home burglaries and motor vehicle theft; 4.3 million (22%) were violent crimes such as rape, sexual assault, robbery, and assault; and 133,000 (1%) were personal theft crimes. Also in 2009, for every 1,000 individuals who were 12 years or older, one rape or sexual assault occurred, two robberies, three aggravated assaults, and 11 simple assaults. Homicide occurred less frequently, with approximately five murders for every 100,000 individuals. Among all violent crimes against men, 45% knew the offender. Among women, 70% knew the offenders, who were friends or acquaintances (Bureau of Justice Statistics, 2011).

Victim impact statements are prepared statements that victims present during the sentencing phase of a trial. These statements detail the effects the crime has had on the victim, family members, or others. Most states have developed a victim bill of rights that articulates the rights of crime victims within their jurisdictions. Box 7.1 shows the *Wyoming crime victim bill of rights* (Wyoming Office of the Attorney General Division of Victim Services, n.d.). As seen, the bill of rights includes the right to be informed about the opportunity to make a victim impact statement at sentencing and parole hearings. According to the Office for Victims of Crime (OVC) (n.d.a) the majority of states have included crime victims' right in their state constitutions, and among these rights is the right to participate during the sentencing phase of a trial.

Box 7.1 Wyoming Crime Victim Bill of Rights

- The right to be treated with compassion, respect, and sensitivity within the criminal justice system
- The right to know the whereabouts of the offender and the current status of the case
- The right to receive restitution from offenders
- The right to know all rights under this law, including information about services and victims assistance at the local level
- The right to know about victim compensation

- The right to reasonable protection and safety and the right to know of legal recourse if threatened
- The right to prompt return of property
- The right to preservation of employment while participating in the criminal justice process
- The right to be informed about the opportunity to make a victim impact statement at sentencing and parole hearings
- The right to be present at tria

Source: The Wyoming Office of the Attorney
General Division of Victim Services (n.d.).

Current efforts are under way to improve services provided to crime victims. OVC (n.d.b) has initiated *Vision 21: Transforming victim services* to review current practices relative to crime victim services. The initiative was implemented in October 2010 and will end in March 2012 with a final report that will be used to implement recommendations made in the final report.

Persons with Disabilities

Persons with a disability are more likely to be victims of adult sexual abuse and assault than those who do not have a disability (Grossman & Lundy, 2008). Data from 2007 show that: (1) females with a disability experienced higher rates of violent crime victimization (rape or sexual assault, robbery, aggravated assault) than males with a disability, (2) females were victimized by intimate partners more than males, (3) 56% of disabled individuals who were victims of violent crime had more than one disability, and (4) individuals with a cognitive disability were more likely to be a victim of violent crimes than those with other types of disability such as physical or sensory disabilities (Rand & Harrell, 2009).

As seen in Table 7.3 on p. 117, in 2007 persons with disabilities experienced higher rates of crime victimization than persons without disabilities. This pattern was consistent across ages groups except for persons aged 20 to 24 who experience a very slightly lower rate of victimization. The general pattern across age groups shows that younger persons with and without disabilities are more likely to be victims of violent crimes (Rand & Harrell, 2009).

Inmates with HIV and AIDS

In 1996, approximately 98,500 to 145,000 HIV-positive inmates were released from prisons and jails, of whom approximately 38,500 had AIDS. Among prison and jail inmates in 1997, approximately 34,800 to 46,000 were HIV-positive and 8,900 had

Table 7.3 Violent Crime Victimization against Persons
with and without Disabilities in 2007

Age	Individuals with disabilities (%)	Individuals without disabilities (%)
12–15	81.2	40.0
16–19	82.7	47.0
20–24	35.1	35.4
25–34	30.9	24.9
35–49	31.2	16.1
50–64	12.2	11.6
65 or older	2.1	3.0

Source: Adapted from Rand & Harrell (2009). U.S. Department of
Justice, Office of Justice Programs, Bureau of Justice Statistics.

AIDS. Because jails are characterized by relatively short incarceration periods and constant turnover, the figures describing released inmates who are HIV-positive are greater than the figures describing the numbers of incarcerated inmates who are HIV-positive or who have AIDS (National Commission on Correctional Health Care, 2002). Former inmates who are HIV-positive or who have AIDS represent both a public health and a public safety concern.

It is not atypical that former offenders experience a gap in health care services upon reentry. Nearly all Texas state prisoners who were HIV-positive experienced a disruption in their HIV treatment upon release. During this time the disease may progress or be transmitted to others. Assisting prisoners with applying for free HIV treatment prior to release can minimize these disruptions. In Texas, a federally funded program, the AIDS Drug Assistance Program (ADAP), provides released prisoners with six items on their release date. Planning begins 30 days prior to a prisoner's release date, and on the release date prisoners are given a copy of their recent HIV test results, a ten-day supply of antiretroviral medication, a list of community-based service providers who provide HIV treatment and are located in the prisoner's community, an ADAP application form to apply for a 30-day supply of antiretroviral medication, an ADAP medication certification that has been signed by a physician, and a toll-free telephone number to contact an ADAP caseworker for assistance with locating a pharmacy in the prisoner's community (Whitten, 2011).

Six and 12 months after participating in case management, day-treatment, outreach, and HIV/AIDS and substance abuse education services, former inmates reported less alcohol, cocaine, crack, and heroin use; and fewer sex partners and criminal behaviors. Former offenders who completed the substance abuse and HIV harm reduction program also reported committing fewer criminal offenses than those who did not complete the program, and were incarcerated fewer days (Bowser, Jenkins-Barnes, Dillard-Smith, & Lockett, 2010).

Sex Offenders

Grady (2009a) reported that the term *sex offender* is a legal term and as such does not incorporate diagnostic or clinical implications. However, sex offender assessment and treatment are guided by ethical standards and valid and reliability assessment instruments, although mixed evidence supports the validity and reliability of these instruments. Levenson (2009) noted that, although mixed evidence supports the efficacy and accuracy of polygraph examinations for assessing and treating sex offenders, polygraph examinations can be useful when used by social workers in assessment and treatment of sex offenders.

The responses of the criminal justice system for managing sex offenders include incarcerating offenders, extending incarceration past an offender's original sentence through civil commits or other means, and sex offender registration and notification laws (Grady, 2009b). Generally, sex offender registration and notification laws require that upon reentry former sex offenders register with an authority and community residents receive notification that the former offender is residing within the community. A study conducted in South Carolina investigated the affects of sex offender registration and notification laws on recidivism, further sexual offending, and possible unintended consequences of the laws. Study results show that laws were effective for deterring some first-time offenders but did not reduce recidivism for sex offenses, an increase was observed in the numbers of sex offenders who plead guilty to non-sex offenses, former sex offenders who did not register did not pose a greater threat to public safety than those who did, and on-line registration did not reduce sex offenses (Letourneau, Levenson, Bandyopadhyay, Sinha, & Armstrong, 2010)

The treatment of sex offenders also includes assessment, particularly a consideration of the risks for reoffending. After the assessment of risks, a variety of treatment approaches are provided to sex offenders. These include in-prison and community-based programs that focus on psychological, cognitive-behavioral, and medical interventions (Grady, 2009a). Providing interventions to sex offenders can be challenging because of the nature of the offense. This work can also be emotionally exhausting for workers. Pais (2001) summarized interviews conducted with two sex therapists in which they described the need to understand the cognitions and behaviors of sex offenders, the usefulness of individual and group supervision, and the skills to work through offenders' defenses such as denial and minimization and use confrontation effectively. Workers also require effective coping strategies to manage their emotional reactions that arise from this work.

Immigrants

The U.S. is presently experiencing the enactment of harsh immigration legislation particularly at state levels. In June 2011, the governor of Alabama signed into law legislation that makes it illegal for a person to give a ride to an illegal immigrant if it is known that the passenger is an illegal immigrant, authorizes public schools to inquire about the immigration status of students, and authorizes police officers to inquire about an individual's immigration status if the officer stopped the person with reason to suspect that the person might be an illegal immigrant. This legislation is more stringent than legislation recently passed in Arizona (Preston, 2011). NASW has opposed the Arizona immigration legislation (NASW, n.d.). Law enforcement officials and the ACLU also oppose the Arizona legislation. Law enforcement officials are concerned that the law will redirect law enforcement functions and diminish police relationships in immigrant communities, and the ACLU has filed a lawsuit (ACLU, 2011).

In addition to stricter immigration legislation, the U.S. has seen an increase in immigration offenders who are involved in the criminal justice system. In 2000, more than 16,000 individuals were referred to attorneys for assistance with immigration offenses. This figure is more than twice the number referred in 1996. The number of prosecutions for immigration offenses also more than doubled from 1996 to 2000 (Scalia & Litras, 2002).

In an interesting study of a sample of 51 MSW students and 27 BSW students, Furman, Langer, Sanchez, & Negi (2007) asked the students to read a scenario involving a domestic violence victim and her children seeking services in an agency that provides services to many undocumented individuals. Students were asked to identify the practice dilemmas that might arise as a result of the Arizona state immigration legislation which requires that social workers who are employed in public human service agencies deny services to individuals who are undocumented and, once this determination is made, to report that individual to immigration authorities. More students reported they would provide the services and ignore the reporting requirement of the legislation, and some students reported creative ways to provide services by not asking the client about her immigration status. Students identified numerous ethical issues including confidentiality and resolving social work ethics with the law.

Persons with Chronic Mental Illness

Persons with chronic mental illness experience unique problems in the criminal justice system. Lamb, Weinberger, & Gross (1999) indicated that a large number of individuals who experience chronic mental illness also have criminal justice system involvement, and community-based treatment considerations are different for offenders than for non-offenders. Primarily, offenders may have to contend with sanctions, be a risk to the community, and resist treatment, and the mental health system may be reluctant to treat offenders owing to their criminal justice system involvement and for some offenders a history of violence.

Lamb, Weinberger, & Gross suggest that successful treatment of chronic mentally ill offenders requires that service providers collaborate with mental health and criminal justice systems, resolve issues related to using authority, manage violence, and involve family and other support systems. Indeed, both the mentally ill offender and the community are important considerations upon reentry (Draine, Wolff, Jacoby, Hartwell, & Duclos, 2005). Inmates who experience chronic mental illness should be prepared for reentry prior to release. Preparation should include assisting inmates with applying for federal entitlement programs such as Medicaid, Medicare, Social Security Disability

Insurance (SSDI), and Social Security Disability Insurance (SSDI), as well as veterans' benefits (Conly, 2005). Some of the same 16 types of non-psychiatric mental health services that Young (2002) found were provided by social workers in a county jail are the same types of services that are required for those with chronic mental illness and criminal justice system involvement. These services include crisis intervention, individual counseling, assessment, follow-up, and discharge planning, among others.

Older Inmates

Over the nine-year period between 1992 and 2001, the number of prisoners aged 50 and older who were incarcerated in state and federal prisons increased 172.6% (Camp & Camp, 2001) owing to demographic trends and the adverse impact of sentencing laws that have resulted in increased incarceration rates for older offenders (Glaser, Warchol, D'Angelo, & Gutterman, 1990). It is anticipated that as more individuals in this age group are sentenced to prison and release policies become more restrictive (Anno, 2001) the number of older prisoners will continue to increase. An age of 50 might seem below the age range of an older person, but "correctional health professionals generally agree that the onset of geriatric conditions usually occurs at a younger age among inmates than the general population" (p. 29) as a result of poverty, less healthy lifestyles, lack of access to health care, the use of tobacco, alcohol and drugs, and high-risk sexual practices with multiple partners (Anno, Graham, Lawrence, Shansky, Bisbee, & Blackmore, 2004).

Aging within a prison environment is different from aging outside of a prison environment (Smyer, Gragert, & LaMere, 1997). Correctional administrators suggested that aging will be among the most significant factors to address in the correctional system throughout the twenty-first century (Aday, 2003). However, no standardized definition of an older inmate exists in the U.S. correctional system. States have developed their own criteria which have resulted in age ranges of 50, 55, 60, or 65 (Aday, 2003). Some states do not define an older inmate (Anno, Graham, Lawrence, Shansky, Bisbee, & Blackmore, 2004). In a national study of state corrections departments, Aday (1999) reported that correctional officials frequently identified age 50 as an older inmate. Others have also defined age 50 and older as an older inmate (Anderson, 1997; Flynn, 1992; Hillerman, 2008). Moreover, longitudinal studies investigating the health status of older prisoners in state correctional facilities used samples of prisoners aged 50 and older (Aday, 1994; Colsher, Wallace, Loeffelholz, & Sales, 1992; Morton & Jacobs, 1992).

Health care costs for older prisoners are estimated to be three times the cost for younger inmates (Faiver, 1998). Older prisoners also experience higher morbidity and utilize more medical services (Lindquist & Lindquist, 1999). For example, Colsher, Wallace, Loeffelholz, & Sales (1992) surveyed prisoners aged 50 and older incarcerated in Iowa state correctional facilities and found that they reported the following health concerns: missing teeth (97%), smoking (70%), physical functional impairments (42%), hypertension (40%), myocardial infarction (19%), and emphysema (18%).

Prior to release older inmates should participate in release planning that provides at least one appointment or referral to a community-based service provider, a short supply of medication if required, informational classes focused on submitting an application for entitlement benefits such as Medicaid and Medicare, and a social worker or case manager to coordinate the release plan with the inmate, family members, correctional staff, parole officers, and community-based service providers (Anno, Graham, Lawrence, Shansky, Bisbee, & Blackmore, 2004).

Emerging Issues in the Criminal Justice System

In addition to the aforementioned populations who are adversely impacted by crime and criminal justice policies and practices, numerous issues such as the types and nature of crimes are also important to understand. Emerging issues in the criminal justice system are connected to both the types of crimes committed and the treatment of both victims and offenders in the criminal justice system. Albanese and Pursley (1993) categorized emerging issues in criminal justice into three areas: (1) issues that affect economic arrangements (e.g., white collar crime, computer crimes, and organized crimes), (2) issues that affect political arrangements (e.g., domestic and international terrorism, political and government corruption, and hate crimes), and (3) issues that affect social arrangements (e.g., youth gangs, domestic violence, child abuse, family and drug crimes, and environmental crimes such as pollution). Whereas all of these categories are of importance to the social work profession, the latter category benefits from more social work involvement.

While this list is not exhaustive of the emerging issues that have been acknowledged, some relevant emerging issues include: bullying, school, campus, and workplace violence, violent offenders, juvenile sex offenders, police misconduct, racial profiling, teen dating violence, releasing low-level offenders, and public notification laws and registration of sex offenders. A resource for learning more information about current and emerging issues is the National Criminal Justice Reference Service (NCJRS) administered by the Office of Justice Programs, U.S. Department of Justice. NCJRS maintains a topical index website that provides information on many emerging issues.

Racial Profiling

A bill introduced before the 107th Congress on June 6, 2001 (*S. 989: End Racial Profiling Act* of 2001), proposed to make it illegal for a law enforcement officer to engage in the practice of racial profiling. The bill states:

> Racial profiling violates the Equal Protection Clause of the Constitution. Using race, ethnicity, or national origin as a proxy for criminal suspicion violates the constitutional requirement that police and other government officials accord to all citizens the equal protection of the law. *Arlington Heights v. Metropolitan Housing Development Corporation, 429 U.S. 252 (1977).*
>
> (s. 989, n.d., p. 3)

Furthermore, the *End Racial Profiling Act* of 2001 did not become law although according to GovTrack.us the last action on the bill occurred in 2011 when a committee hearing was held. The bill defined *racial profiling* as

The practice of a law enforcement agent relying, to any degree, on race, ethnicity, or national origin in selecting which individuals to subject to routine investigatory activities, or in deciding upon the scope and substance of law enforcement activity following the initial routine investigatory activity, except that racial profiling does not include reliance on such criteria in combination with other identifying factors when the law enforcement agent is seeking to apprehend a specific suspect whose race, ethnicity, or national origin is part of the description of the suspect.

(p. 7)

The Racial Profiling Data Collection Resource Center at Northeastern University collects data on law enforcement racial profiling. As Box 7.2 shows, numerous benefits can be obtained from collecting and analyzing racial profiling data. These benefits include opening a discussion between community residents and the police.

Box 7.2 Benefits of Racial Profiling Data Collection Efforts for Law Enforcement Agencies and Communities

1   Send a strong message to the community that the department is against racial profiling and that racial profiling is inconsistent with effective policing and equal protection
2   Build trust and respect for the police in the communities they serve
3   Provide departments with information about the types of stops being made by officers, the proportion of police time spent on high-discretion stops, and the results of such stops
4   Help shape and develop training programs to educate officers about racial profiling and interactions with the community
5   Enable the development of police and community dialogue to assess the quality and quantity of police–citizen encounters
6   Allay community concerns about the activities of police
7   Identify potential police misconduct and deter it, when implemented as part of a comprehensive early warning system
8   Retain autonomous officer discretion and allow for flexible responses in different situations

Source: Racial Profiling Data Collection Resource Center at Northeastern University (n.d.).

Numerous challenges are also associated with collecting racial profiling data, and these are shown in Box 7.3. As can be imagined, merely developing protocols does not ensure that they will be followed, and in this case officers may not comply with racial profiling data collection or other protocols. As a case in point, the ACLU (2010) traces a 15-year period in which it engaged in legislation focused on racial profiling or "driving while black." In 1993, the ACLU filed a class-action lawsuit against the Maryland State

Police (MSP) for stopping and searching an African American motorist on a Maryland highway. The lawsuit was settled in 1995, but in 1997 the federal court ruled that the MSP was continuing its practices of racial profiling, leading to the ACLU filing another lawsuit in 1998. In April 2008, 15 years after the initial lawsuit was filed, it was settled. The Maryland NAACP has also filed several lawsuits against the MSP to compel the MSP to share racial profiling data.

Box 7.3 Challenges of Racial Profiling Data Collection Efforts for Law Enforcement Agencies and Communities

1   Concerns about extra-budgetary expenditures associated with collecting data
2   Developing a benchmark against which the data can be compared
3   The potential burden an improved data collection procedure will have on individual officers in the course of a normal shift
4   The potential for police disengagement from their duties, which may lead to officers scaling back on the number of legitimate stops
5   The challenge of ensuring that officers will fully comply with a directive to collect stop data
6   Ensuring that data is recorded on all stops made, and that the data collected is correct
7   The difficulty of determining the race or ethnicity of the persons stopped
8   Once data is collected and analyzed, the difficulty of making a definite conclusion about whether racial profiling exists or not, as this question requires more than a "yes" or "no" answer

Source: Racial Profiling Data Collection Resource Center at Northeastern University (n.d.).

Racial Disparities

The term *racial disparities* refers to different treatment based on an individual's race although individuals share similar situations and occur within each of the four components of the criminal justice system. The impact of race on disparities in the criminal justice system is cumulative as individuals have contact with each component of the system. Racial disparities arise from numerous factors: different crime rates among groups, the focus of law enforcement activities in specific communities, the adverse impact of legislation, decisions that impact racial groups made in one or more components of the system, unequal access to resources, class differences, and racial bias (The Sentencing Project, 2008).

Racial disparities result from implementing law enforcement procedures in racial and ethnic minority communities differently than in non-minority communities. Social workers should be aware that residents living in racial and ethnic minority communities, particularly those characterized by high crimes rates, may themselves be fearful of crime and demand that police provide an increased presence. While community residents demand a strong police presence they do not want what they perceive as abuses of police powers. The challenges then are to provide law enforcement services in high-crime communities in ways that protect civil rights and treat community residents fairly, while simultaneously ensuring public safety.

Police Misconduct

Police misconduct not only affects the individual(s) and police officer(s) involved, it also affects their families and communities as well as society. Morales & Sheafor (1995) described police brutality victims as a special population because of the human and civil rights violations that they experience. They commented that the role of the social work profession has developed into one in which social workers provide assistance to police officers with individuals experiencing social problems as opposed to advocating for victims of police brutality. Unquestionably, as we have seen in Chapter 3, police social workers are not involved in these matters.

Similar arguments suggest that the social work profession has not been involved in police brutality situations, which is particularly surprising given the profession's large presence in urban areas providing social work services (Ellis, 1981). Ellis recommends that the social work profession become involved in efforts through NASW and the American Bar Association to address police brutality.

Suicide-by-Cop

A recently discussed phenomenon is *suicide-by-cop*, a phrase used to refer to a situation that occurs when an individual intentionally does not follow a police officer's orders to put down a weapon. The person may threaten an officer with the weapon, and the officer then shoots in self-defense resulting in death (Lindsay & Lester, 2004; Lindsay & Lester, 2008). Lindsay & Lester (2008) provide a checklist of behaviors that may indicate a suicide-by-cop situation. Examples from among the 17 behaviors are initiating aggressive behaviors, prior suicidal attempts, psychiatric or chronic medical illness, and becoming involved in a situation that guarantees a police response, among others. More research is needed in this area.

Bullying

Sampson (2009) provided examples of bullying in schools that consists of behaviors such as "assault, tripping, intimidation, rumor-spreading and isolation, demands for money, destruction of property, theft of valued possessions, destruction of another's work and name-calling" (p. 2). In the U.S., sexual harassment, isolation based on sexual orientation, and acts of hazing are also considered bullying as well as some of these behaviors being illegal. Numerous interventions have been proposed to address bullying, and Sampson outlined a total of 16 interventions for use in schools (see Sampson, 2009).

Cyberbullying is a unique form of bullying in which cellphones or other technologies are used in the behaviors discussed above. Cyberbullying is such an important problem that a hearing titled *Cyberbullying and other online safety issues for children* was held on September 30, 2009, before the Subcommittee on Crime, Terrorism, and Homeland Security of the Committee on the Judiciary House of Representatives 111th Congress (Committee on the Judiciary, 2009).

School, Campus, and Workplace Violence

Recent attention has been given to violence that occurs in educational and workplace settings. In 2009, nearly 572,000 nonfatal violent offenses were committed against workers, although the rates of these offenses have continued to decline since 1993 (Harrell, 2011). Some study results show that violent and nonviolent offenses are increasing in schools and colleges, while other studies show that these offenses are decreasing. These studies showing mixed results sampled the same time periods (Noonan & Vavra, 2007).

In some educational and workplace settings, after an incident of mass violence occurs a team of counselors responds to provide crisis intervention and support. Some of these counselors are social workers who provide immediate services after having received pre-training on how to handle a crisis situation. To be sure, incidents of mass violence can be traumatic for individuals involved. Survivors of these crimes may be in need of ongoing counseling or other services to cope with the aftermath of the violence. Social workers providing such services should be knowledgeable about the psychological and physiological reactions of survivors of these violent crimes so that appropriate services are provided.

Client violence toward social workers is also an important concern, particularly for those who provide services to violent offenders. Spencer & Munch (2003) recommended tasks for agency policies and procedures for client violence directed toward psychiatric outreach workers. These areas include client assessment (history of violence, mandated to treatment), environmental assessment (community violence, drug areas, safe travel routes), and worker-related tasks (cell phones programmed with emergency police numbers).

Violent Offenders

Violent offenders are individuals who have committed violent crimes such as homicide and assault or have used guns, knives and other weapons during the commission of a crime. Although violent offenders represent a minority of all offenders, when combined with those released from psychiatric hospitals and mentally disabled persons the number of violent offenders becomes much larger (Quinsey, Harris, Rice, & Cormier, 2006). Policymakers spend a great deal of energy seeking ways to address violent crimes.

For instance, the rise in violent juvenile crime has led to processing juveniles in the adult criminal justice system as opposed to the juvenile justice system (BJA, 1998).

Several medical and psychosocial interventions are recommended for violent offenders, in particular those who also experience mental illness (Lamb, Weinberger, & Gross, 1999). The SAMSHA National GAINS Center (2005) produced a report titled *The Nathaniel Project: An alternative to incarceration program for people with serious mental illness who have committed felony offenses.* The program provides a variety of services to persons with serious mental illness facing felony charges. In many instances, individuals have a history of violence. Services include court advocacy, prison pre-release planning, and post-release case management services. The report notes that it is "politically safer" to attend to low-level misdemeanor offenders but more difficult to address the needs of the serious mentally ill offender with a history of violence.

Juvenile Sex Offenders

One of every eight juvenile sex offenders is under the age of 12; females make up 7% of juvenile sex offenders; juveniles most often commit a sex offense in groups and while at school; and juveniles represent 35.6% of perpetrators who commit sex offenses against minors (Finkelhor, Ormrod, & Chaffin, 2009). Some states include juvenile sex offenders in their sex offender registration and notification laws whereas others do not.

Very little is known about the efficacy of the wide of range of treatment options that exists for juvenile sex offenders. Treatment options include residential and outpatient services that focus on addressing the denial associated with the offense, accepting responsibility for the offense, and expressing empathy toward the victim (Ertl & McNamara, 1997).

Teen Dating Violence

The juvenile justice system, unlike the adult criminal justice system, is not prepared to handle teen dating violence. Zosky (2010) observes that the primary reason is because the juvenile justice system was established to provide rehabilitation to youth instead of punishment. Consequently, how states define "domestic" (p. 366) in their domestic violence legislation excludes teen dating violence, and minor victims of domestic violence can not be granted orders of protection in some states. Zosky suggests that the juvenile justice system adopt policies similar to those found in the adult criminal justice system to address teenage dating violence while simultaneously maintaining the focus on rehabilitation.

Release of Low-level Offenders

Owing to the high costs associated with incarceration, particularly at a time when many states are experiencing fiscal deficits, policymakers have been exploring ways to reduce criminal justice expenditures, particularly those associated with incarceration. Most of these efforts are focused on first-time offenders and nonviolent offenders convicted of low-level misdemeanor offenses. Examples of low-level misdemeanor offenses include: (1) driving after revocation of driver's license, (2) driving after cancellation of driver's license, (3) driving without a valid driver's license, (4) disorderly conduct, (5) loitering with the intent to prostitute, (6) loitering with the intent to sell narcotics, and (7) lurking with the intent to commit a crime (Council on Crime and Justice, 2004).

In some states, individuals are being released from prisons because it is too costly to incarcerate them (Cohen, 2009), whereas in other states individuals are being incarcerated because they have not paid fines (Schwartz, 2009). In either case, these actions are driven by the need to increase state revenue and reduce costs.

Gerrymandering

In this context, gerrymandering is a practice in which prison inmates are counted in the U.S. Census in the district where they are incarcerated, not the districts that encompass their residences. According to Correct the Count (2010), this practice gives more political representation to some legislative districts, while reducing political power in others. Prisoners are counted in the district's census but are unable to vote. As a result of disparities in incarceration rates, gerrymandering has resulted in racial disparities in political power for African Americans and Latinos. So insidious is gerrymandering that some New York State legislative districts met their population numbers only because they counted prisoners, whereas in other districts prisoners made up half of the population. At present, only three states have ended the practice of gerrymandering (Delaware, Maryland, and New York).

Implications for Social Work Practice

Social workers should be knowledgeable about the intersectionality between group status and criminal justice outcomes among vulnerable populations. These populations are characterized by ethnic, racial, cultural, and other forms of diversity. They also experience disparities in the criminal justice system. If not addressed during the early stages of involvement in the criminal justice system, these disparities will exacerbate as individuals interact with the various components of the criminal justice system.

Effective practice interventions require communication and relationship-building skills, and the ability to consider individuals' needs as well as their experiences in the criminal justice system. It is also important to have the skills necessary to locate and retrieve information about local, state, and federal initiatives and legislation that addresses emerging issues. Such information can be used to guide planning and implement of these initiatives in communities. Social workers should be aware of emerging issues in criminal justice and how they affect individuals who are both victims and offenders. Moreover, attending to emerging issues requires that social workers possess meso and macro skills aimed at promoting human rights and social justice. Organizing and collaborating with civil rights and other organizations can be useful in this regard.

Chapter Summary

This chapter presented some populations who because of their statuses experience unique challenges when they have criminal justice system involvement. They require special considerations. The NASW *Code of ethics* directs social workers to challenge discrimination, oppression and social injustice. Each of these issues affects the populations discussed in this chapter. This chapter also examined numerous emerging issues in the criminal justice system with implications for social work practice.

Key Terms

Bullying	Gerrymandering	Social exclusion
Crime victim bill of rights	Juvenile	Status offense
Delinquency	Low-level offenders	Suicide-by-cop
Emerging issues	Racial disparity	Victim impact statement
Felon	Racial profiling	Violent offenders

Questions for Review

1. Define the term *status offense* and provide several examples. What do you think about status offenders being placed under the jurisdiction of the criminal justice system?
2. Select a special population with criminal justice system involvement presented in this chapter. Conduct further research and identify additional considerations for this population.
3. Select an emerging issue in the criminal justice system presented in this chapter. Conduct further research and identify additional considerations for the emerging issue you have selected.
4. Why is it important to collect data identifying incidents of racial profiling? Describe how racial profiling data can be used. List 5 limitations to data collection regarding racial profiling. Do you think that the benefits that can be derived from the data outweigh the limitations? Why or why not?

Further Reading

Ellis, R. A., & Sowers, K. M. (2001). *Juvenile justice practice: A cross-disciplinary approach to intervention*. Belmont, CA: Wadsworth, Brooks/Cole.

Reviere, R., & Young, V. D. (2004). Aging behind bars: Health care for older female inmates. *Journal of Women and Aging, 16(1/2)*, 55–69.

8 | Social Work Practice in the Criminal Justice System

Chapter Overview

Social work practice in the criminal justice system or with individuals having criminal justice involvement can be challenging. Social work functions include direct or clinical practice, administration, advocacy, research, and training and consultation provided to criminal justice professionals. Social workers also intervene at micro, meso, and macro environmental levels.

Social work practice in the criminal justice system is specialized social work practice, as opposed to generalist practice. This chapter examines six categories of criminal justice interventions: incapacitation, deterrence, rehabilitation, community restraints, structure and discipline, and combining rehabilitation and restraints. In addition, whereas each of the previous chapters included a summary of the social work practice implications relevant for that chapter topic, this chapter provides a more detailed examination of criminal justice practice issues. These issues include: practicing within authoritarian and host settings, providing services to mandated clients, individuals' right to self-determination, and social control. Each issue should be considered within the context of culturally relevant practice. Social workers should also be aware of the possibility of being co-opted when working in law enforcement, probation, parole, and correctional settings. Finally, this chapter is grounded in the NASW *Code of ethics*, and, like the focus of the book, emphasizes balancing public safety with social work ethics. Employment in the criminal justice system is considered by examining relevant job announcements.

Introduction to Social Work Practice

A key feature of the social work profession is its emphasis on changing lives as well as social environments. Another feature is the view that environmental factors influence social problems. Professional social work practice has its basis in the NASW *Code of ethics*, and as declared in the Preamble the mission of the profession is to enhance individual and societal well-being, meet needs, and empower vulnerable and oppressed populations, all within a social environmental context.

Social work practice therefore focuses on both individuals and their social environments. These principles are applicable to social work practice in a wide variety of settings such as schools, hospitals, the military, and correctional facilities; populations such as children, adults, and the elderly; and social problems such as poverty, homelessness, and unemployment. Systems theory supports assessment of the interactions between these factors. In Chapter 1, we described the criminal justice system as a system comprised of subsystems and examined the utility of the ecosystems framework for understanding the transactional interactions between individuals and their social and physical environments.

The *problem-solving model* is a useful framework for conceptualizing social work practice. The model focuses on identifying and implementing appropriate solutions to social problems. Compton, Galaway, & Cournoyer (2005) identified four major components associated with the problem-solving model and generalist social work practice. (1) Engagement refers to establishing a relationship with a client, defining problem areas, and working together on goals and problems. (2) Assessment involves joint efforts between the social worker and client aimed at identifying problem areas and solutions. Assessment also includes an examination of the etiology of the problem, and resources, skills, and supports available for problem-solving. (3) Intervention refers to those mutually agreed upon activities aimed at changing a problem area. Interventions can occur at micro, meso, and macro levels. Interventions focus on programs, policies, and practices, or services. (4) Evaluation activities involve assessing whether goals and outcomes were met, and what progress was made, and developing plans to continue services, provide a referral, or terminate services.

Whereas Compton, Galaway, & Cournoyer (2005) offered the problem-solving model as a framework for generalist social work practice, the model can also be utilized as a framework for specialist social work practice in the criminal justice system. For instance, engagement, assessment, intervention, and evaluation are essential functions that are used across all types and levels of social work practice. Furthermore, the model components are similar to those found in other practice areas. Similarities are apparent in the six steps Hoefer (2006) identified for policy practice: (1) getting involved, (2) understanding the issues, (3) planning, (4) advocating, (5) evaluating, and (6) ongoing monitoring.

The problem-solving model is also applicable for social work intervention at micro, meso, and macro levels. These environmental practice levels can be thought of as a hierarchy from smallest to largest. The smallest level of intervention is the micro level. Interventions at this level focus on individual, families, and groups. The next level is the meso level. The object of interventions within this level includes organizations, neighborhoods, and communities. Examples include educational institutions, employment organizations, and criminal justice agencies. The final and largest level of intervention is the macro level. Large-scale interventions that focus on local, state, federal, or global interventions are situated at the macro level. For example, an intervention intended to support state crime legislation is macro-level practice. As social workers intervene with individuals and their social environments, social workers engage in social change efforts to impact all of these levels either individually or simultaneously.

Generalist Social Work Practice

The first year of study in the majority of MSW (graduate) programs places emphasis on generalist social work education practice. In the second year, students learn specialized social work practice within a specific *field of practice*. A field of practice refers to specialized knowledge and skills within a specific practice area. Examples of fields of practice include criminal justice, aging, child welfare, health, mental health, substance abuse, children, youth and families, and immigration. Whereas BSW (undergraduate) programs focus exclusively on generalist practice, MSW programs focus on both generalist and specialist social practice. *Generalist practice* is a holistic approach to practice in which services and interventions are determined based on client needs (Hepworth, Rooney, Rooney, Strom-Gottfried, & Larsen, 2010).

Specialized Social Work Practice

Social workers require specialized training to practice in the criminal justice system (Sarri & Shook, 2005). *Specialized social work practice* refers to possessing an area of expertise and knowledge relative to a specific population or social problem. Commonly reported illustrations used to describe the differences between generalist and specialized social work practice are taken from the field of medicine. Physicians may be generalist practitioners who first examine a wide variety of ailments, and then refer to a specialist physician who possesses specialized knowledge and skill in treating a particular ailment. A specialist physician is much more qualified and experienced to treat the ailment since it is their exclusive area of practice. Readers may be familiar with medical insurance plans which stipulate that insured individuals must first schedule a visit with a generalist practitioner, and receive a referral to a specialist. This is required for medical reimbursement and without the referral the insurance company may refuse to pay for the treatment. A social worker who testifies as an expert witness is an example of specialty social work practice.

Social Work Practice Methods and Roles

As mentioned, social work students, as well as experienced social workers, are often interested in a field of practice and seek training in a particular field. Regardless of the field of practice, social work practice methods are used across these fields. *Practice methods* are areas of concentration such as administration, clinical practice, community organizing, and policy and research. A social worker specializing in the child welfare field of practice could use any of these practice methods. A social worker in the criminal justice field of practice could also employ any of the aforementioned practice methods. Likewise, the same social work roles are employed in both generalist and specialized practice and across fields of practice. Social workers involved in clinical practice (the largest area of social work practice in the criminal justice system) perform tasks such as: direct service roles (work with individuals, couples, families, groups, and educators);

system linkage roles (broker, case management, coordinator, mediator, arbitrator, and advocate); system developer (program developer, planner, policy and procedure developer, advocate); researcher and research consumer; and systems maintenance roles (organizational assessor, facilitator, expediter, team member, consultant, and consultee) (see Hepworth, Rooney, Rooney, Strom-Gottfried, & Larsen, 2010, pp. 26–31).

Criminal Justice as a Field of Practice

Social workers have been interested and employed in the criminal justice system as theoreticians and practitioners prior to social work formally developing into a professional occupation (Chaiklin, 2007). Criminal justice is a field of practice that requires specialized knowledge and skills. Frequently, it requires knowledge and skills in a second field of practice. Lamb, Weinberger, & Gross (1999) conducted a literature review and identified numerous differences in community-based treatment for mentally ill offenders and nonoffenders. Notably, mentally ill offenders are often required to comply with sanctions, resist treatment, and experience barriers in the mental health system owing to their criminal justice system involvement and oftentimes a history of violence. In this instance, social work practice necessitates elements from both criminal justice and mental health fields of practice.

Social workers intervene in response to offending behavior, but it is also vital to provide interventions for other problems such as substance abuse, poverty, poor parenting skills, child abuse and neglect, inadequate housing, poor social relationships, anti-social and criminal peer relationships, poor impulse control, aggression, and low levels of education. Each of these problems affects the possibility that former offenders will commit new offenses (McNeill, Batchelor, Burnett, & Knox, 2005). Furthermore, incarceration and other criminal justice system involvement not only affect the individuals involved but also negatively affect their family members, friends, and community. Iguchi, London, Gorge, Hickman, Fain, & Riehman (2002) observed that offenders returning to vulnerable communities high in substance abuse and crime-fighting efforts, and low in resources to address these issues, weaken the social organization within these communities.

Unfortunately, few social work educational programs offer criminal justice as a field of practice. Social work interns are often unprepared to practice in correctional settings (Ivanoff, Smyth, & Finnegan, 1993), and social work educational programs do not offer students courses in corrections due to inadequate resources to provide such courses (Young & Lomonaco, 2001). As we have seen throughout this book, social work practice in the criminal justice system encompasses more than corrections. Social work educational programs need to carefully consider what content to teach in this field of practice and how to best prepare students for practice. These issues are raised in Chapter 10.

Criminal Justice Interventions

In addition to specialized expertise and skills, social workers should also be knowledge about the interventions used in the criminal justice system. MacKenzie (1997) categorized criminal justice interventions into six broad types:

1. *Incapacitation* refers to eliminating an offender's ability to commit future crimes. This is most often achieved through incarceration in a correctional facility.
2. *Deterrence* refers to activities that are used to discourage individuals from committing crimes. An example is death penalty legislation. It is intended to deter or discourage individuals from committing homicide. As discussed in Chapter 4, NASW opposes death penalty legislation.
3. *Rehabilitation* refers to interventions that change an offender's thoughts, feelings, or behavior. Changing these areas of individual functioning has the potential to reduce future criminal behavior. Rehabilitation includes treatment and counseling interventions and is most suited to social work education and training. Social workers will feel more comfortable providing this category of intervention more than the others.
4. *Community restraints* refers to monitoring individuals. Monitoring can occur through supervision, physically wearing a monitor that tracks an individual's location, and surveillance methods. Social workers may be less comfortable engaged in practice which involves community restraints methods.
5. *Structure, discipline, and challenge* refers to physical or mental activities that provide structure and discipline for individuals. These activities are intended to challenge a person in such a way that they change their attitudes toward criminal behavior. These interventions are designed to deter criminal behavior.
6. *Combining rehabilitation and restraint* represents a combination of interventions focused on individual functioning and community monitoring such as parole supervision.

Criminogenic Needs

The risk–needs–responsivity model postulates that the risk for reoffending must first be assessed. Once risk level has been assessed, interventions should be matched to the level of risk (Andrews, 1989; Andrews & Bonta, 2010). The model is comprised of three principles: the risk principle, the need principle, and the responsivity principle. The risk principle assumes that recidivism rates are reduced when interventions and services provided to offenders match their assessed risk level for reoffending. This necessitates an assessment that results in categorization of high-risk and low-risk offenders. Conversely, the need principle stipulates that interventions focus on criminogenic needs. *Criminogenic needs*, also referred to as dynamic risk factors, are those factors associated with criminal behavior. By reducing dynamic risks (thereby decreasing criminogenic needs) we should observe decreased reoffending and recidivism among offenders.

These dynamic risks should therefore be a component of treatment planning. Static risk factors are those that can not be changed. A list of seven criminogenic needs that can be changed through intervention include: (1) anti-social personality; (2) pro-criminal attitudes; (3) social supports for criminal behavior; (4) substance abuse; (5) poor family and marital relationships; (6) inadequate school and work performance; and (7) lack of pro-social recreational activities. The responsivity principle suggests that cognitive-social learning interventions are the most effective interventions for reducing criminal behavior (Andrews & Bonta, 2010).

Using Data to Inform Interventions

One of the primary interventions provided to incarcerated and reentering offenders is substance abuse treatment. Visher & Courtney (2007) found that, one year after being released, former prisoners in Cleveland used the following services: substance abuse treatment (38%), employment skills/job training (37%), counseling (22%), life skills training (16%), anger management (13%), parenting skills (8%), and educational programs (8%). More than half (66%) indicated that they used at least one program. This study shows that substance abuse treatment was the most often utilized program. Over time the number of former offenders reentering communities with substance abuse problems has increased. The percentage of state prisoners reentering communities who were drug offenders increased from 11% in 1985 to 33% in 1999. Similarly, the percentage of parolees convicted of a drug offense increased from 27% in 1990 to 35% in 1999. Among state prisoners released in 1999, 84% reported drug or alcohol involvement at the time they committed the crime that resulted in incarceration, and 21% reported committing a crime to obtain money to buy drugs. In 2004, approximately one-third of state prisoners and one-quarter of federal prisoners committed a crime while under the influence of drugs. Interestingly, while incarcerated only 40% of state prisoners and 49% of federal prisoners with substance abuse problems received treatment, representing less than half of those in need (Mumola & Karberg, 2006).

Data such as these can inform the need for substance abuse services and programs. Also needed are protocols for ensuring that treatment is relevant for individuals with criminal justice system involvement. Fletcher & Chandler (2006) identified 13 principles of substance abuse treatment relevant for criminal justice populations. These include the following:

1. Drug addiction is a brain disease that affects behavior.
2. Recovery from drug addiction requires effective treatment, followed by management of the problem over time.
3. Treatment must last long enough to produce stable behavioral changes.
4. Assessment is the first step in treatment.
5. Tailoring services to fit the needs of the individual is an important part of effective drug abuse treatment for criminal justice populations.
6. Drug use during treatment should be carefully monitored.
7. Treatment should target factors that are associated with criminal behavior.

8. Criminal justice supervision should incorporate treatment planning for drug abusing offenders, and treatment providers should be aware of correctional supervision requirements.
9. Continuity of care is essential for drug abusers reentering the community.
10. A balance of rewards and sanctions encourages pro-social behavior and treatment participation
11. Offenders with co-occurring drug abuse and mental health problems often require an integrated treatment approach
12. Medications are an important part of treatment for many drug abusing offenders.
13. Treatment planning for drug abusing offenders who are living in or reentering the community should include strategies to prevent and treat serious, chronic medical conditions, such as HIV/AIDS, hepatitis B and C, and tuberculosis.

Anti-oppressive Practice in the Criminal Justice System

Criminal justice populations often associate power, oppression, control, and punishment with service providers. When social workers and other service providers define their problems for them, this has the negative effect of validating their perceptions about service providers (Compton, Galaway, & Cournoyer, 2005). Anti-oppressive practice has been offered as an approach to social justice that acknowledges power and oppression. Larson (2008) summarized the principles of anti-oppressive practice as a framework for social justice that supports equal relationships and power, encourages awareness of personal power, questions social structures that assign power to certain groups, and employs interventions that support equal power.

More attention has been given to mental health settings and anti-oppressive practice, although the similarities with criminal justice settings are evident. Larson (2008) characterized mental health settings as hierarchical, patriarchal, and having unequal power relationships. Implementing anti-oppressive practice in criminal justice settings and with criminal justice populations is not an easy task. Law enforcement agencies, courts, and correctional settings are by design hierarchical, unequal in power, and in some instances such as law enforcement and institutional correctional facilities the settings follow a paramilitary model. It is doubtful that anti-oppressive practice efforts as presently articulated will improve social justice within the criminal justice system. Measures such as impact legislation and other legal activities, as well as ongoing monitoring, have the potential to make significant inroads in this area.

Social workers employed in criminal justice settings are hired to provide services or other functions, thereby making anti-oppressive practice principles difficult to implement since these are a part of social work functions. Moreover, Larson (2008) noted that social workers employed in mental health settings reported that there was insufficient time while performing their jobs and few opportunities to engage in anti-oppressive practice to pursue social justice.

Specifically referring to anti-oppressive social work practice, Wilson & Beresford (2000) provided a debate in which they suggested that clients and agencies have not played a significant role in the development of anti-oppressive practice, the goals of social justice may be unobtainable among certain populations and systems, and anti-oppressive practices may themselves be oppressive. More research is needed that investigates the application and efficacy of anti-oppressive practice in the criminal justice system and with criminal justice populations.

Restorative Justice

Restorative justice is an approach that has been applied to juvenile crime and the juvenile justice system (Bazemore & Walgrave, 1999). Restorative justice has also been offered as an approach in the adult criminal justice system. Restorative justice is an approach to criminal justice in which those affected by the offense including the victim, offender, and community residents participate in discussions aimed at healing victims and restoring justice (van Wormer, 2009). This approach also presents opportunities for social workers to practice in the criminal justice system utilizing a model based on healing instead of the typical adversarial model found in the criminal justice system. Social workers employing a restorative approach use (1) victim–offender conferencing, (2) family group conferencing, (3) healing circles, and (4) community reparations methods (van Wormer, 2008).

Social Control

Functioning as a social control agent is a social work role (Burman, 2004). This role is sometimes neglected in introductory social work practice texts. Barker (2003) defined social control as "1. The organized effort of a society or some of its members to maintain a stable social order and to manage the process of social change. 2. Efforts to constrain people requiring them to adhere to established norms and laws" (p. 403). Whereas social workers might agree with the first part of Barker's definition and support the need to maintain social order, it is the second part of the definition that may make social workers a bit uneasy. Because of the values of the profession, social workers reject attempts to constrain an individual's ability to make choices, although they would agree that individuals should obey laws.

Criminal justice agencies carry out functions that require their practitioners to exert social control. For example, police officers maintain social order through limiting behavior that violates laws. Courts impose sanctions on those who violate laws, and probation and parole officers monitor the behavior of individuals to ensure they are law-abiding and comply with sanctions.

Some would argue that social workers are engaged in social control when providing social work services because oftentimes the service outcomes demand adaptation to societal norms, values, and behaviors. As a case in point, Cowger & Atherton (1974) argued that societies maintain social control through the use of police or providing social services, or both. They suggest that the U.S. relies on both police authority and the provision of social services, particularly in response to social problems such as substance and alcohol abuse, mental illness, and juvenile delinquency.

Consequently, social workers and other social service providers apply social control in the helping process. To function effectively in criminal justice and human service settings, social workers must resolve these issues of social control. At the same time as resolving these issues, social workers must thoroughly understand the mission, goals, and objectives of the particular criminal justice setting or agency in which they are employed. Whether or not social workers perceive themselves as agents of social control, individuals with criminal justice involvement will perceive the social worker as an agent of social control. This is particularly so among individuals who are mandated to participate in services under court order or other sanctions. Effective practice calls for social workers to be accepting of this role and its relevance to social work principles. It also necessitates that social workers not abuse their authority.

Social Work Practice in Authoritarian Settings

Criminal justice agencies are authoritarian settings. *Authoritarian settings* are those agencies in which the workforce is authorized to exert a great deal of power and authority over individuals in their charge. In these settings social workers must be able to balance legal authority and psychological authority (Hutchison, 1987). Hutchison asserted that social work practice characteristically involves authority. For instance, determining which issues to explore during interviews and which treatment approach to employ are presented as examples where social workers exercise authority in practice. Hutchison and others have noted that social workers perceive practice in such settings to be inconsistent with social work values and question whether social workers should assume practice roles in these settings. Finally, Hutchison also provided 13 principles to guide social work practice with mandated clients in authoritarian settings, suggesting that these settings are appropriate for social workers who possess considerable skills for resolving authority issues.

Similarly to the challenges that arise in host settings, authoritarian settings present numerous challenges for social workers. These challenges include resolving ethical issues concerning an individual's right to self-determination, working with mandated clients, confidentiality, and establishing professional relationships with colleagues from other disciplines.

Social Work Practice in Host Settings

Criminal justice agencies are host or secondary settings. *Host settings* are agencies in which social work is not the primary profession. For example, in law enforcement agencies social workers are not the primary profession. Other examples of host settings within the criminal justice system include correctional facilities, courts, and probation and parole departments. Examples of host settings outside of the criminal justice system include hospitals, schools, and the military.

Social workers should be aware of several matters when employed in host settings. Social workers employed in host settings often perceive the profession to be marginalized within these settings. Indeed resources are first allocated to the primary profession or occupation and because they represent the largest numbers of employees they have the greatest influence. Within host settings policies and procedures may be contrary to social work values. Dealing with the organizational bureaucracy may be challenging. Without a doubt even the primary occupation may find these procedures frustrating.

Not all criminal-justice-related practice occurs in host settings. Some human service agencies may operate innovative programs that provide criminal justice services within the context of a broader agency mission. In other situations the entire agency and its various programs focus on servicing individuals with criminal justice involvement.

Social Work Practice with Mandated Clients

Mandated or *involuntary* clients are individuals who by court order or other sanctions are required to comply with specific conditions such as being enrolled in and attending a treatment program. Examples of services that clients can be mandated to participate in are substance abuse, anger management, or counseling programs. Not attending service appointments for a person mandated to do so can result in a violation. A judge or other authority that imposed the initial conditions can consider alternative sanctions. Sanctions imposed on individuals who do not comply with court orders may include incarceration, fines, or loss of certain rights.

Providing services to mandated clients requires acknowledgement that clients are coerced to participate in services. Consequently, clients may not be motivated to participate in services. In other instance their motivations to participate are driven by a desire not to improve their situations but only to fulfill sanctions. Sanctions can have an adverse impact on the helping relationship that social workers develop with clients (Burman, 2004).

Some of the practice activities with mandated clients are the same that would be used with voluntary clients, and are basic to social work practice. The following guidelines are suggested for mandated criminal justice populations:

- Openly discuss individuals' mandated status.
- Explore the meaning that mandated status holds for individuals.
- Explore individuals' concerns about being violated for not complying with sanctions or conditions.
- Expect individuals to fully participate in the process of written or verbal reports that will be provided to authorities.
- Use a perspective that acknowledges attendance, punctuality, participation, and growth among other qualities.
- If informed that participation is occurring only to fulfill conditions, do not take this information personally or let it arouse anger. This information should be explored and discussed openly.

Social Work Practice with Voluntary Clients

While many individuals seen by social workers who have criminal justice system involvement are mandated clients, there are also those who are voluntary clients. Social work practice in the criminal justice system will also involve providing services to voluntary clients. *Voluntary clients* are individuals who are motivated to participate in services and do so on their own volition. Social work practitioners prefer to provide services to clients who voluntarily seek services and are motivated to participate (Hutchison, 1987). Although clients voluntarily seek services, it is plausible that they have been referred by a police officer, attorney, or other criminal justice practitioner. For example, a youth who is beginning to infrequently engage in status offense behaviors may be referred by a police officer to counseling.

Right to Self-determination

As we have established, social workers and other practitioners in the criminal justice system (e.g, police officers, judges, probation officers, and parole officers) are viewed by criminal justice populations as agents of social control. Social workers have an ethical responsibility to help individuals exercise their right to self-determination and to appreciate the choices they make. Social workers also consider social control as contrary to an individual's right to self-determination. Barker (2003) defined the *right to self-determination* as

> An ethical principle in social work that recognizes the rights and needs of clients to be free to make their own choices and decisions. Inherent in the principle is the requirement for the social worker to help the client know what the resources and choices are and what the consequences of selecting any one of them will be. Usually, self-determination also includes helping the client implement the decision made. Self-determination is one of the major factors in the helping relationship.
>
> (p. 387)

Central to this definition is the need to provide individuals with the information they require to make informed choices and subsequently provide assistance that individuals may require to implement their choices. It can be argued that, by not complying with mandated conditions that have been imposed for law violations, and being willing to face alternatives such as incarceration, a person is exercising the right to self-determination.

Confidentiality

Most readers have perhaps watched the local evening news and noticed that a great number of the lead news stories cover a crime or an arrest. These news reports often show a video of the individual(s) who was arrested, describe their crime(s), and provide details about the crime and/or arrest and charges all before a trial has been held. Obviously these events are not confidential. While the media can make these details public information, the NASW *Code of ethics* requires that social workers maintain confidentiality when interacting with the media.

Social workers have an ethical obligation to maintain confidentiality in other areas as well. *Confidentiality* refers to keeping private the information obtained about a client. Clients must give a social worker permission, often through signed consent, to share private information with other individuals or organizations. Oftentimes in the criminal justice system, particularly in probation and parole settings, individuals are required to consent. In social work practice, some situations do exist in which the conditions of confidentiality do not apply. These situations should be mentioned at the onset of interventions and include the mandated reporting of child abuse, and other situations in which individuals threaten to harm themselves or others (see *Tarasoff v. Regents of the University of California*, 1976). The NASW *Code of ethics* does not specify these situations. Therefore, social workers must consult relevant laws and agency policies.

Maintaining confidentiality in criminal justice settings presents unique challenges. As an illustration, Curtis and Lutkus (1985) surveyed 41 police social workers regarding their views about confidentiality and the challenges associated with maintaining confidentiality in police department settings. They concluded: "information that might be confidential in other circumstances can not be confidential. Information must be shared with the police and paramedics when it is related to a valid concern about physical safety" (p. 359).

Social Work Employment in Criminal Justice

Fewer social work positions are found in the legislative arena. More social work positions exist in law enforcement, courts, and corrections. The order of employment positions among the four components of the criminal justice system, from fewest to most, is legislation, law enforcement, courts, and corrections. A key point made throughout this book is the fact that social work practitioners need not be employed in a criminal justice setting or agency to provide services to individuals with criminal justice system involvement. As mentioned, some entire human service agencies provide services to criminal justice populations. An example is an agency that exclusively focuses on reentry services. Other agencies may only maintain specialized programs that provide services to criminal justice populations. In these situations criminal justice populations receive services together with non-criminal justice populations.

A Sample Job Announcement

A job announcement appeared in the *NASW News* for the position of probation officer with the U.S. Probation Department. Box 8.1 illustrates a number of the employment details that were contained in the job announcement for this federal position. As discussed in Chapter 2, federal crimes are those that violate federal laws and are prosecuted in federal courts. The federal government also administers a probation department. Box 8.1 shows that social workers were specifically sought after for this position. The type of clientele, services, and goals of the position are mentioned. Interestingly, the announcement mentions that the "job is not for everybody" and the dangerous circumstances of the position.

A licensure requirement is also not mentioned in the announcement. Interestingly, many positions in the criminal justice system do not require social work licensure. Some positions are civil service positions whereas others are not. Social work practice is regulated through licensing in the 50 states, the District of Columbia, Puerto Rico, and the Virgin Islands. In general a BSW or MSW degree is required to become a licensed social worker although some states allow practitioners who have studied other fields to obtain social work licensure. Such regulations give the social work profession a protected title and also protect from unregulated social work practice (Ginsberg, 2001). In addition to obtaining licensure, social workers practicing in the criminal justice system may opt to join some of the professional associations that are associated with criminal justice practice. These include the National Association of Forensic Counselors (NAFC) or the National Organization of Forensic Social Work (NOFSW), among others. A sample of criminal justice organizations is provided in the Resources section located at the end of this book.

Box 8.1 Sample Job Announcement for Probation Officer

You never thought of this as a social work job did you?

Some of our most successful officers have an M.S.W.

Our clientele have been convicted of federal crimes. It is your job to prevent them from engaging in any further criminal activity.

We assist them with: finding employment; securing suitable housing; intervening in domestic violence; providing counseling and therapy for a myriad of problems.

We have specialists in substance abuse treatment, mental health treatment, community service, electronic monitoring, sex offender treatment, as well as special units for career criminals.

This job is not for everybody.

It is classified as a Hazardous Duty position for pay and retirement purposes (you can retire with half pay after 20 years).

Source: *NASW News* (2000). November 45(1), 15.

Box 8.2 illustrates a number of conditions intended for probation supervision identified from the U.S. Probation Department website. A review of this partial list provides a picture of some of the difficulties that a probation officer and an individual on probation supervision might experience. For instance, interventions should address recidivism so that probationers will not commit further crimes; substance and alcohol abuse treatment to prevent relapse; and opportunities for employment, educational, or training programs so that probationers can support their dependants and fulfill family responsibilities.

If these areas are not addressed, fulfilling probation conditions may be difficult. In some communities the lack of evidence-based treatments or employment, educational, and training opportunities is a consideration. This is compounded by the lack of health insurance and access to health and mental health care. Moreover, as a result of the declining economic climate and high unemployment rates in the U.S., such opportunities may be becoming increasingly difficult for former offenders. Unemployment rates and educational success are not equal among racial and ethnic groups. This situation is compounded when considering criminal justice involvement.

Box 8.2 Conditions of Probation Supervision

- The defendant shall not commit another federal, state, or local crime.
- The defendant shall support his or her dependants and meet other family responsibilities.
- The defendant shall work regularly at a lawful occupation, unless excused by the probation officer for schooling, training, or other acceptable reasons.
- The defendant shall refrain from excessive use of alcohol and shall not purchase, possess, use, distribute, or administer any controlled substance or any paraphernalia related to any controlled substances, except as prescribed by a physician.
- The defendant shall not frequent places where controlled substances are illegally sold, used, distributed, or administered.
- The defendant shall not associate with any persons engaged in criminal activity and shall not associate with any person convicted of a felony, unless granted permission to do so by the probation officer.

Source: Adapted from U.S. Probation Department (2007).
Conditions of supervision: Standard conditions.

Ethical Responsibilities Relevant for Practice in the Criminal Justice System

All of the ethical standards contained in the NASW *Code of ethics* have relevance for social work practice in the criminal justice system. However, three ethical standards comprising five areas are particularly relevant for addressing challenging issues that are likely to occur. These are:

1. Social Workers' Ethical Responsibilities to Colleagues (2.01—Respect; 2.03—Interdisciplinary Collaboration; and 2.04—Disputes Involving Colleagues);

2. Social Workers' Ethical Responsibilities in Practice Settings (3.09—Commitments to Employers);
3. Social Workers' Ethical Responsibilities as Professionals (4.01—Competence).

When one is carrying out social work functions in criminal justice settings or with individuals having criminal justice system involvement, ethical dilemmas are inevitable. These dilemmas arise in relation to work with clients, the agency, and the broader society as well as with colleagues. The source for many dilemmas is a consequence of the criminal justice system as a complex and multi-faceted system characterized by racial disparities, frequently competing philosophies that drive the system, injustices, and legislation that has an adverse impact on specific demographic groups.

Whistleblowing has been described as an advocacy activity for dealing with ethical dilemmas (Greene & Latting, 2004). Greene & Latting provide guidelines designed to inform the whistleblowing process for both social workers and agencies. Westmarland (2001) discusses the ethical dilemmas that arise in research, describing situations in which researchers may observe police officers to use excessive force. The ethical issues that arise are whether to whistleblow, inform the officer, or notify supervisors or other bodies. Westmarland noted that the first difficulty encountered is determining whether the use of force was justified or excessive. After making this determination, decisions about which options to pursue are based "on the moral and ethical beliefs and feelings of the individual" (p. 533).

Responsibilities to Colleagues

Because of the different professional groups who are employed in the criminal justice system and the complex social problems of criminal justice populations, practitioners have varied qualifications, worldviews, and responsibilities. While these issues are not unique to social work practice settings, they are exacerbated in the criminal justice system because of crime and justice issues. These differences also include different perspectives on the causes of crime and the best approaches for treating individuals involved in the criminal justice system. The NASW *Code of ethics* provides guidance for social workers' ethical responsibilities toward other colleagues when such differences arise, indicating that colleagues should be treated with respect and social workers should cooperate with other practitioners to enhance the services that clients receive. The guidelines are shown in Box 8.3.

Box 8.3 Social Workers' Ethical Responsibilities to Colleagues (2.01 Respect)

(a) Social workers should treat colleagues with respect and should represent accurately and fairly the qualifications, views, and obligations of colleagues.

(b) Social workers should avoid unwarranted negative criticism of colleagues in communications with clients or with other professionals. Unwarranted negative criticism may include demeaning comments that refer to colleagues' level of competence or to individuals' attributes such as race, ethnicity, national origin, color, sex, sexual orientation, gender identity or expression, age, marital status, political belief, religion, immigration status, and mental or physical disability.

(c) Social workers should cooperate with social work colleagues and with colleagues of other professions when such cooperation serves the well-being of clients.

Clearly, in criminal justice settings as well as human service settings that involve criminal justice populations a great deal of social work collaboration occurs with other disciplines. Box 8.4 describes social work conduct during interdisciplinary collaboration. During the course of collaborations social work must maintain a viewpoint that is consistent with professional values.

Box 8.4 Social Workers' Ethical Responsibilities to Colleagues (2.03 Interdisciplinary Collaboration)

(a) Social workers who are members of an interdisciplinary team should participate in and contribute to decisions that affect the wellbeing of clients by drawing on the perspectives, values, and experiences of the social work profession. Professional and ethical obligations of the interdisciplinary team as a whole and of its individual members should be clearly established.

(b) Social workers for whom a team decision raises ethical concerns should attempt to resolve the disagreement through appropriate channels. If the disagreement cannot be resolved, social workers should pursue other avenues to address their concerns consistent with client wellbeing.

Disputes between social workers and colleagues from other disciplines may be inescapable as professional values compete with strong personal worldviews regarding crime and punishment, individual responsibility, and access or the lack of access to opportunities. Indeed when one is working with colleagues from different professions in the criminal justice system, different worldviews and orientations regarding crime, public safety approaches, and interventions readily arise. These differences are also certain to arise on the basis of the mission and values of the social work profession. As seen in Box 8.5, when such disputes arise social workers have an ethical responsibility to avoid pursuing self-interests or including clients in these disputes in an improper manner.

Box 8.5 Social Workers' Ethical Responsibilities to Colleagues (2.04 Disputes Involving Colleagues)

(a) Social workers should not take advantage of a dispute between a colleague and an employer to obtain a position or otherwise advance the social workers' own interests.
(b) Social workers should not exploit clients in disputes with colleagues or engage clients in any inappropriate discussion of conflicts between social workers and their colleagues.

Copyrighted material reprinted with permission from the
National Association of Social Workers, Inc.

Responsibilities in Practice Settings

Social work practice in the criminal justice involves practice in authoritarian and host settings where individuals in social work care have limited self-determination and are often mandated to receive services, and where practitioners have a great deal of power and authority over them. Box 8.6 illustrates social workers' ethical responsibilities in practice settings. Ideally, social workers should be knowledgeable about criminal justice practice prior to assuming employment so that job functions and other commitments can be fulfilled without sentiments that agency policies and practice are oppressive, discriminatory, or at odds with social work values. This requires the ability to distinguish between criminal justice functions and actual injustices that occur in practice settings. Burman (2004) noted that the NASW *Code of ethics* offers insufficient guidance regarding ethical standards for providing services in the context of social control and with mandated clients.

Box 8.6 Social Workers' Ethical Responsibilities in Practice Settings (3.09 Commitments to Employers)

(a) Social workers generally should adhere to commitments made to employers and employing organizations.

(b) Social workers should work to improve employing agencies' policies and procedures and the efficiency and effectiveness of their services.

(c) Social workers should take reasonable steps to ensure that employers are aware of social workers' ethical obligations as set forth in the NASW Code of Ethics and of the implications of those obligations for social work practice.

(d) Social workers should not allow an employing organization's policies, procedures, regulations, or administrative orders to interfere with their ethical practice of social work. Social workers should take reasonable steps to ensure that their employing organizations' practices are consistent with the NASW Code of Ethics.

(e) Social workers should act to prevent and eliminate discrimination in the employing organization's work assignments and in its employment policies and practices.

(f) Social workers should accept employment or arrange student field placements only in organizations that exercise fair personnel practices.

(g) Social workers should be diligent stewards of the resources of their employing organizations, wisely conserving funds where appropriate and never misappropriating funds or using them for unintended purposes.

Copyrighted material reprinted with permission from the
National Association of Social Workers, Inc.

Responsibilities as Professionals

Box 8.7 outlines numerous ethical responsibilities related to practice competence. Noteworthy are social workers' ethical responsibilities to include empirical evidence in practice as well as to remain current through continuing education opportunities and reading literature. In criminal justice this includes the "what works, what doesn't and what's promising" literature.

Box 8.7 Social Workers' Ethical Responsibilities as Professionals (4.01 Competence)

(a) Social workers should accept responsibility or employment only on the basis of existing competence or the intention to acquire the necessary competence.

(b) Social workers should strive to become and remain proficient in professional practice and the performance of professional functions. Social workers should critically examine and keep current with emerging knowledge relevant to social work. Social workers should routinely review the professional literature and participate in continuing education relevant to social work practice and social work ethics.

(c) Social workers should base practice on recognized knowledge, including empirically based knowledge, relevant to social work and social work ethics.

Copyrighted material reprinted with permission from the National Association of Social Workers, Inc.

Implications for Social Work Practice

This chapter examined social practice in criminal justice in greater detail than previous chapters. Preceding chapters examined social work practice relative to crime legislation, law enforcement agencies, courts, and correctional agencies. Several alternative criminal justice programs and reforms were also examined. Highly specialized knowledge and skills are required for practice in the criminal justice system. Oftentimes, an additional field of practice area (e.g., mental health, substance abuse, or child welfare) is also required. Whereas criminal justice is a field of practice area, other fields of practice interface with the criminal justice system.

Important decisions need to be made regarding the best approaches for preparing students and professionals for a criminal justice field of practice. Cases assigned to students for student field work learning opportunities are highly selective. Some cases such as those that involve violence may be deemed unsuitable for student learning. Consequently, in most instances students acquire practice experience on the basis of a small, highly selective caseload. Once employed in criminal justice settings, social workers will be expected to provide services in a much wider range of case situations.

An important issue worth mentioning again is that job announcements and descriptions delineate the tasks that social workers will perform in criminal justice settings. For instance, a social worker may be committed to social change efforts that deal with racial disparities in sentencing. It is improbable that this goal can be achieved in a position created to provide administrative or clinical practice services. This does not mean that social workers should not challenge racial disparities or other forms of social injustice. Practical options such as collaborating with NASW, professional associations, or community-based and grassroots organizations can provide fruitful opportunities to challenge social injustice.

A distinction was made in this book between employment *within* a criminal justice setting (legislative office, law enforcement agency, courts, or corrections) and the provision of services to clients with criminal justice involvement by a social worker who is employed *outside* of a criminal justice setting (e.g., outpatient or inpatient mental health setting, nonprofit human service agency). Individuals having criminal justice system involvement require a range of services such as alcohol and substance abuse treatment or anger management services. These services are often not provided in criminal justice settings and are more likely to be provided outside of some criminal justice settings such as law enforcement, courts, probation, or parole. The experiences of a social worker employed in an outpatient mental health clinic that provides services to an individual under probation or parole supervision are very different from those of a social worker who is employed as a probation or parole officer.

Chapter Summary

Criminal justice is a field of practice. Other fields of practice include child welfare, mental health, health, and aging, among others. This chapter explored key issues that arise for social workers in the criminal justice field of practice. Some of these issues can also occur in noncriminal justice settings. The issues discussed included working in authoritarian and host settings, social control, working with mandated or involuntary clients, and working with colleagues who may hold different worldviews regarding causes of crime, punishment, and rehabilitation. The NASW *Code of ethics* was drawn upon to provide guidance for social workers.

Key Terms

Anti-oppressive social work practice	Generalist social work practice	Right to self-determination
Confidentiality	Host settings	Social control
Criminogenic needs	Mandated clients	Specialist social work practice
Field of practice	Practice methods	Voluntary clients

Questions for Review

1. Why is social work practice in the criminal justice system considered specialized social work practice? What is a field of practice? Provide several examples.
2. Summarize the 6 areas of criminal justice intervention. Which intervention(s) do you feel most comfortable with? Why? Which intervention(s) do you feel least comfortable with, and why?
3. Do you feel that social control limits social workers' ability to help criminal justice populations? Why or why not?
4. Define the right to self-determination. Provide an example in which criminal justice populations can not exercise this right and an example where they can.
5. What were your reactions when you read the sample job announcement? On the basis of the announcement can you anticipate the issues that might arise in these positions? Describe the issues.

Further Reading

Alexander, R., Jr. (2000). *Counseling, treatment, and interventions methods with juvenile and adult offenders*. Belmont, CA: Wadsworth, Brooks/Cole.

Congress, E. (2007). Ethical practice in forensic social work. In Albert R. Roberts & David W. Springer (eds.) *Social work in juvenile and criminal justice settings* (3rd ed.) (pp. 75–86). Springfield, IL: Charles C. Thomas.

Hendricks, J. E. (ed.). (2002). *Crisis intervention in criminal justice/social service* (3rd ed.). Springfield, IL: Charles C. Thomas.

Kratcoski, P. C. (2004). *Correctional counseling and treatment* (5th ed.). Long Grove, IL: Waveland Press, Inc.

Raynor, P. (1985). *Social work, justice and control*. New York: Basil Blackwell Ltd.

Reamer, F. G. (1998). *Ethical standards in social work: A critical review of the NASW Code of Ethics*. Washington, DC: NASW Press.

Rooney, R. H. (1992). *Strategies for work with involuntary clients*. New York: Columbia University Press.

Roseman, C. P., Ritchie, M., & Laux, J. M. (2009). A restorative justice approach to empathy development in sex offenders: An exploratory study. *Journal of Addictions & Offender Counseling, 29*, 96–109.

Stein, T. J. (2004). *The role of law in social work practice and administration*. New York: Columbia University Press.

Trotter, C. (2004). *Working with involuntary clients*. Thousand Oaks, CA: Sage Publications Inc.

9 | Evidence-based Practice in the Criminal Justice System

Chapter Overview

Social work practice issues that arise in the criminal justice system were addressed in the previous chapter. In this chapter, we examine the concept of evidence-based practice (EBP), and its applications in both the social work profession and the criminal justice system. Recently, criminal justice practitioners have adopted the use of EBP in an attempt to improve public safety and criminal justice outcomes such as reduced recidivism rates. EBP underscores the use of science. Consequently, the utilization of scientific principles to categorize criminal justice interventions has resulted in three groupings: what works (interventions that are effective), what does not work (interventions that are not effective), and what is promising (tentatively effective but more evidence is needed).

In this chapter, we discuss basic research principles necessary to understand the principles of EBP. We will also review examples of interventions that have been demonstrated to be effective with criminal justice populations. This chapter provides a brief description of several standardized instruments to illustrate how science can make meaningful contributions in the criminal justice system. Standardized instruments are presented to illustrate their utility for conducting an organizational assessment, and to characterize meso-level social work intervention as well as the use of research skills.

What Is Evidence-based Practice?

Shlonsky & Gibbs (2006) credit the Evidence-based Medicine Working Group with coining the phase "evidence-based" in 1992 (see Evidence-based Medicine Working Group, 1992). The phrase refers to the intersection between current empirical evidence demonstrating the effectiveness of an intervention, the values and expectations of clients who receive the interventions, and the expertise of the practitioner who provides the intervention. Shlonsky & Gibbs cite the work of Sackett, Straus, Richardson, Rosenberg, & Haynes (2000) when describing the intersection between these three areas as a component of EBP. When evidence is weak or absent, the values and expectations of clients who receive the interventions and the expertise of the practitioner who provides the intervention are dominant aspects of practice. On the other hand, when evidence is strong and compelling, the other two areas play a lesser role in practice.

Evidence-based practice has been defined in several ways. McNeill (2006) defined EBP as the use of "clinical expertise and values with the best available evidence from systematic research while simultaneously considering the client's values and expectations—all within the parameters of the agency mandate and any legislative or environmental considerations" (p. 147). EBP relies on the use of evidence that has been obtained from a planned, systematic, and organized environment, and requires practitioners to work in a regimented, systematic, and routine fashion (Webb, 2001). Webb further suggested that EBP utilizes statistical analysis of data collected from random controlled trials, single case experimentation, double-blind cohort studies, and crossover designs. Other research methods such as cultural studies, ethnography, discourse analysis, actor network theory, semiotics, and psychoanalysis are not utilized in EBP studies. Opponents of EBP are disheartened that the approach relies exclusively on scientific evidence and quantitative data.

Opponents are also discouraged by what they perceive to be inflexible practices. As the above definitions of EBP have shown, practitioners can use their judgment in providing EBPs. However, judgment should be based on professional judgment, and not personal judgments of EBP and research methodology. In order to formulate professional judgments and assess evidence, social workers require an understanding of research concepts.

A Primer of Research Concepts

Oftentimes social work students are not as passionate about the research course(s) as they are about practice courses, or pursuing social justice. "No other part of the social work curriculum has been so consistently received by students with as much groaning, moaning, eye-rolling, bad-mouthing, hyperventilation, and waiver-strategizing as the research courses" (Epstein, 1987, p. 71). This is understandable given that most social work students desire to become practitioners and are not pursuing careers in research (Adam, Zosky, & Unrau, 2004).

Nevertheless, to fully appreciate the principles of EBP and the relationships between research and practice requires an understanding of research and how the evidence demonstrating effectiveness is obtained. For instance, it requires an understanding of the various types of research designs, outcome measures, and principles of meta-analysis. Weinbach and Grinnell (2007) observed that while an appreciation of research does not necessarily mean that EBPs will be implemented, such an appreciation can produce more informed social work practitioners.

Data Collection

Data should be collected in an objective and systematic manner. Objective data are as free of bias as possible. This is essential because biased data may show that an intervention is effective when in actuality it is ineffective. Standardized instruments are the most common objective measures. *Standardized instruments* are questionnaires containing numerous items that measure the extent of a concept such as depression or anxiety. Standardized instruments should be reliable and valid. Developing one's own scale without attention to reliability and validity analysis may overlook items that assess a concept. *Reliability* refers to the ability of a standardized instrument to provide consistent or similar results each time that it is administered. *Validity* refers to the standardized instrument assessing what it is intended to measure. These are known as the *psychometric properties* of the standardized instrument.

A general limitation of standardized instruments is that they rely on self-report. This means that individuals must be willing and able to recall the items contained in the standardized instrument, and be able to understand the items. Strengths include less expense, and ease of administration and scoring.

Social workers should be knowledgeable about how the instrument was used in prior research studies and clinical settings, possess the ability to locate and understand scoring information, strengths and limitations of the instrument, psychometric properties, the number of items, and time needed to complete the instrument, among other important pieces of information. Among lay persons, as well as some professionals, standardized instruments are typically associated with the field of psychology. With proper training and practice these instruments can also be administered by social workers. Administering a standardized instrument may require purchasing a copyright to reproduce a specific number of instruments, or if the instrument is in the public domain no cost is associated with its use.

Several printed volumes are available that contain standardized instruments. One example of a source that can be used to locate standardized instruments is *Measures for clinical practice: A sourcebook*, third edition, by Kevin Corcoran and Joel Fisher, published in 2000 by the Free Press. Another example is the *Commissioned reviews of 250 psychological tests* edited by John Maltby, Christopher A. Lewis, and Andrew Hill published in 2000 by the Edwin Mellon Press. The latter source provides information and a description of standardized instruments.

Databases can be used to locate standardized instruments although some databases are available only by subscription for a fee. The Buros Center for Testing publishes the Mental Measurement YearBook and Tests in Print editions. The former can be accessed through a university library subscribing to the database. Test Reviews Online (found at www.unl.edu/buros) catalogs standardized instrument reviews and information for more than 3,500 instruments. Box 9.1 illustrates the use of Mental Measurement YearBook for locating standardized instruments.

Box 9.1 Using Mental Measurement YearBook to Locate Standardized Instruments

Step 1: Open the Mental Measurement YearBook database.
Step 2: Enter the search term(s) using keywords, author, or title of the instrument.
Step 3: From the list of hits search for the relevant hit.
Step 4: Click the search returned result of interest.

Using the search terms, Hare Psychopathy Checklist Revised in the Mental Measurement YearBook database yielded six hits. One hit was the Hare Psychopathy Checklist, revised second edition. The database provides detailed information regarding the instrument. For instance, standardized instruments are not only used to assess treatment outcomes but they can also be used to obtain forensic assessment information, and this instrument is intended only for use with assessing psychopathy. It is not intended for use to assess treatment outcomes. The instrument is appropriate for use in both research and clinical as well as forensic settings.

The database also includes information about the instrument title, acronym, author, purpose, publisher and publication date, the population for which the instrument is intended, scores, a 231-page information manual, cost for use, and the time required to administer the instrument, among other information. The instrument should be administered only by a licensed mental health clinician with expertise in forensics and psychopathy. Clinicians should also have training in statistics, psychometrics, and psychopathology. These qualifications are not required by individuals who administer the instrument solely as part of research.

Several other measurement approaches used with criminal justice populations do not rely on self-report. These objective measures include blood tests, breathalyzers, urine analysis, and hair analysis. These approaches are more costly than self-report standardized instruments. Strengths and limitations are also associated with each of these approaches.

Research Designs

In order to assess the efficacy of an intervention it is important to utilize research designs that are capable of ruling out *extraneous factors* (factors other than the intervention which can make it appear that the intervention was effective, such as higher levels of substance abuse among the control group than the experimental group). A *pre-experimental design* is the weakest type of design in this regard. Pre-experimental designs collect only pre-test and/or post-test data without random assignment to an experimental or control group.

Quasi-experimental designs may or may not utilize an experimental or control group. However, the key feature is the lack of random assignment. These designs are an improvement over pre-experimental designs, but owing to the lack of random assignment they do not rule out extraneous factors. For example, in a study designed to assess the effectiveness of residential substance abuse treatment among high-risk individuals on probation, Perez (2009) used a quasi-experimental design. Perez created a control group by matching demographic characteristic such as sex, age, race, and criminal history of 83 probationers participating in a residential drug treatment program with 82 research participants who did not participate in the program. Thus, while the study did include a comparison group, the two groups were not equivalent owing to lack of random assignment.

True experimental designs use random assignment to allocate research participants to experimental and control groups. Because the two groups are equivalent, whatever extraneous factors affect the experimental group will also affect the control group.

Randomized controlled trials (RCTs) (the use of random assignment to a control group which does not receive the treatment of interest, and to an experimental group which does receive the treatment of interest) are true experimental designs that provide the strongest evidence of treatment effectiveness.

In many criminal justice and human service settings RCTs are impractical because they require either that treatment be withheld or that an alternative treatment be offered. Moreover, the use of RCTs may be viewed as unethical in settings that receive funding to provide treatment. Withholding the treatment from active clients is inconsistent with funding guidelines. Often in these situations individuals are offered a comparable intervention which is not the intervention of interest in the research study.

Three primary methods are used in research studies. *Quantitative methods* emphasize numbers and statistical analysis. *Qualitative methods* focus on narratives and analysis of verbal communication. *Mixed methods* utilize both quantitative and qualitative methods. In this way, the qualitative data are used to contextualize the quantitative data.

A method for determining treatment effectiveness on the basis of statistical data is meta-analysis. *Meta-analysis* is a research method in which quantitative research findings are synthesized. Only study findings that have similar concepts and statistical analyses can be synthesized (Lipsey & Wilson, 2001). Lipsey & Wilson write that the synthesis of data in a meta-analysis "is based on only the 'best' evidence" (p. 9). As we have just seen, RCTs provide the best evidence of treatment effectiveness because of their ability to rule out extraneous factors and the use of random assignment to a control group and a treatment group. As a result, studies that do not employ RCTs may or may not be excluded from a meta-analysis.

When one is considering the evidence and making decisions regarding which studies to include in a meta-analysis, a decision needs to be made about whether to include studies in which participants were not randomly assigned to control and experimental groups. For instance, as mentioned earlier, the study conducted by Perez (2009) employed a quasi-experimental design to create a control group by matching demographic characteristics among individuals on probation. Because the control group and experimental group were not created using random assignment, a researcher conducting a meta-analysis will need to make a determination about whether or not to include this study in the meta-analysis.

A few international research organizations are sources for systematic reviews that utilize meta-analysis. A *systematic review* is a summary of research studies that address a specific research topic. The Campbell Collaboration provides resources to develop systematic reviews in the areas of crime and justice, social welfare, and education. The reviews are disseminated through The Campbell Library. The Cochrane Collaboration provides resources to develop systematic reviews in the area of health care. The reviews are published in The Cochrane Library.

Patterson, Chung, & Swan (in press) conducted a meta-analysis to assess the effectiveness of stress management interventions for police officers and recruits. Social workers provide a variety of stress management interventions to police officers, and, owing to the potential negative effects of stress on officers, this research question warrants examination. As Box 9.2 illustrates, the steps for conducting a systematic review are planned in advance and follow a sequential order. The results suggest that stress management interventions had no significant effect on psychological, physiological, or behavioral stress outcomes, but owing to the weakness of the research designs included in the study these results are inconclusive.

Box 9.2 A Meta-Analysis of Police Officer Stress Management Programs

Step 1: The objectives of the systematic review were determined (to assess the effects of officer stress management interventions on stress outcomes).

Step 2: The criteria for inclusion and exclusion of retrieved studies were determined. Inclusion criteria included population characteristics and sampling strategies, interventions, study methods and designs, data analysis, and outcome results. Studies were excluded from the review if the research design did not include both a control and an experimental group.

Step 3: The search strategy involved searching electronic databases and internet websites; handsearching journals, books, and conference proceedings; scanning reference lists; contacting major organizations and authors to inquire about police stress management program evaluations.

Step 4: Retrieved studies were compared to the inclusion criteria and were either included in or excluded from the analysis, and coded.

Step 5: A meta-analysis was performed using the control and experimental group sample sizes, means, and standards deviations.

Step 6: Results and conclusions were written.

Evidence-based Social Work Practice

EBPs have been implemented in many fields including medicine, criminal justice, social work, and psychology. A lot of recent attention has been given to the topic of evidence-based social work practice (Howard, Himle, Jenson, & Vaughn, 2009; McBeath, Briggs, & Aisenberg, 2010; Murdoch 2010; Oancea, 2010; Roberts & Yeager, 2006).

The social work profession does not embrace the use of evidence in practice. Murdach (2010) suggested that, despite the current movement in social work to utilize science and evidence in practice, practitioners continue to utilize "soft data" (qualitative evidence derived from nonscientific sources). It may be that, in addition to having only a moderate or no interest in research, social workers feel that they must provide interventions in a regimented fashion that does not take into account individual differences among clients. EBP does require that fidelity be maintained. *Fidelity* refers to adhering to protocols.

Whatever the reasons for social workers' views toward EBP, Wheeler & Goodman (2007) articulated: "We reject the idea that practitioners should be passive recipients of practice directives when other health professionals are actively engaged in critical evaluation of the literature in their fields" (p. 236). Wheeler & Goodman maintain that three information literacy skills are essential for social work practitioners to possess: retrieval (using search strategies and techniques to locate printed and electronic information), evaluation (critical appraisal of retrieved information), and synthesis (the ability to include information in written reports).

So important is the need to disseminate EBP approaches in the social work profession that the *Journal of Evidence-based Social Work* is committed to this purpose. The aim of the journal is to disseminate evidence-based interventions and issues associated with EBP. In their edited book *Social work in mental health: An evidence-based approach*, Thyer & Wodarski (2007) observe that the social work profession is the largest group of mental health service providers in the U.S., and EBP is more developed in the area of mental health than any other area. Consequently social workers should be knowledgeable about EBPs used in the mental health field.

Moreover, Box 9.3 describes some of social workers' ethical responsibilities to make use of evaluation and research. As the Box shows, social workers should monitor and evaluate policies, the implementation of programs, and practice interventions; promote and facilitate evaluation and research to contribute to the development of knowledge; critically examine and keep current with emerging knowledge relevant to social work, and fully use evaluation and research evidence in their professional practice

---

Box 9.3 Social Workers' Ethical Responsibilities to the Social Work Profession: 5.02 Evaluation and Research

(a) Social workers should monitor and evaluate policies, the implementation of programs, and practice interventions.
(b) Social workers should promote and facilitate evaluation and research to contribute to the development of knowledge.
(c) Social workers should critically examine and keep current with emerging knowledge relevant to social work and fully use evaluation and research evidence in their professional practice.

Copyrighted material reprinted with permission from the National Association of Social Workers, Inc.

Evidence-based Practice in the Criminal Justice System

A lot of recent attention has also been given to EBPs within the criminal justice system (Aos, Mayfield, Miller, & Yen, 2006; Aos, Miller, & Drake, 2006; Belenko & Wexler, 2007; Friedmann, Taxman, & Henderson, 2007; Reitzel, 2005). Best practice approaches in the criminal justice system are based on the use of research principles, EBP approaches, and empirically supported treatments (ESTs) (Reitzel, 2005). For example, motivational interviewing is an effective intervention with juvenile and adult offenders (Feldstein & Ginsburg, 2007), and multi-systemtic therapy has been demonstrated to be an effective intervention for violent and chronic juvenile offenders (Henggeler, Sheidow, & Lee, 2007). These interventions were ascertained on the basis of empirical evidence.

Much of the EBP attention in the criminal justice system has concentrated on treatments provided to offenders to reduce recidivism, and treat substance abuse and mental illness, or co-occurring disorders. The use of EBP in jails and prisons also improves inmate classification systems as well as interventions, thereby increasing safety within prisons and preparing inmates for reentry. These are two primary goals of prisons (Serin, 2005).

Increased interest concerning the use of EBP within the criminal justice system arose when a conference was held in Philadelphia, PA, on December 6–7, 2006. The goal of the conference was to examine the challenges associated with identifying, implementing, disseminating, and sustaining evidence-based drug treatments in the criminal justice system. The report, *Implementing evidence-based drug treatment in criminal justice settings: Final conference report* (Belenko & Wexler, 2007), summarizes the conference results.

The Washington State legislature was so concerned about how publicly funded mental health and substance abuse treatment programs were operating that the legislature passed the *Omnibus Treatment of Mental and Substance Abuse Disorders Act* in 2005. The Act recognized that "Persons with mental disorders, chemical dependency disorders, or co-occurring mental and substance abuse disorders are disproportionately more likely to be confined in a correctional institution" (E2SSB 5763, Chapter 504, Laws of 2005, Section 101 as cited in Aos, Mayfield, Miller, & Yen, 2006). The aims of the Act were to "Improve treatment outcomes by shifting treatment, where possible, to evidence-based treatment practices and by removing barriers to the use of those practices" (E2SSB 5763, Chapter 504, Laws of 2005, Section 101(3) as cited in Aos, Mayfield, Miller, & Yen, 2006).

The Office of Justice Programs (OJP) has a strong interest in EBPs. The *Second Chance Act* of 2007 *(Pub. L. 110-199)* Section 211 contains provisions for funding provided to nonprofit agencies as well as to Indian tribes. The funding announcement articulates the OJP conceptualization of evidence-based programs or practices:

> OJP considers programs and practices to be evidence-based when their effectiveness has been demonstrated by causal evidence (generally obtained through one or more outcome evaluations). Causal evidence documents a relationship between an activity or intervention (including technology) and its intended outcome, including measuring the direction and size of a change, and the extent to which a change may be attributed to the activity or intervention. Causal evidence depends on the use of scientific methods to rule out, to the extent possible, alternative explanations for the documented change. The strength of causal evidence, based on the factors described above, will influence the degree to which OJP considers a program or practice to be evidence-based.

(p. 4)

In order to assess the effectiveness of a program or intervention, the measurement of an objective outcome is essential. Establishing an appropriate outcome measure is a critical component to measuring intervention effectiveness. The outcomes measure should be related both to the goals of the criminal justice system and to the factors that contribute to criminal behavior. The outcomes should also be replicable. In this way programs that adopt an EBP can anticipate that their program will produce similar outcomes. Within the same funding announcement OJP draws on recidivism as an example of an outcome measure. OJP conceptualizes *recidivism* as "a return to prison and or/jail with either a new conviction or as the result of a violation of the terms of supervision within 12 months of initial release" (p. 4).

EBP outcomes investigated among criminal justice populations are often linked to the goals of the criminal justice system. These goals include reducing recidivism and criminal behavior, and improving mental health, substance abuse, employment, and educational outcomes. Providing effective treatments can improve social problems such as substance abuse and mental health issues and improve social functioning, thereby eliminating some of the contributing factors that result in recidivism. Such an improvement can also improve public safety as such individuals are less likely to reoffend.

Aos, Miller, & Drake (2006) conducted a meta-analysis and found empirical support for treatment effectiveness among offenders. Some of their most salient findings among programs for individuals with substance abuse disorders were that: substance abuse community-based treatment reduced recidivism by 12.4%; adult drug courts reduced recidivism by 10.7%; in-prison TC linked to community-based treatment reduced recidivism by 6.9%; and in-prison TC that was not linked to community-based treatment reduced recidivism by 5.3%.

The authors also found that among programs for sex offenders: when provided separately, psychotherapy and behavioral therapy showed a 0% change in recidivism; in-prison cognitive-behavioral treatment reduced recidivism by 14.9%; and cognitive-behavioral treatment provided to low-risk sex offenders on probation reduced recidivism by 14.9%. Sanctions requiring intensive supervision that were in effect simultaneously with treatment reduced recidivism by 21.9%, whereas sanctions that provided intense supervision through surveillance, adult boot camps, electronic monitoring, and restorative justice for low-risk adults showed a 0% change in recidivism rates. In other words, these later programs did not reduce recidivism rates.

Overall, their results show that substance abuse, work, and education programs demonstrated a greater reduction in recidivism rates when compared with standard treatment:

- In-prison correctional industries programs reduced recidivism by 7.8%.
- Adult education programs reduced recidivism by 5.1%.
- Community-based employment training and job assistance reduced recidivism by 4.8%.
- In-prison vocational education reduced recidivism by 12.6%.

Aos, Mayfield, Miller, & Yen (2006) investigated whether evidence-based treatment provided for alcohol and substance abuse and mental illness reduced the seriousness of these disorders. They also investigated the cost benefits associated with evidence-based treatment for these disorders. Overall evidence-based treatments reduced the seriousness of alcohol disorders by 15%, substance abuse disorders by 22%, and mental illness by 22%. They also found that, for each dollar spent on evidence-based treatment for these disorders, Washington State residents received $3.77 (or a 56% return rate) in cost-effective benefits.

Hanley (2006) used research principles to investigate relationships between levels of risk, service participation, and reoffending. Utilizing a dataset from the Intensive Supervision Programs, Hanley found that, when high-risk offenders received services that matched their level of risk, they were less likely to be rearrested. Although results were not statistically significant, services provided to low-risk offenders that were more appropriate for high-risk offenders were ineffective. These results support prior research findings in this area, and Hanley contended that correctional programs should use risk levels to determine which group of offenders should receive services that are insufficient to meet the demand. Thus, offenders at highest risk for committing future crimes should receive services, as opposed to those who present lower levels of committing future crimes.

If insufficient services are available to meet the demand, should these services be offered to offenders who pose the highest risk for reoffending instead of those who are at lower risk? What should happen if a low-risk offender requests services? Would the offender be denied services because of risk level? This amounts to risk level representing criteria upon which to establish service eligibility. Moreover, on the basis of a risk assessment which classifies the offender at low risk, what if the offender was denied services and reoffends? These are important questions that warrant ethical considerations when allocating services. They are, however, questions that do arise when available resources are scarce and the demand for services is greater than the ability to provide services.

Assessing Treatment Effectiveness on the Basis of Study Designs and Methods

Contemplate the following example in which Seiter & Kadela (2003) described an approach for determining the effectiveness of reentry programs. Their approach involved several steps used to assess study designs and methods. As shown in Box 9.4, the approach entails defining the area of interest, locating and retrieving studies, ranking each study on a scale of 1 (weakest) to 5 (strongest) using the Maryland Scale of Scientific Methods (Sherman, Gottfredson, MacKenzie, Eck, Reuter, & Bushway, 1998), rating studies according to: (1) what works, (2) what does not work, and (3) what is unknown, and finally developing conclusions.

Box 9.4 Assessing Reentry Programs Using Evidence

Step 1: Prisoner reentry programs were defined (as correctional programs that focus on transitioning from prison to community, and prison-based programs that are linked to a community-based program).

Step 2: Thirty-two published studies that met this definitional criterion were retrieved, representing 32 programs.

Step 3: Using the Maryland Scale of Scientific Methods (Sherman, Gottfredson, MacKenzie, Eck, Reuter, & Bushway, 1998), each study was ranked on a scale of 1 (weakest) to 5 (strongest). Retrieved studies were also categorized based on five levels ranging from Level 1 (correlational analysis) to Level 5 (research involving random assignment).

Step 4: The 32 programs were rated according to: (1) what works, (2) what does not work, and (3) what is unknown.

Step 5: Conclusions were drawn that vocational training and work release programs were effective for reducing recidivism and improving job readiness skills. Individuals who completed drug treatment were less likely than those on parole to be rearrested, commit a drug-related crime, use drugs, or violate parole conditions. Educational programs increased educational achievement scores, but did not decrease recidivism. Halfway house programs reduced involvement in severe crimes, pre-release programs reduced recidivism, and sex and violent offender programs showed promising results.

In a similar approach, Reyes (2009) examined nine studies conducted in five countries to assess the utility of an international approach toward corrections-based substance abuse treatment programs. The studies were also rated using the Maryland Scientific Methods Scale (Sherman, Farrington, Welsh, & MacKenzie, 2002). Reyes found inconclusive evidence that the programs reduced recidivism. Using the model of what works, what does not work, or what is promising, Reyes concluded that such programs are promising and require further investigation.

Challenges to Implementing Evidence-based Practice in Criminal Justice Settings

Several challenges are associated with the implementation of EBPs in criminal justice settings. The challenges encountered when implementing EBP in correctional facilities include: an organizational culture within correctional facilities that resists change, political administrators who may be reluctant to implement new approaches that have the potential for failure, and gaining support from administrators and correctional officers who must be convinced to realize that EBP will improve correctional safety and management of inmates (Latessa, 2004).

Welsh, Sullivan, & Olds (2010) used an example based on early crime prevention trials to report the numerous challenges that exist when "scaling-up" interventions. First, during research trials a program may have been provided to higher-risk children and adults. When it is scaled up, program participants may not be representative of the high-risk trial group, resulting in reduced intervention effectiveness. Second, research study participants tend to be homogeneous in research trials. When the program is scaled up, program clients who receive services are likely to be different from those who participated in the research trial. Third, when programs are implemented on a larger scale, inadequate funding to keep the program operating, insufficient staff trained to implement the intervention, or other problems often surface. Fourth, when programs are no longer implemented within a closely controlled environment, fidelity can be a problem. As previously mentioned, fidelity refers to adhering to protocols. When these factors are no longer considered, such as when the program is scaled up, a decrease in intervention effectiveness may be observed.

Another challenge to implementing EBPs in criminal justice settings is the fact that not all settings provide evidence-based treatments, particularly drug treatment. In spite of evidence demonstrating the effectiveness of interventions for criminal justice populations, and suggestions for the use of EBPs in criminal justice settings, clearly many criminal justice settings still do not utilize EBPs. Friedmann, Taxman, & Henderson (2007) found that, among correctional facilities and community-based substance abuse treatment programs for adults, most of the programs included in their study provided fewer than 60% of the established EBPs recommended for substance abusing offenders. Among their findings were that prison settings utilized more EBPs than did jails or probation and parole; prisons used more standardized substance use/abuse instruments than jails, probation, or parole; prisons were less likely to coordinate services with community-based service providers than jails, probation, or parole; probation and parole settings used more standardized risk-assessment instruments and drug testing procedures than prison and jails; community-based treatment programs used more engagement techniques, treated co-occurring disorders, involved family members in treatment, and employed more qualified substance abuse treatment staff than prisons, jails, probation, or parole.

Inmates and offenders experience co-occurring disorders. The goals of intervention among this population are also to reduce recidivism and increase well-being. EBP can enhance these goals. Numerous challenges have been reported that impact the implementation of EBP to individuals with co-occurring disorders. Chandler, Peters, Field, & Juliano-Bult (2004) offer the following challenges: the contrasting goals between the criminal justice system (which emphasizes punishment and public safety) and treatment (which focuses on improved functioning and well-being); unfamiliarity with EBPs; incarcerating inmates in special units where EBPs are not available; little continuity of EBPs from institutional to community-based settings; limited funding and other resources needed to sustain EBPs; and ethical issues that arise in criminal justice settings.

Program Evaluation

As articled in the NASW *Code of ethics*, social workers have an ethical responsibility to monitor and evaluate programs. This is particularly relevant when considering EBP in criminal justice settings. Some agencies may not have developed the capacity to implement EBPs. An important consideration is the capacity of criminal justice and human services agencies to provide evidence-based treatments. In order to become an "evidence-based organization" (p. 13), organizations must be prepared to integrate EBP, and first conduct an organizational assessment (Guevara, Loeffler-Cobia, Rhyne, & Sachwald, 2011). Lehman, Greener, & Simpson (2002) noted that it is important to "assess motivation and personality attributes of program leaders and staff, institutional resources, and organizational climate as an important *first step* in understanding organizational factors related to implementing evidence-based drug treatment into a reentry program" (p. 197).

One method for assessing organizational capacity is to conduct a program evaluation. *Program evaluation* is the process of examining program outcomes and other indicators of effectiveness to learn whether programs are achieving their intended outcomes, but more specifically whether programs are effective. A social worker conducting an organizational assessment, or program evaluation, is engaging in meso-level practice while at the same time utilizing research skills.

Sample Standardized Instruments for Program Evaluation

Standardized instruments have been developed that can be used to conduct a program evaluation, in this case an organizational assessment. The Organizational Readiness for Change (ORC) examines the most salient variables for investigating change efforts in substance abuse treatment organizations: motivation for change, institutional resources of the program, personality attributes of the staff, and the organizational climate of the program. Specifically the instrument assesses the motivational readiness (perceived need and pressure for change) among directors and staff, personality attributes (personal growth, efficacy, influence, and adaptability), the organizational climate (clarity of mission and goals, staff cohesion, communication, and openness to change), and institutional resources (staffing levels, physical resources, training levels, and computer usage) within programs (Lehman, Greener, & Simpson, 2002).

The *Organizational Readiness for Change (TCU ORC) Treatment Staff Version (TCU ORC-S)* is a self-administered instrument that contains 129 items. These items assess: motivation for change (perceived program needs for improvement, immediate training needs, and pressures for change); program resources (staffing levels, physical resources, training levels, and computer usage); staff attributes (personal growth, efficacy, influence, and adaptability); and organizational climate (clarity of mission and goals, staff cohesion, autonomy, communication, stress, and openness to change) among staff. The instrument contains 18 scales and a 5-point Likert scale with anchors (1) disagree strongly to (5) strongly agree and demonstrates acceptable reliability. This instrument also solicits demographic information such as gender, age, race and ethnicity, education, certification status, and length of experience and employment in present position (Lehman, Greener, & Simpson, 2002). Information about the instrument is located at the Institute of Behavioral Research at Texas Christian University website (www.ibr.tcu. edu) (retrieved from www.ibr.tcu.edu/pubs/datacoll/Forms/orc-s.pdf).

The *Organizational Readiness for Change (TCU ORC) Treatment Director Version (TCU CJ ORC-D)* is similar to the staff version, but is self-administered to program directors. The instrument contains 115 items that assess: motivation for change (perceived program needs for improvement, immediate training needs, and pressures for change); program resources (staffing levels, physical resources, training levels, and computer usage); staff attributes (personal growth, efficacy, influence, and adaptability); and organizational climate (clarity of mission and goals, staff cohesion, autonomy, communication, stress, and openness to change) among program directors. The instrument contains 18 scales and a 5-point Likert scale with anchors (1) disagree strongly to (5) strongly agree and demonstrates acceptable reliability. Demographic information is also solicited such as gender, age, race and ethnicity, education, certification status, and length of experience and employment in present position. Additional information solicited includes information about the substance abuse treatment unit such as the primary setting, types of clients served, and whether the setting is a program located in a larger agency context (Lehman, Greener, & Simpson, 2002). Information about this instrument is also located at the Institute of Behavioral Research at Texas Christian University website (www.ibr. tcu.edu) (retrieved from www.ibr.tcu.edu/pubs/datacoll/Forms/cj-orc-d.pdf).

Advocacy Research

Social workers can combine advocacy practice with research skills to measure the size and scope of a social problem, and to engage in advocacy efforts to ameliorate the problem. Barker (2003) defined this combination of practice and skills as advocacy research. Barker noted that *advocacy research* consists of "systematic investigation of specific social problems and objective measurement of their extent, progression, and response to corrective actions. This type of research also heightens public awareness of the social problems and recommends possible solutions" (p. 11).

For example, the research process described by The Sentencing Project (2008) is useful for empirically assessing whether racial disparities occur within the four components of the criminal justice system. The process requires the skills to identity reasons for racial disparities, and design, implement, and monitor the effectiveness of strategies to reduce disparities. Applying this research process, social workers use research skills to investigate the extent of racial disparities, and engage in advocacy practice to bring attention to this social problem and its solutions.

These activities are consistent with the ethical mandate to challenge social injustice and pursue social change related to discrimination and oppression based on racial diversity. Equality for persons involved in the criminal justice system is also assumed. An advocacy research approach enhances advocacy practice because such efforts are based on empirical evidence, and go beyond gut feelings and assumptions about racial disparities and racism in the criminal justice system.

Implications for Social Work Practice

Whereas the majority of BSW and MSW students aspire to become practitioners and not researchers, social workers have an ethical responsibility to possess the skills necessary to retrieve, evaluate, and synthesize research findings, and to integrate research findings into professional practice. In addition, the NASW *Code of ethics* states that social workers have an ethical responsibility to monitor and evaluate programs and practice interventions. Implicit in this statement is the notion that, should evaluation results uncover that a program or practice intervention is ineffective, modifications should be employed to increase effectiveness. Otherwise ineffective programs and practice interventions should be replaced with those that are effective. If modifications are not made to new or existing programs or practices, then monitoring and evaluation activities are meaningless.

This implicit assumption suggests that EBP is congruent with the values of social work. Knowledge of EBP can assist social workers in the mission of the profession, as well as providing effective interventions to criminal justice populations. Monitoring and evaluation also assume that, subsequent to implementing EBPs, social workers will engage in these activities. Monitoring activities should focus on assessing whether the EBP is achieving its intended outcomes. For example, if the EBP has been shown to reduce recidivism, social workers should engage in monitoring and evaluation efforts to assess whether after implementation recidivism is indeed reduced.

Social workers should and do participate in the development of EBPs for a wide range of social problems. Contributing to the development of EBPs specifically for criminal justice populations has the potential to benefit this group and fulfill the ethical responsibilities of the social work profession. Finally, social workers should strive to decrease the challenges associated with implementing EBPs in criminal justice settings. This can be achieved by addressing some of the challenges described in this chapter.

Chapter Summary

This chapter summarized the basic principles of EBP and discussed some of the challenges associated with EBPs in social work practice and criminal justice settings. The chapter provided a brief overview of basic research principles necessary for understanding EBP. Finally, types of interventions demonstrated to be effective for treating criminal justice populations were reviewed and an organizational assessment model was presented as an example of meso-level social work practice.

Key Terms

Advocacy research	Meta-analysis	Randomized controlled
Database	Outcome measure	trials
Evidence-based practice	Program evaluation	Standardized instrument
Fidelity	Psychometric properties	Systematic review

Questions for Review

1. Describe the basic principles of evidence-based practice. Summarize proponent and opponent views of EBP.
2. Locate a standardized instrument using a strategy presented in this chapter. What concept does the instrument measure? Briefly describe the psychometric properties of the instrument. Do you think the instrument would be appropriate for criminal justice populations? Why or why not?
3. Describe the basic principles of meta-analysis. Summarize the strengths and limitations of meta-analysis.
4. Locate and retrieve 5 studies describing evidence-based practice and a criminal justice population. Rank the studies using the Maryland Scale of Scientific Methods (locate the scale). On the basis of this rating scale and what you have read in the articles, do you agree with the ratings that positioned some studies lower? Why or why not?
5. This chapter reprinted only a portion of the NASW *Code of ethics* statement outlining social workers' ethical responsibilities with regard to evaluation and research. Summarize the statement. Specifically, what are social workers' ethical responsibilities toward the contributions of evaluation and research in professional practice? Does this ethical obligation change your views toward evaluation and research? Why or why not?

Further Reading

Carter, M. M., Gibel, S., Giguere, R., & Stroker, R. (2007). *Increasing public safety through successful offender reentry: Evidence-based and emerging practices in corrections.* Silver Spring, MD: Center for Effective Public Policy.

Crime and Justice Institute (2004). *Implementing evidence-based practice in community corrections: The principle of effective intervention.* Washington, DC: Department of Justice, National Institute of Corrections.

Gibbs, L. E. (2003). *Evidence-based practice for the helping professions: A practical guide with integrated multimedia.* Pacific Grove, CA: Brooks/Cole—Thompson Learning.

Listwan, S. J., Cullen, F. T., & Latessa, E. J. (2006). How to prevent prisoner re-entry programs from failing: Insights from evidence-based corrections. *Federal Probation, 70(3)*, 19–25.

National Institutes of Health (2004). *Report of the blue ribbon task force on health services at the National Institute on Drug Abuse.* Bethesda, MD: Author.

Taylor, B. J., Dempster, M., & Donnelly, M. (2003). Hidden gems: Systematically searching electronic databases for research publications for social work and social care. *British Journal of Social Work, 33*, 423–439.

10 The Future of Social Work Practice in the Criminal Justice System

Chapter Overview

This final chapter presents a number of issues that will be pertinent for the future of social work practice in the criminal justice system. These issues include the use of technology, science and research, the influence of global trends, and interdisciplinary collaboration. Earlier in this book we established the decline of social work involvement in the criminal justice system. Despite declining involvement, social workers continue to practice in the criminal justice system. Notably, the future of social work practice in the criminal justice system will involve much more interdisciplinary collaboration and research than in the past. This is already beginning to occur in the area of funding given to agencies for criminal-justice-related programs and services. Therefore criminal justice practice will necessitate that social workers possess skills in collaboration and research in addition to criminal-justice-specific knowledge. This chapter also reviews the lessons learned from social work practice models in the criminal justice systems found in the Netherlands and Scotland.

What Do the Experts Say?

Three experts in the field of criminal justice—Bryan J. Vila, Christopher E. Stone and David Weisburd—addressed the question "What will criminal justice look like in 2040?" (Ritter, 2006, p. 8) at the National Institute of Justice Annual Research and Evaluation Conference held in 2004.

Bryan J. Vila suggested that the future of criminal justice will require an understanding of the evolving nature of crime and innovative ways to address it. Vila added that technology will play a prominent role in addressing crime. Specific technological approaches include DNA evidence, intelligence databases, biometrics, and interoperability systems that can be utilized during public emergencies to facilitate communication among emergency responders.

Christopher E. Stone discussed the effects that increased racial and ethnic diversity will have in the U.S. and internationally. Stone asked "What will foreign-born Americans expect of the U.S. justice system, given their experiences in their native countries? How will they regard the roles of the defense lawyer, prosecutor, and judge?" (p. 9). Stone further commented that empirical evidence demonstrating which practices are effective, which are not, and why they are not will play a major role in the criminal justice system of 2040, particularly in three areas: civilian oversight of law enforcement, the role of prosecutors, and new approaches to defending the poor at trial.

Finally, David Weisburd commented that the criminal justice system is presently juxtaposed between two viewpoints. The first view is the clinical experience model based on the insights of practitioners. The second view is the evidence-based model. This model stresses the importance of empirical research results for demonstrating practice effectiveness. Weisburd notes that the clinical experience model is currently the prevailing model in which practitioners' experiences define effective practices. This is due in part to the expense, time, and expertise required to implement the evidence-based model. Five strategies are proposed for increasing use of the evidence-based model: (1) streamline the evidence-based research process within agencies, (2) ensure that research studies make the most of prior study findings indicating effective methods, (3) develop strategies to expedite the development and implementation of research studies, (4) develop an organizational culture in which practitioners consider whether interventions are effective or ineffective, and (5) increase federal funding to support the evidence-based model.

Because of these influences the future of social work practice in the criminal justice system will be much more interdisciplinary than it has been in the past. Social workers will have increased interactions with professionals who are knowledgeable in the abovementioned topics. A precedent has already been established for other disciplines to assume activities that are consistent with social work values utilizing the skill base of their disciplines. For example, when social work involvement in the criminal justice system declined, human rights attorneys advocated for federal legislation that ruled in favor of the rights for individuals to receive treatment (Sarri & Shook, 2005).

The U.S. Attorney General Eric Holder in a speech made on March 7, 2011 to the National Association of Counties Legislative Conference emphasized two issues that will be the focus of DOJ in the future: legal representation for youth in the juvenile justice system, and equal access to legal services for all citizens. First, Attorney General Holder noted that countless juveniles either do not have legal representation, are unaware that they can request it, can not afford it, and in some jurisdictions unnecessarily waive their rights to an attorney. Consequently, many plead guilty to an offense without legal representation (U.S. Department of Justice, 2011a).

The juvenile justice system was established on the premise that troubled youth were in need of services and rehabilitation instead of punishment. Consequently, as we saw in Chapter 4, the juvenile court system uses different terminology from adult courts. As mentioned, the social work profession was very influential in establishing the first juvenile court, which became a model for the juvenile court system. The adversarial nature of adult criminal courts is relatively absent in juvenile courts. A shift towards ensuring more legal representation for youth would establish an adversarial juvenile court system. The Attorney General remarked that the juvenile justice system is not functioning effectively and does not improve outcomes among troubled youth. More legal representation is proposed to improve outcomes and cost efficiency of the system. These developments will require that social workers rethink the future of the juvenile justice system, the direction the system will take, and the future role of the social work profession.

Second, Attorney General Holder told the audience that the adult criminal justice system is presently undergoing an "indigent-defense crisis" in which the poor many times only have access to unacceptably operated public defenders' offices. Inadequate legal representation has implications for social and economic justice. In the future, as the DOJ moves toward implementing strategies to resolve this crisis, social workers and their professional organizations can provide support and advocacy for these solutions. Seeking solutions to this crisis is consistent with social work values although the solutions are not led by social workers.

Research and Evaluation

Funding is a key component for implementing programs that provide services to criminal justice populations. Without financial resources, fewer programs can operate. Increasingly, funding sources are insisting on the use of research and evaluation as a condition for funding. For example, the *Second Chance Act Adult Mentoring Grants to Nonprofit Organizations FY 2011 Competitive Grant Announcement* describes the requirements for funding provided to nonprofit agencies and Indian tribes. The grant announcement also contains an evaluation component. Because human service agencies endeavor to submit competitive applications, the process requires a thorough understanding of research and project evaluation methods. Importantly, after the funding period ends, resourceful approaches are necessary to sustain programs. If programs are not sustained, needed services may no longer be provided.

Of primary interest to the DOJ is the ability of an agency or program to replicate the funded project if it is demonstrated to be effective, a plan to sustain the project after the funding period ends, and a justification of research and evidence-based methods that form the basis of the interventions. To assist applicants in this process, the *Second Chance Act* grant announcement (U.S. Department of Justice, 2011b) provides a definition of research: "Research, for the purposes of human subjects protections for OJP-funded programs, is defined as, 'a systematic investigation, including research development, testing, and evaluation, designed to develop or contribute to generalizable knowledge' 28 C.F.R. § 46.102(d)" (p. 15).

The *Second Chance Act* grant announcement also outlines the criteria involved in the project evaluation process:

> Applicants that propose to use funds awarded through this solicitation to conduct project evaluations should be aware that certain project evaluations (such as systematic investigations designed to develop or contribute to generalizable knowledge) may constitute "research" for purposes of applicable DOJ human subject protec-

tions. However, project evaluations that are intended only to generate internal improvements to a program or service, or are conducted only to meet OJP's performance measure data reporting requirements likely do not constitute "research."

(p. 15)

Pace (2009) anticipated that the social work profession would participate in this funding opportunity. Social workers were asked to explore their roles as well as the roles of the human service agencies that employ them in response to *Second Chance Act* funding.

The NASW *Code of ethics* offers guidance in this area. Included in the ethical standards titled "Social workers' ethical responsibilities to the social work profession," section 5.02—Evaluation and Research—are specific ethical obligations for conducting research and evaluation activities. One ethical mandate requires that social workers consult with Institutional Review Boards (IRBs) to protect human subjects participating in research. Most human service agencies do not have internal IRBs. They oftentimes also lack research and evaluation expertise. Social work faculty can and often do provide research and evaluation expertise to these agencies, and because academic institutions have IRBs, faculty submit applications, and engage in approved research. This also creates opportunities for social work students to become involved in the research process. As a result students learn research and evaluation skills specific to criminal justice practice.

Additional ethical responsibilities include obtaining written informed consent from volunteer research participants, maintaining the confidentiality of research participants, and recording and reporting results accurately. Altogether 16 distinct ethical responsibilities exist pertaining to research and evaluation.

Lessons Learned from Other Models

The Scottish Criminal Justice Social Work Model

Criminal justice social work emerged in Scotland as a result of two significant developments. First, the Kilbrandon Report published in 1964 was influential in removing juveniles from the jurisdiction of the adult criminal courts. Second, the Scottish Probation Service (adult program) was abolished in 1969. This provided opportunities for social workers to form social work departments that would provide services to criminal offenders. Criminal justice social work was under way in the late 1970s and funded by the Scottish Office in 1989. Criminal justice social work presently constitutes an agency in Scotland (McNeill, 2005).

In Scotland, the *Social Work Act 1968* authorized that services for criminal offenders be placed under the jurisdiction of social work departments. The *National objectives and standards for social work services in the criminal justice system*, first published in 1991, and updated in a 2001 report titled *Criminal justice social work services national priorities for 2001–2002 and onwards* identifies objectives and standards for social work treatment of offenders. These were articled in three key areas: (1) a commitment to public safety; (2) emphasis on the rehabilitation perspective; and (3) reducing future criminal offending by integrating offenders into society.

The Scottish Executive's Social Work Services Inspectorate sponsored the 21st Century Social Work Review Group to examine the future of criminal justice social work, and to identify essential skills for social work practice relative to community-based supervision of offenders. The group conducted a literature review to examine effective practices and concluded that four principal skills were useful to reduce reoffending. These were: developing effective relationships with offenders as a foundation for interventions; accurately assessing offenders' needs and strengths, and risks for reoffending; implementing interventions that have been demonstrated to be effective on the basis of research findings; and the ability to coordinate the many systems and services that offenders use (McNeill, Batchelor, Burnett, & Knox, 2005).

Wilson (2010) noted that the Scottish criminal justice social work model can inform social work practice in the U.S. criminal justice system on the basis of the many strengths of the model. These strengths include several decades of existence, an extensive research component describing effective practices, and policies and procedures that are an established component of the Scottish criminal justice system.

The Dutch Drug Policy Model

A second model for social work practice in the criminal justice system comes from the experiences of social workers in the Netherlands surrounding the Dutch drug policy. The policy was implemented on the premise of tolerance and permissiveness despite criticisms from countries such as the U.S. The policy also regarded drug use as a social and medical problem that was best treated accordingly. Drug use was not viewed as criminal behavior. Although hundreds of social workers were employed in institutional and community-based drug treatment settings, social workers were historically marginalized in the development and implementation of Dutch drug policy. This occurred for several reasons. (1) Throughout the history of the drug policy, the role of social work had never been articulated. (2) Drug policy was developed and implemented on the basis of a medical model which focused on public health, harm reduction, and health and mental health services. This view was seen as the domain of physicians, psychiatrists, epidemiologists, and nurses, and not social work. (3) The harm reduction model used in the Netherlands did not include social work services; instead this model emphasized drug use, demand, and supply. Drug policy viewed drug use as normal. Consequently, social work efforts aimed at sobriety were inconsistent with the policy. (4) The policy stressed detoxification treatment as medical treatment and did not include rehabilitation services. After receiving detoxification treatment, individuals did not participate in social work services. (5) The social work profession itself also contributed to the marginalization of social work. Social work educational programs prepared students for generalist practice as opposed to specialty practice (which is necessary in the substance abuse field). Social work had not developed practice standards in the area of substance abuse, which made it difficult to define the role of social work in this field (Koning & Kwant, 2002).

As a result of mounting criticisms and increased drug-related crimes, the Dutch drug policy shifted towards a more punitive approach. For example, only recently has legislation been enacted that makes it illegal to sell alcohol to minors in the Netherlands. The shift in the drug policy now places emphasis on public safety, punishment, and rehabilitation for drug offenders. Ironically this has created new opportunities for social workers. At the same time increased unemployment and social change in urban communities have provided additional social work opportunities (Koning & Kwant, 2002).

What Can We Learn?

This book has addressed social work roles and practices that are far-reaching in the four components of the U.S. criminal justice system. Criminal justice social work evolved from changes in the Scottish probation system, and social work experiences with the Dutch drug policy focused exclusively on drug offenders. Consequently, the Scottish and Dutch models are narrower in scope to the extent that they focus on a specific social problem or reducing criminal offending.

Given the enormous size and complexity of the U.S criminal justice system, it is unlikely that such a narrow focus will be adopted. The tasks performed by social workers in each of the four components of the system are too varied. Moreover, the U.S. criminal justice system is characterized by racial disparities, death penalty legislation, and other forms of social injustice. Social workers intervene at a variety of levels including influencing legislation (including treatment policies) at the macro level, and the provision of clinical services at the micro level.

While these two models may be narrower in scope than the U.S. model, they do provide implications for social work practice in the criminal justice system. Foremost is the need to develop standards for social work practice in the criminal justice system. At present, no practice standards have been developed that describe social work practice in the criminal justice system. NASW has developed social work practice standards relevant for populations that include older adults and adolescents, and settings which include schools, health care, and long-term care facilities. The 14 practice standards are available from NASW. Lacking are standards for criminal justice practice. Such standards, if developed, will require recognition of practice in the four components of the criminal justice system in addition to both juvenile and adult systems. This will be an ambitious task indeed but a necessary one that can complement state licensing laws and state legislation identifying the scope of social work practice in the criminal justice system. Indeed, professional advocacy is required to increase the recognition of the social work profession in the criminal justice, as is granted to other disciplines.

These practice standards should be developed together with a representative committee composed of social workers, and criminal justice practitioners from law, legislation, law enforcement, courts, and corrections, so that the standards capture the full scope of social work practice.

As we saw in Chapter 8, social work educational programs in the U.S. already prepare students for both generalist and specialty practice. This approach to social work education is a relatively recent development in the Netherlands.

A relatively recent event in the U.S. social work educational system is the development of practice standards for substance abuse. The Council on Social Work Education (CSWE) in collaboration with the Commission for Curriculum and Educational Innovation (COCEI), the Commission for Accreditation (COA), the CSWE Office of Social Work Accreditation and Educational Excellence and Institutional Research developed the resource titled *Advanced social work practice in the prevention of substance use disorders*. The resource is a model that can be applied to other practice areas. In the report knowledge and practice behaviors are described which are tied to the ten core competencies articulated in the 2008 Educational Policy and Accreditation Standards (EPAS). The EPAS describes educational policies and accreditation standards that must be met in order for a BSW or MSW social work education program to become accredited or reaccredited (CSWE, 2008).

The abovementioned resource proposes that social work students should have knowledge about the relationship between substance abuse and crime, how substance abuse treatment is provided in the criminal justice system, and the role of legislation. The practice behaviors are exclusive for substance abuse disorders, and were not developed for criminal justice settings. Similarly, the knowledge component addresses a wide range of practice settings. Consequently, despite having these standards, students will continue to require criminal-justice-specific knowledge and competencies. Next we will explore approaches to field and classroom instruction that can provide students with criminal justice knowledge and practice competencies.

Classroom Instruction and Field Placement

Social work programs lack concentrations in criminal justice as a field of practice. Few programs offer criminal justice courses. Addressing these concerns requires modifications in two educational components, coursework and field instruction. By exploring innovative methods in these two areas, social work education programs can explore ways to increase social work involvement in the criminal justice system in the future. In addition to the previously mentioned need for criminal justice practice standards, social work educational programs can consider the following approaches.

Classroom Instruction

The varied tasks that social workers perform in the four components of the criminal justice raise questions regarding what content should be emphasized in criminal justice courses offered in social work education programs. Consider the following questions. Should courses focus on the juvenile or adult criminal justice system? Which of the four criminal justice system components should a course address? What types of skills and tasks should be taught? Should the course focus on mitigation specialists, police social workers, restorative justice, mediation and arbitration activities or social work expert testimony, for example? Finally, what types of social problems should be covered: domestic violence, child abuse, substance abuse, criminal offending, juvenile delinquency? Should the most frequently addressed social problems that social workers deal with in the criminal justice system be covered? Indeed these are not insignificant issues which must be resolved when developing a course.

One approach to this vast area under discussion is to allow students to select a topic of their own choosing based on their interests. This approach does not limit students to the course content and provides opportunities to expand their knowledge base in a particular area. A second approach is to develop a criminal justice institute in which Blackboard, an academic online course program, or a similar program, is used to allow students to post questions, create wikis, and engage in topical discussions and link to resources. The program can also be used to post the syllabus, assignments, and other course materials. Hybrid and on-line instructional methods can be especially valuable for students whose schedules make it difficult to attend face-to-face classes, seminars, or workshops.

Internal or external institutional funding can be sought to support the development and implementation of a "criminal justice institute" which brings together all of the student body completing a criminal justice field placement. In this way, students can focus exclusively on criminal justice matters and field placement issues that arise because they are separated from students in non-criminal-justice field placements. Consequently they are not contending with students in non-criminal-justice settings and the focus can remain solely on criminal justice issues. A large number of students can be managed using Blackboard.

Field Instruction

Much of the discussion throughout this book has focused on social work practice in public (governmental) agencies primarily at local and state levels. Ginsberg (2001) asserted that colleagues employed in governmental agencies can lack motivation and enthusiasm, and perform poorly, although these situations can occur in other types of agencies as well. Civil service regulations make it difficult to terminate these employees. Ginsberg suggested that social workers prepare in advance for these situations. Moreover, issues can arise between colleagues with and without social work degrees while performing the same tasks. Field instruction can be particularly useful in this regard as students learn practice skills, and how to address these issues within a social work educational program integrating coursework, field learning, and faculty expertise.

Indeed, employment with colleagues who exhibit these characteristics can be challenging. The NASW *Code of ethics* outlines social workers' ethical responsibilities towards colleagues in 11 areas such as respect, confidentiality, and participation in interdisciplinary collaboration. Other areas include impairment, incompetence, and unethical conduct of colleagues. Options for ethically addressing the later issues range from discussing the behavior with the colleague to following agency or professional association protocols.

The CSWE 2008 EPAS describe the standards for the accreditation of social work programs and the academic degrees that social work faculty, including field supervisors, must have. A social work degree is required, the BSW or MSW for undergraduate programs, and the MSW or Ph.D. for MSW programs. Only bachelor's and master's degree programs are accredited by CSWE. Consequently, in the field practicum the primary supervisor is required to hold a social work degree, either a BSW or MSW (Ginsberg, 2001). In some criminal justice settings this may be difficult to achieve because the agency does not employ social workers.

CSWE (2008) identifies the social work credentials and practice experience required by field instructors within accredited educational programs in section 2.1.6 of the *2008 educational policy and accreditation standards*. These standards require that BSW field instructors hold a BSW or MSW degree from a CSWE-accredited educational program, and MSW field instructors hold a MSW degree from a CSWE-accredited educational program. In situations where it is not possible to meet these requirements, CSWE allows educational programs to develop and describe alternative methods for ensuring that students are supervised within the framework of a "social work perspective."

Because BSW and MSW student interns require a field supervisor with a social work degree, alternative models can be explored. Social work educational programs can explore and pursue models in which a task supervisor is utilized. A task supervisor can provide the day-to-day supervision and acclimation to the setting. A field supervisor social worker can consult with the agency and provide social work supervision to the student intern, either a faculty member or a field instructor from another agency.

This method can increase the number of field placements in criminal justice settings and provide students with practice opportunities that otherwise would not exist. However, this requires time to prepare all individuals involved. For example, a small local law enforcement agency expressed interest in having a social work student intern not aware of the aforementioned issues. Planning between the social work field placement department and law enforcement agency resulted in exploring a model in which an MSW social work supervisor who was already a consultant with the agency was asked to provide the social work supervision. A sergeant was asked to provide the task supervision. In the end, the field placement did not happen because of the lack of time to adequately prepare a new placement before the beginning of the academic year. Planning and preparation must consider the academic calendar.

Knowledgeable faculty are also a key component in the field education process. Students should be prepared in advance for field placement in correctional settings by providing orientation and information to students, involving field instructors, and allowing students to visit the correctional facility (Ivanoff, Smyth, & Finnegan, 1993). Faculty with expertise in social work practice in correctional settings, for example, can educate students concerning the type of knowledge they require in advance of visiting the facility and prior to beginning field placement.

Some agencies hire BSW-level social workers to perform the same tasks as MSW-level social workers (Ginsberg, 2001). This is very likely to occur in criminal justice agencies, particularly governmental agencies. For instance, the author is personally aware of a situation in which a BSW-level and an MSW-level police social worker both performed the same tasks. In this instance, the title *social worker* was not employed. This raises several questions for professional social work practice which delineates BSW and MSW level practice. Furthermore, state licensing laws distinguish between the types of practice licensed social workers can perform. Some government criminal justice agencies may not require social work licensure. These are all important issues that need to be addressed as the social work profession looks to the future of practice in the criminal justice system.

Benefits for the agency participating in field education are obtaining student interns who are skilled in retrieving, evaluating, and synthesizing up-to-date information, and who bring up-to-date knowledge to the field. Benefits for the profession include social work professionals who graduate with entry-level skills and are realistically prepared for practice in criminal justice settings.

Implications for Social Work Practice

This chapter has raised questions about whether a narrower focus for social work practice would increase social work involvement in the U.S. criminal justice system in the future. Would such a narrow focus be feasible given the widespread involvement of social work in the adult and juvenile criminal justice systems? These questions are posed after a review of social work practice in the criminal justice systems found in the Netherlands and Scotland. One certainty is that the future contributions of the social work profession in the U.S. criminal justice system will involve interdisciplinary practice. Efforts to challenge social injustice and racial disparities will require that social work collaborate with other disciplines.

The profession does not have all the tools necessary to change criminal justice conditions alone. Elsewhere in this book numerous social justice initiatives were presented that have been implemented within agencies and communities that are not social-work-driven, although these initiatives are compatible with social work values. These initiatives have the potential to significantly change criminal justice procedures and practices. In addition, technological advances and global trends will require that social workers remain current regarding these developments and possess the necessary skills to acquire up-to-date knowledge. Interdisciplinary communication skills will be essential to enhance social work practice in the criminal justice system in the future.

Societal conditions will also require consideration and monitoring. Tonry (2009) suggested that increasing U.S. crime rates, harsh attitudes toward criminal offenders, and political posturing were not the basis for tough-on-crime legislation. Instead, Tonry suggested that fundamentalist religious views, an obsolete constitution, and poor race relations have all contributed to harsher punishment policies. Social work practice will necessitate ongoing consideration of these factors as they shape the future of criminal justice policies and practices. At present, these factors, combined with a conservative approach to social issues, appear to permeate American politics.

Of course all of these suggestions are contingent upon student desire and demand for criminal justice courses and field placements, and professional social workers' interest in criminal justice employment. In 2007, only 1% of the NASW membership identified criminal justice as their principal social work practice area (Whitaker & Arrington, 2008), which means that 99% of the membership are not employed primarily in criminal justice settings.

Chapter Summary

This final chapter looked at the future of social work practice in the criminal justice system. It highlighted the fact that the future will hold more interdisciplinary practice, necessitate that social workers employ EBP, science, and research, and understand the effects of technological advances and global trends on criminal justice policies and practices. The Dutch and Scottish models describing social work practice in their criminal justice systems were reviewed. The lessons learned from these models raise numerous questions about the future of social work practice in the U.S. criminal justice system. Finally, options were examined for social work educational programs, particularly field and classroom instruction, to explore methods that have the potential to increase social work involvement in criminal justice settings.

Key Terms

Council on Social Work Education
  Educational Policy and
  Accreditation Standards
Criminal justice social work
Dutch drug policy

Field placement
NASW standards for social work
  practice
Project evaluation
Research

Questions for Review

1. Identify the challenges that face the criminal justice system in the twenty-first century.
2. What specialized knowledge do social workers require for criminal justice practice in the twenty-first century?
3. What skills do social workers require for criminal justice practice in the twenty-first century?
4. Summarize the lessons learned from international models that can inform the future of social work practice in the criminal justice system. Do you think that the lessons learned from these models are applicable to the U.S. criminal justice system? Why or why not?

Further Reading

Mason, M. A. (1991). The McMartin case revisited: The conflict between social work and criminal justice. *Social Work, 36(5)*, 391–395.

O'Malley, P. (2000). Criminologies of catastrophe? Understanding criminal justice on the edge of the new millennium. *Australian & New Zealand Journal of Criminology, 33(2)*, 153–167.

Reamer, F. G. (1992). The impaired social worker. *Social Work, 37(2)*, 165–170.

Tomita, M. (2010). Multidisciplinary exploration of the social environment for effective criminal justice system. *Social Work Review, 9(3)*, 121–128.

Resources

American Correctional Association (ACA)

www.aca.org

The ACA website describes it as the oldest and largest international correctional association in the world. The ACA provides professional development, correctional standards, accreditation, consultation, conferences, workshops, and publications.

American Jail Association (AJA)

www.aja.org

The AJA is a national nonprofit organization. AJA focuses on the operations of local correctional facilities and offers technical assistance, the *American Jails* magazine, and certifications in jail officer, jail management, and jail training.

American Probation and Parole Association (APPA)

www.appa-net.org

The APPA is an international association with a focus on community-based corrections, probation, and parole in both the juvenile and adult criminal justice systems. APPA provides advocacy, and education and training for direct staff, supervisors, and administrators.

Amnesty International

www.AmnestyUSA.org

Amnesty International is the largest grassroots human rights organization in the world. Previously awarded the Nobel Peace Prize, Amnesty International provides human rights investigations, education, and activities focused on challenging human rights abuses.

Bureau of Justice Assistance (BJA)

www.ojp.usdoj.gov/BJA

BJS provides training, technical assistance, resources, and funding focused on law enforcement, courts, corrections, crime victims, crime prevention, and the use of technology in the criminal justice system.

Bureau of Justice Statistics (BJS)
www.bjs.gov
BJS collects, analyzes, and disseminates data on crime, crime victims, and the operations of criminal justice systems at tribal, local, state, and federal levels.

The Center for Court Innovation
www.courtinnovation.org
The Center for Court Innovation is a public/private partnership that focuses on victim services, crime reduction, and improving public perceptions of the criminal justice system. The organization also focuses on specialty or problem courts, and in New York State conducts research in the court system designed to test court innovations.

Correctional Corporation of America (CCA)
www.cca.com/about
CCA established the private corrections industry. It is the largest corrections system in the U.S. after the federal government and three state prison systems. CCA provides management of corrections systems relative to design, construction, and operations.

Death Penalty Information Center (DPIC)
www.deathpenaltyinfo.org
This nonprofit organization provides death penalty information to journalists and others interested in the death penalty. The website contains information such as facts about the death penalty and other resources.

Drop the Rock
www.droptherock.org
This alliance is comprised of a New York State-wide membership focused on reducing the New York State prison population. The website provides current information on the New York State Rockefeller Drug Laws.

Families to Amend California's Three-Strikes Law
www.facts1.org
This website provides personal stories, updates, and resources pertaining to California's Three-Strikes Law.

International Association of Chiefs of Police (IACP)
www.theiacp.org
According to its website the IACP is the oldest and largest nonprofit police executive membership organization in the world. IACP has more than 20,000 members in more than 100 countries representing international, federal, and local law enforcement agencies.

Justice Policy Institute
www.justicepolicy.org
As a national nonprofit organization the Justice Policy Institute provides information concerning criminal justice reform efforts, training, and technical assistance.

Murder Victims' Families for Reconciliation (MVFR)

www.mvfr.org

MVFR focuses its efforts on abolishing the death penalty through recruiting and preparing victims to become involved, and working with the criminal justice system and media.

National Association of Forensic Counselors (NAFC)

www.nationalafc.com

The NAFC is the largest certification body in the U.S. for forensic counselors. The NAFC is a nonprofit organization that provides practice standards, clinical guidelines, and certification for forensic counselors.

The National Criminal Justice Reference Service (NCJRS)

www.ncjrs.gov

The NCJRS is funded by the federal government and provides criminal justice and substance abuse resources focused on policy, programs, and research.

National Institute of Corrections (NIC)

www.nicic.gov

The NIC provides a variety of services to local, state, and federal correctional facilities which include training, technical assistance, and funding.

The National Institute of Justice (NIJ)

www.nij.gov

The NIJ is the research and evaluation agency of the U.S. Department of Justice. As such, NIJ promotes the use of science and technology in criminal justice systems at state and local levels.

National Organization of Forensic Social Work (NOFSW)

www.nofsw.org

The NOFSW provides resources to advance forensic social work practice. These resources include an annual conference, training, publications, networking, and political action activities.

National Organization of Parents of Murdered Children, Inc. (POMC)

www.pomc.org

POMC provides support and other services to survivors of homicide victims.

National Sheriffs' Association (NSA)

www.sheriffs.org

NSA provides training, education, information, and other services to sheriffs, deputies, law enforcement, public safety officials, and citizens aimed at sharing information and improving the functions of sheriffs' offices.

Office of Juvenile Justice and Delinquency Prevention (OJJDP)
www.ojjdp.gov
OJJDP is a component of the Office of Justice Programs, U.S. Department of Justice, focused on improving policies and practices that affect juveniles in the adult and juvenile justice systems. OJJDP provides support to tribal, state, and local jurisdictions through research, training, information, and funding.

U.S. Citizenship and Immigration Services (USCIS)
www.uscis.gov/portal/site/uscis
USCIS is responsible for managing immigration into the U.S. Its efforts focus on improving the immigration system, the provision of immigration and services, and supporting immigration policies and programs.

References

Chapter 1

Albanese, J. S. (2008). *Criminal justice* (4th ed). Boston, MA: Pearson Education, Inc.

Alexander, R., Jr. (2007). Juvenile delinquency and social work practice. In C. A. McNeece & A. R. Roberts (eds.) *Policy and practice in the justice system* (pp. 181–197). Chicago, IL: Nelson Hall.

Alexander, R., Jr. (2008). Criminal justice: Overview. In T. Mizrahi & L. E. Davis (eds.) *Encyclopedia of social work* (20th ed.) (vol. 3, pp. 470–476). Washington, DC: NASW Press, and New York: Oxford University Press.

Andrews, D. A., & Bonta, J. (2010). Rehabilitating criminal justice policy and practice. *Psychology, Public Policy, and Law, 16(1)*, 39–55.

Barker, R. L. (2003). *The social work dictionary* (5th ed.). Washington, DC: NASW Press.

Barker, R. L., & Branson, D. M. (1993). *Forensic social work: Legal aspects of professional practice*. New York: The Haworth Press.

Bazemore, G., & Walgrave, L. (eds.) (1999). Restorative juvenile justice: In search of fundamentals and an outline for systematic reform. In G. Bazemore and L. Walgrave (eds.) *Restorative juvenile justice: Repairing the harm of youth crime* (pp. 45–74). Monsey, NY: Criminal Justice Press.

Bill of rights transcript (n.d.). Retrieved from http://archives.gov/exhibits/charters/bill_of_rights_transcript.html.

Bureau of Justice Statistics (2011). *National crime victimization survey (NCVS)*. Retrieved from http://bjs.ojp.usdoj.gov/index.cfm?ty=dcdetail&iid=245.

Bureau of Justice Statistics (n.d.a). *Total correctional population*. Retrieved from http://bjs.ojp.usdoj.gov/index.cfm?ty=tp&tid=11.

Bureau of Justice Statistics (n.d.b). *Employment and expenditure*. Retrieved from http://bjs.ojp.usdoj.gov/index.cfm?ty=tp&tid=5.

Cole, G. F., & Smith, C. E. (2004). *The American system of criminal justice* (12th ed.). Belmont, CA: Wadsworth, Cengage Learning.

DeLisi, M., Hochstetler, A., Higgins, G. E., Beaver, K. M., & Graeve, C. M. (2008). Toward a general theory of criminal justice: Low self-control and offender noncompliance. *Criminal Justice Review, 33(2)*, 141–158.

Dripps, D. (2002). Criminal justice process. In J. Dressler (ed.) *Encyclopedia of crime and justice* (2nd ed.) (pp. 362–371). New York: Gale Group.

Ellis, R. A., & Sowers, K. M. (2001). *Juvenile justice practice: A cross-disciplinary approach to intervention.* Belmont, CA: Wadsworth, Brooks/Cole.

Federal Bureau of Investigation (2009). *Uniform crime reporting program frequently asked questions.* Retrieved from www.fbi.gov/about-us/cjis/ucr/frequently-asked-questions/ucr_faqs08.pdf.

Federal Bureau of Investigation (2010). *Preliminary semiannual uniform crime report, January–June, 2010.* Retrieved from www.fbi.gov/about-us/cjis/ucr/crime-in-the-u.s/2010/preliminary-crime-in-the-us-2009.

Frase, R. S., & Weidner, R. R. (2002). Criminal justice system. In Joshua Dressler (ed.) *Encyclopedia of crime and justice* (2nd ed.) (pp. 371–393). New York: Gale Group.

Ginsberg, L. H. (2001). *Careers in social work* (2nd ed). Boston, MA: Allyn & Bacon.

Haugen, D., & Musser, S. (2009). *Criminal justice: Opposing viewpoints.* Detroit, MI: Greenhaven Press.

Judah, E. H., & Bryant, M. (2004). Rethinking criminal justice: Retribution vs. restoration. In E. H. Judah and M. Bryant (eds.) *Criminal justice: Retribution vs. restoration* (pp. 1–6). Binghamton, NY: The Haworth Social Work Press.

Langan, P. A., & Levin, D. J. (2002). *Recidivism of prisoners released in 1994.* Washington, DC: U.S. Department of Justice, Office of Justice Programs, Bureau of Justice Statistics.

Minton, T. D. (2011). *Jail inmates at midyear 2010: Statistical tables.* U.S. Department of Justice, Office of Justice Programs, Bureau of Justice Statistics.

National Association of Social Workers (2008). *Code of ethics of the National Association of Social Workers.* Washington, DC: Author.

National Association of Social Workers (n.d.). *Code of Ethics.* Retrieved from http://social workers.org/pubs/code/default.asp.

Perry, S. W. (2005). *Census of tribal justice agencies in Indian country, 2002.* U.S. Department of Justice, Office of Justice Programs, Bureau of Justice Statistics.

Primm, A. B., Osher, F. C., & Gomez, M. B. (2005). Race and ethnicity, mental health services and cultural competence in the criminal justice system: Are we ready to change? *Community Mental Health Journal, 42(5),* 557–569.

Puzzanchera, C., Adams, B., & Sickmund, M. (2010). *Juvenile court statistics 2006–2007.* Pittsburgh, PA: National Center for Juvenile Justice.

Reamer, F. G. (2004). Social work and criminal justice: The uneasy alliance. In E. H. Judah and M. Bryant (eds.) *Criminal justice: Retribution vs. restoration* (pp. 213–231). Binghamton, NY: The Haworth Social Work Press.

Ross, J. I., & Gould, L. (2006). Native Americans, criminal justice, criminological theory, and policy development. In J. I. Ross & L. Gould (eds.) *Native Americans and the criminal justice system: Theoretical and policy directions* (pp. 3–14). Boulder, CO: Paradigm Publishers.

Sarri, R. C., & Shook, J. J. (2005). The future for social work in juvenile and adult criminal justice. *Advances in Social Work, 6(1),* 210–220.

Siegel, L. J. (2010). *Introduction to criminal justice* (12th ed.). Belmont, CA: Wadsworth, Cengage Learning.

Smith, J. (2011). *George Stinney, Jr., was 14 years old.* Retrieved from http://maddowblog.msnbc.msn.com/_news/2011/10/05/8157666-george-stinney-jr-was-14-years-old.

Universal declaration of human rights (n.d.). Retrieved from www.un.org/en/documents/udhr/index.shtml.

U.S. Department of Health & Human Services, Centers for Medicare & Medicaid Services (n.d.). *NHE fact sheet national health expenditure data.* Retrieved from www.cms.gov/NationalHealthExpendData/25_NHE_Fact_Sheet.asp.

U.S. Department of Justice, Office of Justice Programs (n.d.). *Reentry*. Retrieved from www.reentry.gov.

Van Ness, D. W. (2004). Justice that restores: From impersonal to personal justice. In E. H. Judah and M. Bryant (eds.) *Criminal justice: Retribution vs. restoration* (pp. 93–109). Binghamton, NY: The Haworth Social Work Press.

van Wormer, K. (2009). Restorative justice as social justice for victims of gendered violence: A standpoint feminist perspective. *Social Work, 54(2)*, 107–116.

Ward, T., & Langlands, R. (2009). Repairing the rupture: Restorative justice and the rehabilitation of offenders. *Aggression and Violent Behavior, 14*, 205–214.

West, H. C. (2010). *Prison inmates at midyear 2009: Statistical tables*. U.S. Department of Justice, Office of Justice Programs, Bureau of Justice Statistics.

Whitaker, T., & Arrington, P. (2008). *Social workers at work*. NASW Membership Workforce Study. Washington, DC: National Association of Social Workers.

Wikstrom, P. H., Ceccato, V., Hardie, B., & Treiber, K. (2009). Activity fields and the dynamics of crime: Advancing knowledge about the role of the environment in crime causation. *Journal of Quantitative Criminology, 26*, 55–87.

Wilson, M. (2010). *Criminal justice social work in the United States: Adapting to new challenges*. Washington, DC: NASW Center for Workforce Studies.

Winick, B. J. (1997). The jurisprudence of therapeutic jurisprudence. *Psychology, Public Policy, and Law, 3(1)*, 184–206.

Young, D. S., & Lomonaco, S. W. (2001). Incorporating content on offenders and corrections into social work curricula. *Journal of Social Work Education, 37(3)*, 475–491.

Chapter 2

Albanese, J. S. (2008). *Criminal justice*. (4th ed.). Boston, MA: Pearson Education, Inc.

Barker, R. L. (2003). *The social work dictionary* (5th ed.). Washington, DC: NASW Press.

Barlow, H. D., & Decker, S. H. (2010). *Criminology and public policy: Putting theory to work*. Philadelphia, PA: Temple University Press,

Cox, T. (2011). *"Andrea's Law" would track released murders*. Retrieved from www.daily herald.com/article/20110125/news/701259799/.

Ditton, P. M., & Wilson, D. J. (1999). *Truth in sentencing in state prisons*. Washington, DC: U.S. Department of Justice, Office of Justice Programs, Bureau of Justice Statistics.

Drop the Rock (2009). *The campaign to repeal the Rockefeller Drug Laws*. New York: Author.

Drug Policy Alliance (2009). *New York's Rockefeller Drug Laws: Explaining the reforms of 2009*. New York: Author.

Families against mandatory minimums (2010). Retrieved from www.famm.org/Repository/Files/FEDERAL%20MANDATORY%20MINIMUMS%206.2.11.pdf.

Frase, R. S., & Weidner, R. R. (2002). Criminal justice system. In J. Dressler (ed.) *Encyclopedia of crime and justice* (2nd ed.) (pp. 371–393). New York: Gale Group.

Hoefer, R. (2006). *Advocacy practice for social justice*. Chicago, IL: Lyceum Books, Inc.

H.R. 1064: Youth Prison Reduction through Opportunities, Mentoring, Intervention, Support, and Education Act 111th Congress: 2009–2010 (n.d.). Retrieved from www.govtrack.us/congress/bill.xpd?bill=h111-1064.

H.R. 1913: Local Law Enforcement Hate Crimes Prevention Act of 2009 (n.d.). Retrieved from www.govtrack.us/congress/bill.xpd?bill=h111-1913.

H.R. 2418: Mynisha's Law (n.d.). Retrieved from www.govtrack.us/congress/bill.xpd? bill=h111-2418.

H.R. 3355: Violent Crime Control and Law Enforcement Act of 1994 (n.d.). Retrieved from www.govtrack.us/congress/bill.xpd?bill=h103-3355.

H.R. 4055: Honest Opportunity Probation with Enforcement (HOPE) Initiative Act of 2009 (n.d.). Retrieved from www.govtrack.us/congress/bill.xpd?bill=h111-4055.

Kennedy-Ross, S. (2006). *Mynisha's law unveiled.* Retrieved from www.sbsun.com/ci_ 3755886.

King, R. S., & Mauer, M. (2001). *Aging behind bars: 'Three strikes' seven years later.* Washington, DC: The Sentencing Project.

Legislative Analysts' Office (1995). *The three strikes and you're out law.* Retrieved from www.lao.ca.gov/analysis_1995/3strikes.html.

Mondros, J. B. (2009). Principles and practice guidelines for social action. In A. R. Roberts (ed.) *Social workers' desk reference* (2nd ed.) (pp. 901–906). New York: Oxford University Press, Inc.

National Association of Social Workers (2007). *NASW advocacy.* Retrieved from http:// capwiz.com/socialworkers/issues/bills.

National Association of Social Workers (2008). *NASW 2008 legislative agenda.* Washington, DC: NASW Office of Government Relations and Political Action.

National Association of Social Workers (2011). *Social workers in congress.* Retrieved from http://socialworkers.org/pace/swCongress/default.asp.

National Association of Social Workers (n.d.). *Legislative agenda for the 111th Congress: January 2009–December 2010.* Washington, DC: NASW Office of Government Relations and Political Action. Retrieved from www.socialworkers.org/advocacy/images/gr materials/111th%20Legislative%20Agenda.pdf.

National Association of Social Workers Massachusetts (n.d.). *2009–2010 legislative agenda.* www.naswma.org/displaycommon.cfm?an=1&subarticlenbr=201.

National Association of Social Workers / Texas Chapter 2011 Legislative agenda—Texas 82nd Legislative Session (2010). Retrieved from www.naswtx.org/associations/8710/files/ 2011_Legislative_Agenda%20_7_.pdf.

New York State Division of Criminal Justice Services (2010). *Leandra's Law Factsheet.* Retrieved from http://criminaljustice.state.ny.us/pio/press_releases/2010-7-20_pressrelease. html.

Pace, P. R. (2009). Social work and the Second Chance Act. *NASW News, 54(5),* 4.

Pace, P. R. (2010). Political leaders offer inspirational stories. *NASW News, 55(6),* 9.

Pace, P. R. (2011). Report stresses need from criminal reform leadership. *NASW News, 56(1),* 5.

Reentry Policy Council (n.d.). *Second Chance Act.* Retrieved from http://reentrypolicy.org/ government_affairs/second_chance_act.

Reisch, M. (2009). Legislative advocacy to empower oppressed and vulnerable groups. In A. R. Roberts (ed.). *Social workers' desk reference* (2nd ed.) (pp. 893–900). New York: Oxford University Press, Inc.

Robinson, M. (2010). Assessing criminal justice practice using social justice theory. *Social Justice Research, 23,* 77–97.

S. 306: National Criminal Justice Commission Act of 2011 (n.d.). Retrieved from www. govtrack.us/congress/bill.xpd?bill=s112-306.

S. 909: Matthew Shepard Hate Crimes Prevention Act (n.d.). Retrieved from www.gov track.us/congress/bill.xpd?bill=s111-909.

S. 1789: Fair Sentencing Act of 2010 (n.d.). Retrieved from www.govtrack.us/congress/bill.xpd?bill=s111-1789.

S. 2772: Criminal Justice Reinvestment Act of 2010 (n.d.). Retrieved from www.govtrack.us/congress/bill.xpd?bill=s111-2772.

Schwartz, J. (2011). *Thousands of prison terms in crack cases could be eased.* Retrieved from www.nytimes.com/2011/07/01/us/01sentence.html?_r=1.

Sentencing Project, The (2008). *Racial disparity in the criminal justice system: A manual for practitioners and policymakers.* Washington, DC: Author.

Serrano, R. A., Savage, D. G., & Williams, C. J. (2011). *Early release proposed for crack cocaine offenders.* Retrieved from http://articles.latimes.com/2011/jun/01/nation/la-na-holder-crack-20110602.

Shepherd, J. M. (2002). Fear of the first strike: The full deterrent effect of California's two- and three-strikes legislation. *Journal of Legal Studies, 31,* 159–201.

Siegel, Larry J. (2010). *Introduction to criminal justice* (12th ed.). Belmont, CA: Wadsworth, Cengage Learning.

Social Work Reinvestment Initiative (n.d.). Retrieved from www.socialworkreinvestment.org/State.

Squillace, J. (2010). The effect of privatization on advocacy: Social work state-level advocacy with the executive branch. *Families in Society, 91(1),* 25–30.

Teater, B. (2009). Influencing state legislators: A framework for developing effective social work interest groups. *Journal of Policy Practice, 8,* 69–86.

United States Department of Justice, Office of Justice Programs (n.d.). *AMBER Alert—America's missing: Broadcast Emergency response.* Retrieved from www.amberalert.gov/.

USA.gov. *U.S. federal government.* Retrieved from www.usa.gov/Agencies/federal.shtml.

Wilson, A. D. (2000). *Rockefeller drug laws information sheet.* Retrieved from http://prdi.org/rocklawfact.html.

Wilson, M. (2010). Criminal justice reform: Why social workers should care. *Social work & the Courts, 1,* 3–5.

Zimring, F. E., Hawkins, G., & Kamin, S. (2001). *Punishment and democracy: Three strikes and you're out in California.* Oxford, UK: Oxford University Press.

Chapter 3

ATF online—bureau of alcohol, tobacco and firearms (n.d.). Retrieved March 11, 2004, from www.atf.gov/about/mission/htm.

Barker, R. L. (2003). Police social work. *The social work dictionary* (5th ed.) (p. 330). Washington, DC: NASW Press.

Bar-On, A. (1995). They have their job, we have ours: Reassessing the feasibility of police–social work cooperation. *Policing and Society, 5,* 37–51.

Barton, R. (2000). Police officers and the interface with social work. In M. Davies (ed.) *The Blackwell encyclopedia of social work* (p. 257). Malden, MA: Blackwell Publishers Ltd.

Briar, K. H. (1985). Emergency calls to police: Implications for social work intervention. *Social Service Review, 59(4),* 593–603.

Bureau of Investigation—facts and figures 2003 (2003). Retrieved from www.fbi.gov/priorities/priorities.htm.

Callahan, J. (2000). Debriefing the Oklahoma City Police. *Tulane Studies in Social Welfare, XXI–XXII,* 285–294.

Calliantos, C. (2000). Social workers intervene at police stations. *NASW News, 45.1* (November), 14.

Cheung, M., & Boutte-Queen, N. M. (2000). Emotional responses to child sexual abuse: A comparison between police and social workers in Hong Kong. *Child Abuse & Neglect, 24(12)*, 1613–1621.

City of Chicago (2010). *Police mission.* Retrieved from www.cityofchicago.org/cp/Welcome/Mission.html.

Cole, G. F., & Smith, C. E. (2004). *The American system of criminal justice* (12th ed.). Belmont, CA: Wadsworth, Cengage Learning.

Compton, B. R., & Galaway, B. (1994). Social work processes. Belmont, CA: Wadsworth.

Conte, J. R., Berliner, L., & Nolan, D. (1980). Police and social workers cooperation: A key in child sexual assault cases. *FBI Law Enforcement Bulletin, 49(3)*, 7–10.

Cooper, L., Anaf, J., & Bowden, M. (2008). Can social workers and police be partners when dealing with bikie-gang related domestic violence and sexual assault? *European Journal of Social Work, 11(3)*, 295–312.

Coordinating police and social work (1952). *The American City, 67*, 163.

Corcoran, J., Stephenson, M., Perryman, D., & Allen, S. (2001). Perceptions and utilization of a police–social work crisis intervention approach to domestic violence. *Families in Society, 82(4)*, 393–398.

DEA briefs & background, drug policy, DEA mission (n.d.). Retrieved from www.usdoj.gov/dea/agency/mission.htm.

Federal Bureau of Investigation (n.d.a). *Quick facts.* Retrieved from www.fbi.gov/about-us/quick-facts.

Federal Bureau of Investigation (n.d.b). *FBI resources for helping victims.* Retrieved from www.fbi.gov/stats-services/victim_assistance/resources.

Federal Bureau of Investigation (n.d.c). *FBI Comes to aid of victims.* Retrieved from www.fbi.gov/news/stories/2006/november/vic_assist111306.

Federal Bureau of Investigation (n.d.d). *Office for victim assistance.* Retrieved from www.fbi.gov/news/podcasts/inside/office-for-victim-assistance.mp3/view/.

Fielding, N., & Conroy, S. (1992). Interviewing child victims: Police and social work investigations of child sexual abuse. *Sociology, 26(1)*, 103–124.

Findlay, C. (1991). Joint police and social work investigations in child abuse: A practice example from Scotland. *Children & Society, 5(3)*, 225–231.

Fong, K., & Cheung, M. (1997). Developing the interview protocol for video-recorded child sexual abuse investigations: A training experience with police officers, social workers, and clinical psychologists in Hong Kong. *Child Abuse & Neglect, 21(3)*, 273–284.

Garrett, P. M. (2004). Talking child protection: The police and social workers "working together". *Journal of Social Work, 4(1)*, 77–97.

Hickman, M. J. (2003). *Tribal law enforcement, 2000.* Washington, DC: U.S. Department of Justice, Office of Justice Programs, Bureau of Justice Statistics.

Hickman, M. J., & Reaves, B. A. (2003a). *Local police departments 2000.* Washington, DC: U.S. Department of Justice, Office of Justice Programs, Bureau of Justice Statistics.

Hickman, M. J., & Reaves, B. A. (2003b). *Sheriffs' offices 2000.* Washington, DC: U.S. Department of Justice, Office of Justice Programs, Bureau of Justice Statistics.

Holdaway, S. (1986). Police and social work relations—Problems and possibilities. *British Journal of Social Work, 16*, 137–160.

Holmes, S. A. (1982). A Detroit model for police–social work co-operation. *Social Casework, 63(4)*, 220–226.

Home, A. M. (1994). Attributing responsibility and assessing gravity in wife abuse situations: A comparative study of police and social workers. *Journal of Social Service Research*, 19(1/2), 67–84.

Home page of the Atlanta Police Department (2003). Retrieved from www.atlantapd.org.

Houston police online—mission statement (n.d.). Retrieved from www.cihouston.tx.us/departure/police/mission.htm.

Jones, H. 1963. Policemen as social workers. *New Society*, 14 (November), 9–10.

Kelley, S. (1990). Responsibility and management strategies in child sexual abuse: A comparison of child protective workers, nurses, and police officers. *Child Welfare*, LXIX(1), 43–51.

Knox, K., & Roberts, A. R. (2009). The social worker in a police department. In A. R. Roberts (ed.) *Social worker's desk reference* (2nd ed.) (pp. 85–94). New York: Oxford University Press.

Mastrofski, S. (1983). The police and noncrime services. In G. P. Whitaker and C. D. Phillip (eds.) *Evaluating performance of criminal justice agencies* (pp. 33–61). Beverly Hills, CA: Sage.

McMullan, E. C., Carlan, P. E., & Nored, L. S. (2009). Future law enforcement officers and social workers: Perceptions of domestic violence. *Journal of Interpersonal Violence*, XX(X), 1–21.

Michaels, R. A., & Treger, H. (1973). Social work in police departments. *Social Work*, 69, 67–75.

Mission statement (1998). Retrieved from www.cityofchicago.org/cp/Welcome/Mission.html.

Mission statement (2002). Retrieved from www.cssdoorway.org/css/mission_statement.htm.

Morris, P., & Heal, P. (1981). *Crime control and the police.* London: Home Office Research Study, no. 67.

Odem, M. E., & Schlossman, S. (1991). Guardians of virtue: The juvenile court and female delinquency in early 20th-Century Los Angeles. *Crime & Delinquency*, 37(2), 186–203.

O'Keefe, J. (2004). *Protecting the republic: The education and training of American police officers.* Upper Saddle River, NJ: Pearson Education, Inc.

Openshaw, L. (2009). Police officers and their spouses. In A. Gitterman & R. Salmon (eds.) *Encyclopedia of social work with groups* (pp. 228–230). New York: Routledge.

Parkinson, G. C. (1980). Cooperation between police and social workers: Hidden issues. *Social Work*, 25(1), 12–18.

Patterson, G. T. (2004). Police social work crisis teams: Practice and research implications. *Stress, Trauma and Crisis*, 7, 93–104.

Patterson, G. T. (2008a). Police social work: A unique area of practice arising from law enforcement functions. *Currents Newsletter of the NASW, 52(8),* 1, 8–9.

Patterson, G. T. (2008b). A framework for facilitating stress management educational groups for police officers. *Social Work with Groups, 31(1),* 53–70.

Patterson, G. T. (2008c). Police social work. In T. Mizrahi & L. E. Davis (eds.) *Encyclopedia of social work* (20th ed.) (vol. 3, pp. 357–362). Washington, DC: NASW Press, and New York: Oxford University Press.

Penner, L. G. (1959). An experiment in police and social agency co-operation. *Annals of the American Academy of Political and Social Science*, 322, 79–88.

Peterson, D. M. (1974). The police officer's conception of proper police work. *The Police Journal*, 47, 102–108.

Portland Police Bureau—mission, values and goals (n.d.). Retrieved from http://portland policebureau.com/mission.html.

Reaves, B. A. (1992). *State and local police departments, 1990*. Washington, DC: U.S. Department of Justice, Office of Justice Programs, Bureau of Justice Statistics.

Reaves, B. A. (2006). *Federal law enforcement officers, 2004*. Washington, DC: US Department of Justice, Office of Justice Programs, Bureau of Justice Statistics.

Reaves, B. A., & Hickman, M. J. (2002). *Police departments in large cities, 1990–2000*. Washington, DC: US Department of Justice, Office of Justice Programs, Bureau of Justice Statistics.

Richards, K. (1976). Conversation—not confrontation. *Social Work Today, 7(8)*, 232.

Robert Wood Johnson (2001). *The youth service providers network*. Retrieved from http://sasnet.com/bostonstrategy/programs/15_YSProvidersNet.html.

Roberts, A. R. (1978). Training police social workers—A neglected area of social work education. *Journal of Education for Social Work, 14(2)*, 98–103.

Roberts, A. R. (2007a). Police social work: Bridging the past to the present. In A. R. Roberts & D. W. Springer (eds.) *Social work in juvenile and criminal justice settings* (3rd ed.) (pp. 126–129). Springfield, IL: Charles C. Thomas.

Roberts, A. R. (2007b). The history and role of social work in law enforcement. In A. R. Roberts & D. W. Springer (eds.) *Social work in juvenile and criminal justice settings* (pp. 106–112). Springfield, IL: Charles C. Thomas.

Scott, E. J. (1981), *Calls for service: citizen demand and initial police response*. Washington, DC: National Institute of Justice.

Slaght, E. F. (2002). Revisiting the relationship between social work and law enforcement. *Journal of Community Practice, 10(2)*, 23–36.

Stephens, M. (1988). Problems of police-social work interaction: Some American lessons. *The Howard Journal, 27(2)*, 81–91.

Thomas, T. (1988). The police and social workers: Creativity or conflict? *Practice, 2(2)*, 120–129.

Treger, H. (1980). Guideposts for community work in police-social work diversion. *Federal Probation, 44(3)*, 3–8.

Treger, H. (1981). Police social work cooperation: problems and issues. *Social Casework, 61(5)*, 426–433.

Treger, H. (1987). Police social work. In A. Minahan (ed.) *Encyclopedia of social work* (18th ed.) (vol. 2, pp. 263–268). Washington, DC: NASW Press.

Treger, H. (1995). Police social work. In R. L. Edwards & J. G. Hopps (eds.) *Encyclopedia of social work* (19th ed.) (pp. 1843–1848). Washington, DC: NASW Press.

Trojanowicz, R. C., & Dixon, S. L. (1974). *Criminal justice and the community*. Englewood Cliffs, NJ: Prentice-Hall, Inc.

Trute, B., Adkins, E., & MacDonald, G. (1992). Professional attitudes regarding the sexual abuse of children: Comparing police, child welfare and community mental health. *Child Abuse & Neglect, 16*, 359–368.

United States Conference of Mayors (1999). *Rochester police department, victim assistance unit—Comprehensive crime victims program*. Retrieved from www.usmayors.org/best practices/domestic/rochester_ny.htm.

United States Department of Justice, Community Oriented Policing (n.d.). *What is community policing?* (n.d.). Retrieved from www.cops.usdoj.gov/Default.asp?Item =36.

Walker, D. (2006). Lost and forgotten: Early police social workers. *The New Social Worker, 13(2)*, 8–9.

Waterhouse, L., & Carnie, J. (1991). Social work and police response to child sexual abuse in Scotland. *British Journal of Social Work, 21*, 373–379.

Webster, J. A. (1970). Police task and time study. *Journal of Criminal Law, Criminology and Police Science, 61*, 94–100.

Wilson, J. Q. (1968). *Varieties of police behavior*. Cambridge, MA: Harvard University Press.

Zezima, K. (2010). State cuts put officers on front lines of mental care. *The New York Times, CLX, No. 55, 245*, 32.

Zimmerman, S. I. (1998). *Police social work in twenty-three programs: Program description and analysis of interdisciplinary relations* (Unpublished doctorial dissertation). University of Illinois at Chicago, Chicago, IL.

Chapter 4

Administrative Office of the United States Courts (n.d.a). *Understanding federal and state courts*. Retrieved from www.uscourts.gov/EducationalResources/FederalCourtBasics/CourtStructure/UnderstandingFederalAndStateCourts.aspx.

Administrative Office of the United States Courts (n.d.b). *The difference between federal and state courts*. Retrieved from www.uscourts.gov/FederalCourts/UnderstandingtheFederalCourts/Jurisdiction/DifferencebetweenFederalAndStateCourts.

Albanese, J. S. (2008). *Criminal justice* (4th ed.). Boston, MA: Pearson Education, Inc.

Andrews, A. B. (1991). Social work expert testimony regarding mitigation in capital sentencing proceedings. *Social Work, 36(5)*, 440–445.

Ashford, J. B. (2009). Overview of forensic social work: Broad and narrow definitions. In A. R. Roberts (ed.) *Social workers' desk reference* (2nd ed.) (pp. 1055–1060). New York: Oxford University Press, Inc.

Barker, R. L., & Branson, D. M. (1993). *Forensic social work: Legal aspects of professional practice*. New York: The Haworth Press.

Bazemore, G., & Walgrave, L. (1999). Restorative juvenile justice: In search of fundamentals and an outline for systematic reform. In G. Bazemore and L. Walgrave (eds.) *Restorative juvenile justice: Repairing the harm of youth crime* (pp. 45–74). Monsey, NY: Criminal Justice Press.

Bazemore, G., & Walgrave, L. (eds.) (1999). *Restorative juvenile justice: Repairing the harm of youth crime*. Monsey, NY: Criminal Justice Press.

Bertelli, A. (1998). Should social workers engage in the unauthorized practice of law? *The Boston University Public Interest Law Journal*. Retrieved from www.lexisnexis.com.

Birgeden, A. (2004). Therapeutic jurisprudence and responsivity: Finding the will and the way in offender rehabilitation. *Psychology, Crime & Law, 10(3)*, 283–295.

Braye, S. & Preston-Shoot, M. (1990). On teaching and applying the law in social work: It is not that simple. *The British Journal of Social Work, 20(4)*, 333–353.

Braye, S. & Preston-Shoot, M. (2006). Broadening the vision: Law teaching, social work and civil society. *International Social Work, 49(3)*, 376–389.

Brooks, S. L. (2004). Practicing (and teaching) therapeutic jurisprudence: Importing social work principles and techniques into clinical legal education. *St. Thomas Law Review, 17*, 513–530.

Bureau of Justice Assistance (2003). *Juvenile drug courts: Strategies in practice*. Retrieved from www.ncjrs.gov/pdffiles1/bja/197866.pdf.

Bureau of Justice Assistance (n.d.). *Mental health courts program*. Retrieved from www.ojp.usdoj.gov/BJA/grant/MentalHealthCtFS.pdf.

Bynum, R. (2011). *Troy Davis execution fuels eyewitness ID debate*. Retrieved from www.ajc.com/news/nation-world/troy-davis-execution-fuels-1189542.html.

Cole, G. F., & Smith, C. E. (2004). *The American system of criminal justice* (12th ed.). Belmont, CA: Wadsworth, Cengage Learning.

Coleman, B. (2001). Lawyers who are also social workers: How to effectively combine two different disciplines to better serve clients. *Washington University Journal of Law & Policy*. Retrieved from www.lexisnexis.com.

Colledge, D., Zeigler, F., Hemmens, C., & Hodge, C. (2000). What's up doc? Jaffee v. Redmond and the psychotherapeutic privilege in criminal justice. *Journal of Criminal Justice, 28*, 1–11.

Death Penalty Information Center (2010). *States with and without the death penalty*. Retrieved from www.deathpenaltyinfo.org/states-and-without-death-penalty.

Delaware Judicial Information Center (2008). *Reentry court*. Retrieved from http://courts.delaware.gov/Superior/reentry.stm.

Dressler, J. (ed.). (2002). *Encyclopedia of crime and justice* (2nd ed.). New York: Gale Group.

Governor Creates Racial Disparity Commission (2007). Retrieved from www.wi-doc.com/Racial_Disparity_Commission.htm.

Guin, C. C., Nobel, D. N., & Merrill, T. S. (2003). From misery to mission: Forensic social workers on multidisciplinary mitigation teams. *Social Work, 48(3)*, 362–371.

Hamilton, Z. (2010). *Do reentry courts reduce recidivism? New York: Center for Court Innovation*. Retrieved from www.courtinnovation.org/sites/default/files/Reentry_Evaluation.pdf.

Innocence Project (n.d.). *Understand the causes*. Retrieved from www.innocenceproject.org/understand/.

Joslin, K., & Fleming, R. (2001). Case management in the law office. *Journal of Gerontological Social Work, 34(3)*, 33–48.

Kopels, S., & Gustavsson, N. S. (1996). Infusing legal issues into the social work curriculum. *Journal of Social Work Education, 32(1)*, 115–125.

Labriola, M., Bradley, S., O'Sullivan, C. S., & Moore, S. (2009). *A national portrait of domestic violence courts*. Retrieved from www.courtinnovation.org/sites/default/files/national_portrait.pdf.

Latimer, J., Dowden, C., & Muise, D. (2005). The effectiveness of restorative justice practices: A meta-analysis. *The Prison Journal, 85(2)*, 127–144.

Lee, E. (2000). *Community courts: An evolving model*. Washington, DC: U.S. Department of Justice, Office of Justice Programs, Bureau of Justice Assistance.

Madden, R. G. (2000). Legal content in social work education: Preparing students for interprofessional practice. *Journal of Teaching in Social Work, 20(1)*, 3–17.

Madden, R. G. (2003). *Essential law for social workers*. New York: Columbia University Press.

MSN Encarta Dictionary (2009). *Mitigation specialist definition*. Retrieved from http://encarta.msn.com/dictionary_1861678951/mitigation_specialist.html.

National Association of Social Workers (2009). Capital punishment and the death penalty. In *Social work speaks: National Association of Social Workers policy statements 2009–2012* (8th ed.) (pp. 38–41). Washington, D.C: NASW Press.

National Association of Social Workers (2010). NASW legal defense fund: What social work members need to know. *Social Work & the Courts, 1*, 6–7.

National Association of Social Workers (n.d.). *Specialty practice sections*. Retrieved from www.socialworkers.org/sections/default.asp.

National Association of Social Workers Legal Defense Fund (2002). *Are licensed clinical social workers authorized to provide expert witness testimony concerning the diagnosis and treatment of emotional and mental disorders?* Washington, DC: Author.

National Association of Social Workers Legal Defense Fund (2003). *Social workers as death penalty specialists.* Washington, DC: Author.

New York State Problem Solving Courts Brochure (n.d.). Retrieved from www.nycourts. gov/courts/problem_solving/PSC-FLYER4Fold.pdf.

New York State Unified Courts (2004). *Court structure.* Retrieved from www.courts.state. ny.us/courts/structure.shtml.

Office of Justice Programs Drug Court Clearinghouse and Technical Assistance Project. *Juvenile and family drug courts: An overview* (n.d.). Retrieved from www.ncjrs.gov/ html/bja/jfdcoview/dcpojuv.pdf.

Office of National Drug Control Policy (n.d.). *Drug courts.* Retrieved from www.white housedrugpolicy.gov/enforce/DrugCourt.html.

Perry, S. W. (2005). *Census of tribal justice agencies in Indian country, 2002.* U.S. Department of Justice, Office of Justice Programs, Bureau of Justice Statistics.

Phillips, A. (1979). Social work and the delivery of legal services. *The Modern Law Review, 42(1),* 29–41.

Preston-Shoot, M., Roberts, G., & Vernon, S. (1998). Developing a conceptual framework for teaching and assessing law within training for professional practice: Lessons from social work. *The Journal of Practice Teaching in Health and Social Work, 1(1),* 41–51.

Racial Disparity Commission (2007). *Governor Doyle creates commission to reduce racial disparity in Wisconsin's criminal justice system.* Retrieved from www.wi-doc.com/Racial _Disparity_Commission.htm.

Roberts, A. R., & Brownell, P. (1999). A century of forensic social work: Bridging the past to the present. *Social Work, 44(4),* 359–369.

Roche, J. (2001). Social work values and the law. In L. A. Long and J. Roche (eds.) *The law and social work: Contemporary issues for practice.* Basingstoke, U.K.: Palgrave Macmillan.

Rome, S. H. (2008). Forensic social work. In T. Mizrahi & L. E. Davis (eds.) *Encyclopedia of social work* (20th ed.) (vol. 3, pp. 221–223). Washington, DC: NASW Press and New York: Oxford University Press.

Roseman, C. P., Ritchie, M., & Laux, J. M. (2009). A restorative justice approach to empathy development in sex offenders: An exploratory study. *Journal of Addictions & Offender Counseling, 29,* 96–109.

Rottman, D. B., & Strickland, S. M. (2004). *State court organization 2004.* Washington, DC: U.S. Department of Justice, Office of Justice Programs, Bureau of Justice Statistics.

Schroeder, J., Guin, C. C., Pogue, R., & Bordelon, D. (2006). Mitigating circumstances in death penalty decisions: Using evidence-based research to inform social work practice in capital trials. *Social Work, 51(4),* 355–364.

Siegel, D. M. (2008). The growing admissibility of expert testimony by clinical social workers on competence to stand trial. *Social Work, 53(2),* 153–163.

Siegel, L. J. (2010). *Introduction to criminal justice* (12th ed.). Belmont, CA: Wadsworth, Cengage Learning.

Snell, T. L. (2010). *Capital punishment, 200—Statistical tables.* Washington, DC: U.S. Department of Justice, Office of Justice Programs, Bureau of Justice Statistics.

State of Arizona Supreme Court (2010). *Capital sentencing guide.* Retrieved from www. azcourts.gov/ccsguide/MitigatingCircumstances.aspx.

Tyuse, S. W., & Linhorst, D. M. (2005). Drug courts and mental courts: Implications for social work. *Social Work*, *30(3)*, 233–240.

van Wormer, K. (2008). Restorative justice. In T. Mizrahi & L. E. Davis (eds.) *Encyclopedia of social work* (20th ed.) (vol. 3, pp. 531–533). Washington, DC: NASW Press and New York: Oxford University Press.

Weil, M. (1982). Research on issues in collaboration between social workers and lawyers. *Social Service Review*, *56(3)*, 393–405.

Weil, M. O., & Gamble, D. N. (2009). Community practice model for the twenty-first century. In A. R. Roberts (ed.) *Social workers' desk reference* (2nd ed.) (pp. 882–892). New York: Oxford University Press, Inc.

Williams, C. J. (2011). *Death penalty costs California $184 million a year, study says.* Retrieved from http://articles.latimes.com/2011/jun/20/local/la-me-adv-death-penalty-costs-20110620.

Young, D. S. (2008). Criminal justice: Courts. In T. Mizrahi & L. E. Davis (eds.) *Encyclopedia of social work* (20th ed.) (vol. 3, pp. 476–478). Washington, DC: NASW Press and New York: Oxford University Press.

Chapter 5

Abdul-Alim, J. (2010). *It's time to lift the ban on Pell Grants for prisoners.* Retrieved from http://campusprogress.org/articles/its_time_to_lift_the_ban_on_pell_grants_for_prisoners.

Albanese, J. S. (2008). *Criminal justice* (4th ed). Boston, MA: Pearson Education, Inc.

Alexander, R., Young, D. S., & McNeece, C. A. (2008). Criminal justice. In T. Mizrahi & L. E. Davis (eds.) *Encyclopedia of social work* (20th ed.) (vol. 1, pp. 478–484). Washington, DC: NASW Press and New York: Oxford University Press.

Anno, B. J., Graham, C., Lawrence, J. E., Shansky, R., Bisbee, J., & Blackmore, J. (2004). *Correctional health care: Addressing the needs of elderly, chronically ill, and terminally ill inmates.* Washington, DC: U.S. Department of Justice, National Institute of Corrections.

Beck, A. J., & Shipley, B. E. (1989). *Recidivism of prisoners released in 1983.* Washington, DC: U.S. Department of Justice, Office of Justice Programs, Bureau of Justice Statistics.

Binswanger, I. A., Stern, M. F., Deyo, R. A., Heagerty, P. J., Cheadle, A., Elmore, J. G., & Koepsell, T. D. (2007). Release from prison: A high risk of death for former inmates. *The New England Journal of Medicine*, *356*, 157–166.

Butts, J. A. (2008). Probation and parole. In T. Mizrahi & L. E. Davis (eds.) *Encyclopedia of social work* (20th ed.) (vol. 3, pp. 415–418). Washington, DC: NASW Press and New York: Oxford University Press.

Chaiklin, H. (2008). Correctional social work. In A. R. Roberts (ed.), *Correctional counseling and treatment: Evidence-based perspectives* (pp. 277–289). Upper Saddle, NJ: Pearson Prentice Hall.

Conly, C. H. (2005). *Helping inmates obtain federal disability benefits: Serious medical and mental illness, incarceration, and federal disability entitlement program.* Washington, DC: U.S. Department of Justice.

De Leon, G. (1998). *Prison based therapeutic community treatment: What we know, and where we should go.* Retrieved from www.ncjrs.gov/ondcppubs/treat/consensus/deleon.pdf.

District of Columbia Department of Corrections (n.d.). *Halfway-house facilities.* Retrieved from http://doc.dc.gov/doc/cwp/view,a,3,q,491452.asp.

Dominelli, L. (2002). *Anti-oppressive social work theory and practice*. New York: Palgrave Macmillan.

Draine, J., Wolff, N., Jacoby, J. E., Hartwell, S., & Duclos, C. (2005). Understanding community reentry of former prisoners with mental illness: A conceptual model to guide new research. *Behavioral Sciences and the Law, 23*, 689–707.

Durose, M. R., & Langan, P. A. (2007). *Felony sentences in state courts, 2004*. Washington, DC: U.S. Department of Justice, Office of Justice Programs, Bureau of Justice Assistance.

Finn, P. (2000). *Addressing correctional officer stress: Programs and strategies*. Washington, DC: U.S. Department of Justice, Office of Justice Programs, National Institute of Justice.

Freudenberg, N. (2004). Community health services for returning jail and prison inmates. *Journal of Correctional Health Care, 10*, 369–397.

Freudenberg, N., Daniels, J., Crum, M., Perkins, T., & Richie, B. (2005). Coming home from jail: The social and health consequences of community reentry for women, male adolescents, and their families and communities. *American Journal of Public Health, 95 (10)*, 1725–1736.

Gibbons, J. J., & Katzenbach, N. B. (2006). *Confronting confinement: A report of the commission on safety and abuse in American prisons*. Washington, DC: Vera Institute of Justice.

Glaze, L., & Bonczar, T. B. (2007). *Probation and parole in the United States, 2006*. Washington, DC: U.S. Department of Justice, Office of Justice Programs, Bureau of Justice Statistics.

Hairston, C. F. (2001). *Prisoners and families: Parenting issues during incarceration*. Washington, DC: U.S. Department of Health and Human Services, The Urban Institute.

Harrison, P. M., & Beck, A. J. (2006). *Prison and jail inmates at midyear 2005*. Washington, DC: U.S. Department of Justice, Office of Justice Programs, Bureau of Justice Statistics.

Hughes, T., & Wilson, J. (2002). *Reentry trends in the United States*. Washington, DC: U.S. Department of Justice, Office of Justice Programs, Bureau of Justice Statistics.

Hughes, T. A., Wilson, D. J., & Beck, A. J. (2001). *Trends in state parole, 1990–2000*. Washington, DC: U.S. Department of Justice, Office of Justice Programs, Bureau of Justice Statistics.

Iguchi, M. Y., London, J. A., Gorge, N. G., Hickman, L., Fain, T., & Riehman, K. (2002). Elements of well-being affected by criminalizing the drug user. *Public Health Reports, 117*, 146–150.

Inciardi, J. A., Martin, S. S., & Butzin, C. A. (2004). Five-year outcomes of therapeutic community treatment of drug-involved offenders after release from prison. *Crime & Delinquency, 50*, 88–107.

Langan, P. A., & Levin, D. J. (2002). *Recidivism of prisoners released in 1994*. Washington, DC: U.S. Department of Justice, Office of Justice Programs, Bureau of Justice Statistics.

La Vigne, N. G., & Cowan, J. (2006). *Mapping prisoner reentry: An action research guidebook*. Washington, DC: U.S. Department of Justice.

La Vigne, N. G., & Kachnowski, V. (2003). *A portrait of prisoner reentry in Maryland*. Washington, DC: The Urban Institute.

La Vigne, N. G., & Mamalian, C. A. (2004). *Prisoner reentry in Georgia*. Washington, DC: The Urban Institute.

Lipton, D. S. (1998). *Principles of correctional therapeutic community treatment programming for drug abusers*. New York: National Development and Research Institutes, Inc.

Listwan, S. J. (2009). Reentry for serious and violent offenders: An analysis of program attrition. *Criminal Justice Policy Review, 20*, 154–169.

Lynch, J. P., & Sabol, W. J. (2001). *Prisoner reentry in perspective*. Washington, DC: The Urban Institute.

MacKenzie, D. L. (2006). *What works in corrections: Reducing the criminal activities of offenders and delinquents*. New York: Cambridge University Press.

Marbley, A. F., & Ferguson, R. (2005). Responding to prisoner reentry, recidivism, and incarceration of inmates of color: A call to the communities. *Journal of Black Studies, 35*, 633–649.

McDonald, D., Fournier, E., Russell-Einhourn, M., & Crawford, S. (1998). *Private prisons in the United States: An assessment of current practice*. Cambridge, MA: Abt Associates Inc.

Minton, T. D. (2011). *Jail inmates at midyear 2010: Statistical tables*. U.S. Department of Justice, Office of Justice Programs, Bureau of Justice Statistics.

Morse, D. E., & Kerr, A. R. (2006). Disparities in oral and pharyngeal cancer incidence, mortality and survival among black and white Americans. *Journal of the American Dental Association, 137*, 203–212.

Mumola, C. J., & Karberg, J. C. (2006). *Drug use and dependence, state and federal prisons*. Washington, DC: U.S. Department of Justice, Office of Justice Programs, Bureau of Justice Statistics.

Naser, R. L., & La Vigne, N. G. (2006). Family support in the prisoner reentry process: Expectations and realities. *Journal of Offender Rehabilitation, 43*, 93–106.

National Commission on Correctional Health Care (2002). *The health status of soon-to-be-released inmates: A report to Congress, Volume 1*. Chicago, IL: Author.

National Governors Association (2005). *Improving prisoner reentry through strategic policy innovations*. Washington, DC: NGA Center for Best Practices.

National Institute of Corrections (2002). *Transition from prison to community initiative*. Retrieved October 29, 2006, from http://www.nicic.org/pubs/2002/017520.pdf.

National Institute on Drug Abuse (2002). *Therapeutic community*. Washington, DC: National Institute on Drug Abuse, NIH Publication Number 02-4877.

New York City Department of Citywide Administrative Services (2005). *Probation officer, exam 2064*. Retrieved from www.nyc.gov/html/dcas/downloads/pdf/noes/probation officer.pdf.

Office of Justice Programs (n.d.). *Reentry*. Retrieved from http://www.reentry.gov.

Oppel, R. A., Jr. (2011). Private prisons to offer little in savings. *The New York Times*, Vol. CLX, No. 55, 410. A1–A4.

Pace, P. R. (2009). Social work and the Second Chance Act. *NASW News, 54(5)*, 4.

Petersilia, J. (2000). *When prisoners return to the community: Political, economic, and social consequences*. Washington, DC: U.S. Department of Justice, Office of Justice Programs.

Petersilia, J. (2001). Prisoner reentry: Public safety and reintegration challenges. *The Prison Journal, 81*, 360–376.

Petersilia, J. (2003). *When prisoners come home: Parole and prisoner reentry*. New York: Oxford University Press.

Pollack, S. (2004). Anti-oppressive social work practice with women in prison: Discursive reconstructions and alternative practices. *British Journal of Social Work, 34(5)*, 693–707.

Rowland, M. K. (2009). *Family-based reintegration: Effective interventions for juveniles*. El Paso, TX: LFB Scholarly Publications.

Seiter, R. P., & Kadela, K. R. (2003). Prisoner reentry: What works, what does not, and what is promising. *Crime & Delinquency, 49*, 360–388.

Severson, M. M. (1994). Adapting social work values to the corrections environment. *Social Work, 39(4)*, 451–456.

Sherman, L. W., Gottfredson, D. C., MacKenzie, D. L., Eck, J., Reuter, P., & Bushway, S. D. (1998). *Preventing crime: What works, what doesn't, what's promising.* Washington, DC: National Institute of Justice.

Siegel, L. J. (2010). *Introduction to criminal justice* (12th ed.). Belmont, CA: Wadsworth, Cengage Learning.

Solomon, A. L., Kachnowski, V., & Bhati, A. (2005). Does parole work? Analyzing the impact of postprison supervision on rearrest outcomes. Washington, DC: Urban Institute Press.

Solomon, A. L., Palmer, T., Atkinson, A., Davidson, J., & Harvey, L. (2006). *Prisoner reentry: Addressing the challenges in Weed and Seed Communities.* Washington, DC: Urban Institute Press.

Stoesen, L. (2004). Corrections: Public safety, public health. *NASW News, 49(1)*, 4.

Swanson, C. L. (2009). *Restorative justice in a prison community: Or everything I didn't learn in kindergarten I learned in prison.* Lanham, MD: Lexington Books.

Travis, J. (2005). *But they all come back: Facing the challenges of prisoner reentry.* Washington, DC: Urban Institute Press.

Travis, J., Keegan, C. F., Cadora, E., Solomon, A., & Swartz, C. (2003). *A portrait of prisoner reentry in New Jersey.* Washington, DC: The Urban Institute Justice Policy Center.

Urban Institute, The (2008). *The reentry mapping network.* Retrieved from www.urban.org/projects/reentry-rnapping/index.cfm.

U.S. Department of Labor (2007a). *About PRI.* Retrieved from www.doleta.gov/PRI/aboutPRl.cfrn.

U.S. Department of Labor (2007b). *Welcome.* Retrieved from http://www.doleta.gov/pri.

Visher, C. A., & Courtney, M. E. (2007). *One year out: Experiences of prisoners returning to Cleveland.* Washington, DC: The Urban Institute Justice Policy Center.

West, H. C. (2010). *Prison inmates at midyear 2009: Statistical tables.* U.S. Department of Justice, Office of Justice Programs, Bureau of Justice Statistics.

White House. *State of the Union address* (2004). Retrieved from www.whitehouse.gov/news/releases/2004/0l/20040120-7.html.

White House. *Faith-based and community initiatives-prisoner reentry initiative* (n.d.). Retrieved from www.whitehouse.gov/government/fbci/pri .html.

Willmott, D., & van Olphen, J. (2005). Challenging the health impacts of incarceration: The role for community health workers. *Californian Journal of Health Promotion, 3(2)*, 38–48.

Wilson, D. B., Gallagher, C. A., & MacKenzie, D. L. (2000). A meta-analysis of corrections-based education, vocation, and work programs for adult offenders. *Journal of Research in Crime and Delinquency, 37(4)*, 347–368.

Young, D. S. (2002). Non-psychiatric services provided in a mental health unit in a county jail. *Journal of Offender Rehabilitation, 35(2)*, 63–82.

Young, D. S. (2007). Jail mental health services. In D. W Springer & A. R. Roberts (eds.) *Handbook of forensic mental health with victims and offenders: Assessment, treatment, and research* (pp. 425–444). New York: Springer Publishing Company, LLC.

Chapter 6

Allen, T. (2005). Taking a juvenile into custody: Situational factors that influence police officers' decisions. *Journal of Sociology and Social Welfare, XXXII(2)*, 121–129.

American Civil Liberties Union (n.d.). *Criminal justice.* Retrieved from www.aclu.org/ racial-justice/criminal-justice.

Arya, N. (2011). *State trends: Legislative changes from 2005 to 2010 removing youth from the adult criminal justice system.* Washington, DC: Campaign for Youth Justice.

Blair, P., Greifinger, R., Stone, T. H., & Somers, S. (2011). *Increasing access to health coverage insurance coverage for pre-trial detainees and individuals transitioning from correctional facilities under the Patient Protection and Affordable Care Act.* Retrieved from www.cochs.org/files/ABA/aba_final.pdf.

Blakely, C. R. (2007). *Prisons, penology and penal reform: An introduction to institutional specialization.* New York: Peter Lang Publishing, Inc.

Bureau of Justice Assistance (1998). *1996 national survey of state sentencing structures.* Washington, DC: U.S. Department of Justice, Office of Justice Programs, Bureau of Justice Assistance.

Center for Dispute Settlement (2011). *Welcome to the center for dispute settlement.* Retrieved from www.cdsadr.org.

Center for Problem-Oriented Policing (2011). What is POP? Retrieved from http://www.popcenter.org/about/?p=whatiscpop.

Community Capacity Development Office (n.d.). *Weed and Seed.* Retrieved August 17, 2007 from www.ojp.usdoj.gov/ccdo/ws/welcome.html.

Elkin, M. (1987). Joint custody: Affirming that parents and families are forever. *Social Work, 32(1)*, 18–24.

Fowler, D. F., Lightsey, R., Monger, J., Terrazas, E., & White, L. (2007). *Texas' school-to-prison pipeline: Dropout to incarceration the impact of school discipline and zero tolerance.* Retrieved from www.texasappleseed.net/pdf/Pipeline%20Report.pdf.

Fox, A., & Gold, E. (2010). *Daring to fail: First-person stories of criminal justice reform.* New York: Center for Court Innovation.

Goldstein, H. (1990). *Problem-oriented policing.* New York: McGraw-Hill, Inc.

Gottfredson, M. R., & Gottfredson, D. M. (1988). *Decision making in criminal justice: Toward the rational exercise of discretion.* New York: Plenum Press.

Govtrack.us (n.d.). *S. 1789 [111th]—Summary: Fair Sentencing Act of 2010.* Retrieved from www.govtrack.us/congress/bill.xpd?bill=s111-1789&tab=summary.

Indiana Department of Corrections (n.d.). *Transition from prison to community initiative.* Retrieved from http://www.in.gov/idoc/2520.htm.

Innocence Project (n.d.a). *About us: Mission Statement.* Retrieved from www.innocence project.org/about/Mission-Statement.php.

Innocence Project (n.d.b). *About us: Faqs: Are services available to exonerees after release?* Retrieved from www.innocenceproject.org/Content/Are_services_available_to_exonerees _after_release.php.

Innocence Project (n.d.c). *Know the cases: After exoneration.* Retrieved from www.innocenceproject.org/know/After-Exoneration.php.

Kim, C. Y., Losen D. J., & Hewitt, D. T. (2010). *The school-to-prison pipeline: Structuring legal reform.* New York: New York University Press.

Lattimore, P. K., & Visher, C. A. (2009). *The multi-site evaluation of SVORI: Summary and synthesis.* Washington, DC: National Institute of Justice, Office of Justice Programs, U.S. Department of Justice.

Listwan, S. J. (2009). Reentry for serious and violent offenders: An analysis of program attrition. *Criminal Justice Policy Review, 20,* 154–169.

Mayer, B. (2008). Conflict resolution. In T. Mizrahi & L. E. Davis (eds.) *Encyclopedia of social work* (20th ed.) (vol. 1, pp. 415–420). Washington, DC: NASW Press and New York: Oxford University Press.

National Institute of Corrections (2002). *Transition from prison to community initiative.* Retrieved October 29, 2006, from www.nicic.org/pubs/2002/017520.pdf.

Office of Policy and Management (2011). *Juvenile justice system.* Retrieved from www.ct.gov/opm/cwp/view.asp?a=2974&q=383628&opmNav_GID=1797.

Office of the State Attorney 18th Judicial Circuit of Florida (2000). *Community arbitration program.* Retrieved from http://sa18.state.fl.us/prosecute/cap.htm.

Phelps, S. (2002). *World of criminal justice* (vol. 1). Farmington Hills, MI: The Gale Group.

Phoenix House (n.d.). *Criminal justice services.* Retrieved from http://www.phoenixhouse.org/services-for/criminal-justice-services.

Roehl, J. A., Huitt, R., Wycoff, M. A., Pate, A., Rebovich, D., & Coyle, K. (1996). *National process evaluation of operation weed and seed.* Washington, DC: U.S. Department of Justice, Office of Justice Programs, National Institute of Justice.

Sentencing Project, The (2008). *Racial disparity in the criminal justice system: A manual for practitioners and policymakers.* Washington, DC: Author.

Serrano, R. A. Savage, D. G., & Williams, C. J. (2011). *Early release proposed for crack cocaine offenders.* Retrieved from http://articles.latimes.com/2011/jun/01/nation/la-na-holder-crack-20110602.

Shoaf, L. C. (2005). *Akron weed and seed program 2000–2004.* Columbus, OH: Ohio Office of Criminal Justice Services.

Solomon, A. L., Palmer, T., Atkinson, A., Davidson, J., & Harvey, L. (2006). *Prisoner reentry: Addressing the challenges in Weed and Seed Communities.* Washington, DC: Urban Institute Press.

Swanson, C. G. (2009). *Restorative justice in a prison community: Or everything I didn't learn in kindergarten I learned in prison.* Lanham, MD: Lexington Books.

Taylor, C. (2011). *Alternative sentencing slows prison costs increases.* Retrieved from http://dailylocal.com/articles/2011/08/01/news/srv0000012875108.txt.

United Nations Office on Drugs and Crime (2010). *Justice section: Crime prevention and criminal justice reform.* Retrieved from www.unodc.org/documents/justice-and-prison-reform/crimeprevention/10-56655_leaflet_eBook.pdf.

U.S. Department of Labor (2007a). *About PRI.* Retrieved from www.doleta.gov/PRI/aboutPRl.cfrn.

U.S. Department of Labor (2007b). *Welcome.* Retrieved from www.doleta.gov/pri/.

Walgrave, L. (1999). Community service as a cornerstone of a systematic restorative response to (juvenile) crime. In G. Bazemore and L. Walgrave (eds.) *Restorative juvenile justice: Repairing the harm of youth crime* (pp. 129–154). Monsey, NY: Criminal Justice Press.

White House. *State of the Union address* (2004). Retrieved from www.whitehouse.gov/news/releases/2004/0l/20040120-7.html.

White House (n.d.). *Faith-based and community initiatives—prisoner reentry initiative.* Retrieved from www.whitehouse.gov/government/fbci/pri .html.

Wisconsin Department of Corrections (2007). *Governor Doyle creates commission to reduce racial disparity in Wisconsin's criminal justice system.* Retrieved from www.wi-doc.com/Racial_Disparity_Commission.htm.

Women's Prison Association (2009). *Women's voices: Advocacy by criminal justice-involved women.* New York: Author.

Chapter 7

Abudu, N. (2010). *Racial bias is inherent in state felony disfranchisement laws.* Retrieved from www.aclu.org/blog/racial-justice-voting-rights/racial-bias-inherent-state-felony-disfran chisement-laws.

Aday, R. H. (1994). Golden years behind bars: Special programs and facilities for elderly inmates. *Federal Probation, 58,* 48.

Aday, R. H. (1999). *Responding to the graying of American prisons: A 10-year follow-up.* Unpublished report. Murfreesboro: Middle Tennessee State University.

Aday, R. H. (2003). *Aging prisoners: Crisis in American corrections.* Westport, CT: Praeger.

Albanese, J. S., & Pursley, R. D. (1993). *Crime in America: Some existing and emerging issues.* Englewood Cliffs, NJ: Prentice Hall.

American Civil Liberties Union (2010). *"Driving While Black" in Maryland.* Retrieved from www.aclu.org/print/racial-justice/driving-while-black-maryland.

American Civil Liberties Union (2011). *Friendly House et al. v. Whiting et al.* Retrieved from www.aclu.org/print/immigrants-rights-racial-justice/friendly-house-et-al-v-whiting-et-al.

Anderson, D. C. (1997). Aging behind bars. *New York Times Magazine, 146,* 23–33.

Anno, B. J. (2001). *Correctional health care: Guidelines for the management of an adequate delivery system.* Chicago, IL: National Commission on Correctional Health Care.

Anno, B. J., Graham, C., Lawrence, J. E., Shansky, R., Bisbee, J., & Blackmore, J. (2004). *Correctional health care: Addressing the needs of elderly, chronically ill, and terminally ill inmates.* Washington, DC: U.S. Department of Justice, National Institute of Corrections.

Barker, R. L. (2003). *The Social Work Dictionary* (5th ed.). Washington, DC: NASW Press.

Blanchette, K. (2002). Classifying females offenders for effective intervention: Application of the case-based principles of risk and need. *Forum on Correctional Research, 13,* 31–35.

Borger, J. (2005). *US becomes last country to end death penalty for under-18s.* Retrieved from www.guardian.co.uk/world/2005/mar/02/usa.julianborger.

Bowser, B. P., Jenkins-Barnes, T., Dillard-Smith, C., & Lockett, G. (2010). Harm reduction for drug abusing ex-offenders: Outcome of the California Prevention and Education Project MORE Project. *Journal of Evidence-Based Social Work, 7,* 15–29.

Bureau of Justice Assistance (1998). *1996 national survey of state sentencing structures.* Washington, DC: U.S. Department of Justice, Office of Justice Programs, Bureau of Justice Assistance.

Bureau of Justice Statistics (2011) *Victims.* Retrieved from http://bjs.ojp.usdoj.gov/index.cfm?ty=tp&tid=9.

Bureau of Justice Statistics (n.d.). *Victims and offenders.* Retrieved from http://bjs.gov/index.cfm?ty=tp&tid=94.

Camp, G., & Camp, C. (2001). *The 1992–2001 Corrections Yearbook.* Middletown, CT: Criminal Justice Institute.

Child Welfare League of America (2002). *Juvenile offenders and the death penalty: Is justice served?* Washington, DC: Author.

Cohen, A. (2009). *The costs of justice.* Retrieved from www.cbsnews.com/stories/2009/04/07/opinion/courtwatch/main4925174.shtml.

Cohen, T. H., & Kyckelhahn, T. (2010, revised 7/15/2010). *Felony defendants in large urban counties, 2006.* Washington, DC: U.S. Department of Justice, Office of Justice Programs, Bureau of Justice Statistics.

Colsher, P. L., Wallace, R. B., Loeffelholz, P. L., & Sales, M. (1992). Health status of older inmates: A comprehensive survey. *American Journal of Public Health, 82*, 881–884.

Committee on the Judiciary (2009). *Cyberbullying and other online safety issues for children.* Retrieved from http://judiciary.house.gov/hearings/hear_090930.html.

Conly, C. H. (2005). *Helping inmates obtain federal disability benefits: Serious medical and mental illness, incarceration, and federal disability entitlement program.* Washington, DC: U.S. Department of Justice.

Correct the Count (2010). *Prison-based gerrymandering ends in New York!* Retrieved from http://correctthecount.org/2010/08/prison-based-gerrymandering-ends-in-new-york/ 353.

Council on Crime and Justice (2004). *Low level offenses in Minneapolis: An analysis of arrests and their outcomes.* Retrieved from www.crimeandjustice.org/researchReports/ Low%20Level%20Offenses%20in%20Minneapolis-%20An%20Analysis%20of%20 Arrests%20and%20their%20Outcomes.pdf.

Draine, J., Wolff, N., Jacoby, J. E., Hartwell, S., & Duclos, C. (2005). Understanding community re-reentry of former prisoners with mental illness: A conceptual model to guide new research. *Behavioral Sciences and the Law, 23*, 689–707.

Ellis, A. L. (1981). Where is social work? Police brutality and the inner city. *Social Work, 26(2)*, 511–515.

Ertl, M. A., & McNamara, J. R. (1997). Treatment of juvenile sex offenders: A review of the literature. *Child and Adolescent Social Work Journal, 14(3)*, 199–221.

Faiver, K. L. (1998). Special issues of aging. In K. L. Favier (ed.) *Health care management issues in corrections* (pp. 123–132). Lanham, MD: American Correctional Association.

Finkelhor, D., Ormrod, R., & Chaffin, M. (2009). *Juveniles who commit sex offenses against minors.* Washington, DC: U.S. Department of Justice, Office of Justice Programs, Office of Juvenile Justice and Delinquency Programs.

Flynn, E. E. (1992). The graying of America's prison population. *The Prison Journal, 72*, 77–98.

Furman, R., Langer, C. L., Sanchez, T. W., & Negi, N. J. (2007). A qualitative study of immigration policy and practice dilemmas for social work students. *Journal of Social Work Education, 43(1)*, 1–14.

Gaskins, S. (2004). "Women of circumstance"—The effects of mandatory minimum sentencing on women minimally involved in drug crimes. *American Criminal Law Review, 41.4*, 1533–1553.

Glaser, J. B., Warchol, A., D'Angelo, D., & Gutterman, H. (1990). Infectious diseases of geriatric inmates. *Reviews of Infectious Diseases, 12*, 683–692.

Glaze, L. E., & Maruschak, L. M. (2008, revised 3/30/10). *Parents in prison and their minor children.* Washington, DC: U.S. Department of Justice, Office of Justice Programs, Bureau of Justice Statistics.

Gould, L., & Ross, J. I. (2006). Integrating the past, present and future. In J. I. Ross & L. Gould (eds.) *Native Americans and the criminal justice system: Theoretical and policy directions* (pp. 237–241). Boulder, CO: Paradigm Publishers.

Govtrack.us (2011). *H.R. 2212: Democracy restoration act of 2011.* Retrieved from www. govtrack.us/congress/bill.xpd?bill=h112-2212.

Grady, M. D. (2009a). Sex offenders part I: Theories and models of etiology, assessment, and intervention. *Social Work in Mental Health, 7(4)*, 353–371.

Grady, M. D. (2009b). Sex offenders part II: Policies that address sex offenders. *Social Work in Mental Health, 7(4)*, 372–384.

Grossman, S. F., & Lundy, M. (2008). Double jeopardy: A comparison of persons with and without disabilities who were victims of sexual abuse and/or sexual assault. *Journal of Social Work in Disability & Rehabilitation, 7(1)*, 19–46.

Hairston, C. F. (2007). Family programs in state prison. In C. A. McNeece & A. R. Roberts (eds.) *Policy and practice in the justice system* (pp. 143–157). Chicago, IL: Nelson Hall.

Hairston, C. F. (1991). Mother in jail: Parent–child separation and jail visitation. *Affilia, 6(2)*, 9–27.

Harrell, E. (2011). *Workplace violence, 1993–2009*. Washington, DC: U.S. Department of Justice, Office of Justice Programs, Bureau of Justice Statistics.

Hillerman, R. (2008). Older prisoners: Is there life after "life" sentencing? A white paper. In E. T. Jurkowski (ed.) *Policy and program planning for older adults: Realities and visions* (pp. 351–359). New York: Springer.

Justice resource update: Advancing the field of criminal justice (2011). Washington, DC: U.S. Department of Justice, Office of Justice Programs. Retrieved from www.ojp.gov/justiceresourceupdate/february2011/index.htm.

Lamb, H. R., Weinberger, L. E., & Gross, B. H. (1999). Community treatment of severely mental ill offenders under the jurisdiction of the criminal justice system: A review. *Psychiatric Services, 50*, 907–913.

Letourneau, E. J, Levenson, J. S., Bandyopadhyay, D., Sinha, D., & Armstrong, K. S. (2010). *Evaluating the effectiveness of sex offender registration and notification policies for reducing sexual violence against women*. Washington, DC: U.S. Department of Justice.

Levenson, J. S. (2009). Sex offender polygraph examination: An evidence-based case management tool for social workers. *Journal of Evidence-Based Social Work, 6*, 361–375.

Lindquist, C. H., & Lindquist, C. A. (1999). Health behind bars: Utilization and evaluation of medical care among jail inmates. *Journal of Community Health, 24(4)*, 285–303.

Lindsay, M., & Lester, D. (2004). *Suicide-by-cop*. Amityville, NY: Baywood.

Lindsay, M., & Lester, D. (2008). Criteria for suicide-by-cop incidents. *Psychological Reports, 102*, 603–605.

Listwan, S. J. (2009). Reentry for serious and violent offenders: An analysis of program attrition. *Criminal Justice Policy Review, 20*, 154–169.

Michigan guide to compliance with laws governing the placement of juveniles in secure facilities (n.d.). Retrieved from http://michigan.gov/documents/dhs/DHS-BJJJuvenile JusticeBookletWebVersion_292401_7.pdf.

Morales, A. T., & Sheafor, B. W. (1995). *Social work a profession of many faces* (7th ed.). Boston, MA: Allyn & Bacon.

Morales, A. T., Sheafor, B. W., & Scott, M. E. (2007). *Social work: A profession of many faces* (11th ed.). Boston, MA: Pearson Education, Inc.

Morton, J. B., & Jacobs, N. C. (1992). *An administrative overview of the older inmate*. Washington, DC: National Institute of Corrections.

Moses, M. C. (2006). Does parental incarceration increase a child's risk for foster care placement? *National Institute of Justice Journal, 255*, 12–14.

National Association of Social Workers (n.d.). *NASW opposes Arizona immigration law*. Retrieved from www.socialworkers.org/practice/intl/2010/042910.asp.

National Commission on Correctional Health Care (2002). *The health status of soon-to-be-released inmates: A report to Congress, Volume 1*. Chicago, IL: Author.

Noonan, J. H., & Vavra, M. C. (2007). *Crime in schools and colleges: A study of offenders and arrestees reported via national Incident-based reporting system data*. Washington,

DC: U.S. Department of Justice, Federal Bureau of Investigation, Criminal Justice Information Services Division.

Office for Victims of Crime (n.d.a). *What can you do if you are a victim of a crime.* Retrieved from www.ovc.gov/publications/infores/whatyoucando_2010/WhatUCanDo_508.pdf.

Office for Victims of Crime (n.d.b). *Vision 21: Transforming victim services.* Retrieved from http://ovc.ncjrs.gov/vision21/initiative.html.

Pais, S. (2001). Therapist issues in working with sex offenders. *Journal of Clinical Activities, Assignments & Handouts in Psychotherapy Practice, 1(4),* 89–97.

Perry, S. W. (2005). *Census of tribal justice agencies in Indian country, 2002.* U.S. Department of Justice, Office of Justice Programs, Bureau of Justice Statistics.

Preston, J. (2011). Alabama: Tough immigration measure becomes law. Retrieved from www.nytimes.com/2011/06/10/us/10brfs-Alabama.html?_r=1&ref=todayspaper.

Puzzanchera, C., Adams, B., & Sickmund, M. (2010). *Juvenile court statistics 2006–2007.* Pittsburgh, PA: National Center for Juvenile Justice.

Quinsey, V. L., Harris, G. T., Rice, M. E., & Cormier, C. A. (2006). *Violent offenders: Appraising and managing risk* (2nd ed.). Washington, DC: American Psychological Association.

Racial Profiling Data Collection Resource Center at Northeastern University (n.d.). Retrieved from www.racialprofilinganalysis.neu.edu/background/.

Rand, M. R., & Harrell, E. (2009). *Crime against people with disability, 2007.* Washington, DC: U.S. Department of Justice, Office of Justice Programs, Bureau of Justice Statistics.

Reentry Council (2011). *Reentry mythbusters.* Retrieved from www.nationalreentryresource center.org/documents/0000/1090/REENTRY_MYTHBUSTERS.pdf.

S. 989: End Racial Profiling Act of 2001 (n.d.). Retrieved from www.aele.org/s989.html.

Sampson, R. (2009). *Bullying in schools.* Washington, DC: U.S. Department of Justice, Office of Community Oriented Policing Services, Center for Problem-Oriented Policing, Inc.

SAMSHA National GAINS Center (2005). *The Nathaniel Project: An alternative to incarceration program for people with serious mental illness who have committed felony offenses.* Retrieved from http://gainscenter.samhsa.gov/text/jail/TheNathanielProject_Summer_2005.asp.

Sarri, R. C. (2008). Juvenile justice: Overview. In T. Mizrahi & L. E. Davis (eds.) *Encyclopedia of social work* (20th ed.) (vol. 3, pp. 12–21). Washington, DC: NASW Press and New York: Oxford University Press.

Scalia, J., & Litras, M. F. X. (2002, revised 10/23/02). *Immigration offenders in the federal criminal justice system, 2000.* Washington, DC: U.S. Department of Justice, Office of Justice Programs, Bureau of Justice Statistics.

Schwartz, J. (2009). *Pinched courts push to collect fees and fines.* Retrieved from www.nytimes.com/2009/04/07/us/07collection.html?_r=2&hp=&pagewanted=print.

Sentencing Project, The (2008). *Racial disparity in the criminal justice system: A manual for practitioners and policymakers.* Washington, DC: Author.

Siegel, J. A. (2011). Felon disenfranchisement and the fight for universal suffrage. *Social Work, 56(1),* 89–91.

Smyer, T., Gragert, M. D., & LaMere, S. (1997). Stay safe! Stay healthy! Surviving old age in prison. *Journal of Psychosocial Nursing, 35(9),* 10–17.

Spencer, P. C., & Munch, S. (2003). Client violence toward social workers: The role of management in community health programs. *Social Work, 48(4),* 532–544.

Whitten, L. (2011). HIV treatment interruption is pervasive after release from Texas prisons. *NIDA Notes, 23(4),* 4–6.

Wilbanks, W. (1986). Are female felons treated more leniently by the criminal justice system? *Justice Quarterly, 4,* 517–529.

Wyoming Office of the Attorney General Division of Victim Services (n.d.). *Wyoming crime victim bill of rights.* Retrieved from http://victimservices.wyoming.gov/vbor.htm.

Young, D. S. (2002). Non-psychiatric services provided in a mental health unit in a county jail. *Journal of Offender Rehabilitation, 35(2),* 63–82.

Zosky, D. L. (2010). Accountability in teenage dating violence: A comparative examination of adult domestic violence and juvenile justice systems policies. *Social Work, 55(4),* 359–368.

Chapter 8

Andrews, D. A. (1989). Recidivism is predictable and can be influenced: Using risk assessments to reduce recidivism. *Forum on Corrections Research, 1,* 11–18.

Andrews, D. A., & Bonta, J. (2010). Rehabilitating criminal justice policy and practice. *Psychology, Public Policy, and Law, 16(1),* 39–55.

Barker, R. L. (2003). *The social work dictionary* (5th ed.). Washington, DC: NASW Press.

Bazemore, G., & Walgrave, L. (eds.) (1999) Restorative juvenile justice: In search of fundamentals and an outline for systematic reform. In G. Bazemore and L. Walgrave (eds.) *Restorative juvenile justice: Repairing the harm of youth crime* (pp. 45–74). Monsey, NY: Criminal Justice Press.

Burman, S. (2004). Revisiting the agent of social control role: Implications for substance abuse treatment. *Journal of Social Work Practice, 18(2),* 197–210.

Chaiklin, H. (2007). Epilogue: Social work and criminal justice? In D. W Springer & A. R. Roberts (eds.) *Handbook of forensic mental health with victims and offenders: Assessment, treatment, and research* (pp. 573–585). New York: Springer Publishing Company, LLC.

Compton, B. R., Galaway, B., & Cournoyer, B. R. (2005). *Social work processes* (7th ed.). Belmont, CA: Brooks/Cole, Thomson Learning, Inc.

Cowger, C. D., & Atherton, C. R. (1974). Social control: A rationale for social welfare. *Social Work, 19(4),* 456–462.

Curtis, P. A., & Lutkus, A. M. (1985). Client confidentiality in police social work settings. *Social Work, 30(4),* 355–360.

Fletcher, B. W., & Chandler, R. K. (2006). *Principles of drug abuse treatment for criminal justice populations (NIH Publication No. 06-5316).* Rockville, MD: National Institute on Drug Abuse.

Ginsberg, L. H. (2001). *Careers in social work* (2nd ed.). Boston, MA: Allyn & Bacon.

Greene, A. D., & Latting, J. K. (2004). Whistle-blowing as a form of advocacy: Guidelines for the practitioner and organization. *Social Work, 49(2),* 219–230.

Hepworth, D. H., Rooney, R. H., Rooney, G. D., Strom-Gottfried, K., & Larsen, J. (2010). *Direct social work practice: Theory and skills* (8th ed.). Belmont, CA: Brooks/Cole, Cenage Learning.

Hoefer, R. (2006). *Advocacy practice for social justice.* Chicago, IL: Lyceum Books, Inc.

Hutchison, E. D. (1987). Use of authority in direct social work practice with mandated clients. *Social Service Review, 61(4),* 581–598.

Iguchi, M. Y., London, J. A., Gorge, N. G., Hickman, L., Fain, T., & Riehman, K. (2002). Elements of well-being affected by criminalizing the drug user. *Public Health Reports, 117,* 146–150.

Ivanoff, A., Smyth, N. J., & Finnegan, D. J. (1993). Social work behind bars: preparation for fieldwork in correctional institutions. *Journal of Teaching in Social Work, 7(1)*, 137–149.

Lamb, H. R., Weinberger, L. E., & Gross, B. H. (1999). Community treatment of severely mentally ill offenders under the jurisdiction of the criminal justice system: A review. *Psychiatric Services, 50*, 907–913.

Larson, G. (2008). Anti-oppressive practice in mental health. *Journal of Progressive Human Services, 19(1)*, 39–54.

MacKenzie, D. L. (1997). Criminal justice and crime prevention. In L. W. Sherman, D. Gottfredson, D. L. MacKenzie, J. Eck, P. Reuter, & S. Bushway, *Preventing crime: What works, what doesn't, what's promising* (pp. 1–76). Washington, DC: Office of Justice Programs.

McNeill, F., Batchelor, S., Burnett, R., & Knox, J. (2005). *21st century social work: Reducing re-offending: Key practice principles*. Edinburgh, U.K.: Scottish Executive.

Mumola, C. J., & Karberg, J. C. (2006). *Drug use and dependence, State and Federal prisons*. Washington, DC: U.S. Department of Justice, Office of Justice Programs, Bureau of Justice Statistics.

NASW News (2000). *Probation officer*. November *45(1)*, 15.

National Association of Social Workers (2008). *Code of ethics of the National Association of Social Workers*. Washington, DC: Author.

Sarri, R. C., & Shook, J. J. (2005). The future for social work in juvenile and adult criminal justice. *Advances in Social Work, 6(1)*, 210–220.

Tarasoff v. Regents of the University of California, 17 Cal.3d 425; 551 P.2d 334; 131 Cal. Rptr. 14 (1976).

United States Probation Department (2007). *Conditions of supervision: Standard conditions*. Retrieved from www.nyep.uscourts.gov/conditionsofsupervision/standardconditions.html.

van Wormer, K. (2008). Restorative justice. In T. Mizrahi & L. E. Davis (eds.) *Encyclopedia of social work* (20th ed.) (vol. 3, pp. 531–533). Washington, DC: NASW Press and New York: Oxford University Press.

van Wormer, K. (2009). Restorative justice as social justice for victims of gendered violence: A standpoint feminist perspective. *Social Work, 54(2)*, 107–116.

Visher, C. A., & Courtney, M. E. (2007). *One year out: Experiences of prisoners returning to Cleveland*. Washington, DC: The Urban Institute Justice Policy Center.

Westmarland, L. (2001). Blowing the whistle on police violence. *British Journal of Criminology, 41*, 523–535.

Wilson, A., & Beresford, P. (2000). "Anti-oppressive practice": Emancipation or appropriation? *British Journal of Social Work, 30*, 553–573.

Young, D. S., & Lomonaco, S. W. (2001). Incorporating content on offenders and corrections into social work curricula. *Journal of Social Work Education, 37(3)*, 475–491.

Chapter 9

Adam, N., Zosky, D. L., & Unrau, Y. A. (2004). Improving the research climate in social work curricula: Clarifying learning expectations across BSW and MSW research courses. *Journal of Teaching in Social Work, 24*, 1–18.

Aos, S., Mayfield, J., Miller, M., & Yen, W. (2006). *Evidence-based treatment of alcohol, drug, and mental health disorders: Potential benefits, costs, and fiscal impacts for Washington State*. Olympia: Washington State Institute for Public Policy.

Aos, S., Miller, M., & Drake, E. (2006). *Evidence-based adult corrections programs: What works and what does not.* Olympia: Washington State Institute for Public Policy.

Barker, R. L. (2003). *The social work dictionary* (5th ed.). Washington, DC: NASW Press.

Belenko, S., & Wexler, H. K. (2007). Implementing evidence-based drug treatment in criminal justice settings: Final conference report. Retrieved from www.tresearch.org/law_ethics/CEICAFinalReport2006.pdf.

Chandler, R. K., Peters, R. H., Field, G., & Juliano-Bult, D. (2004). Challenges in implementing evidence-based treatment practices for co-occurring disorders in the criminal justice system. *Behavioral Sciences and the Law, 22,* 431–448.

Epstein, I. (1987). Pedogagy of the perturbed: Teaching research to reluctants. *Journal of Teaching in Social Work, 1,* 71–89.

Evidence-based Medicine Working Group (1992). Evidence-based medicine: A new approach to teaching the practice of medicine. *Journal of the American Medical Association, 262,* 2420–2425.

Feldstein, S. W., & Ginsburg, J. I. D. (2007). Sex, drugs and rock 'n' rolling with resistance: Motivational interviewing in juvenile justice settings. In D. W. Springer & A. R. Roberts (eds.) *Handbook of forensic mental health with victims and offenders: Assessment, treatment, and research* (pp. 247–271). New York: Springer Publishing Company, LLC.

Friedmann, P. D., Taxman, F. S., & Henderson, C.E. (2007). Evidence-based treatment practices for drug-involved adults in the criminal justice system. *Journal of Substance Abuse Treatment, 32,* 267–277.

Guevara, M., Loeffler-Cobia, J., Rhyne, C., & Sachwald, J. (2011). *Putting the pieces together: Practical strategies for implementing evidence-based practices.* Washington, DC: U.S. Department of Justice, National Institute of Corrections, Community Resources for Justice.

Hanley, D. (2006). Appropriate services: Examining the case classification principle. *Journal of Offender Rehabilitation, 42,* 1–22.

Henggeler, S. W., Sheidow, A. J., & Lee, T. (2007). Multisystemic treatment of serious clinical problems in youths and their families. In D. W Springer & A. R. Roberts (eds.) *Handbook of forensic mental health with victims and offenders: Assessment, treatment, and research* (pp. 315–345). New York: Springer Publishing Company, LLC.

Howard, M. O., Himle, J., Jenson, J. M., & Vaughn, M. G. (2009). Revisioning social work clinical education: Recent developments in relation to evidence-based practice. *Journal of Evidence-based Social Work, 6,* 256–273.

Latessa, E. J. (2004). The challenge of change: Correctional programs and evidence-based practices. *Criminology & Public Policy, 3(4),* 547–560.

Lehman, W. E. K., Greener, J. M., & Simpson, D. D. (2002). Assessing organizational readiness for change. *Journal of Substance Abuse Treatment, 22,* 197–209.

Lipsey, M. W., & Wilson, D. B. (2001). *Practical meta-analysis.* Thousand Oaks, CA: Sage Publications, Inc.

McBeath, B., Briggs, H. E., & Aisenberg, E. (2010). Examining the premises supporting the empirically supported intervention approach to social work practice. *Social Work, 55(4),* 347–357.

McNeill, T. (2006). Evidence-based practice in an age of relativism: Toward a model for practice. *Social Work, 51(2),* 147–156.

Murdoch, A. D. (2010). What good is soft evidence? *Social Work, 55(4),* 309–316.

National Association of Social Workers (2008). *Code of ethics of the National Association of Social Workers.* Washington, DC: Author.

Oancea, M. (2010). The evidence of evidence-based social work. *Social Work Review, 9(1),* 158–171.

Patterson, G. T., Chung, I. W., & Swan, P. G. (in press). *The effects of stress management interventions among police officers and recruits*. The Campbell Library.

Perez, D. M. (2009). Applying evidence-based practices to community corrections supervision: An evaluation of residential substance abuse treatment for high-risk probationers. *Journal of Contemporary Criminal Justice*, 25(4), 442–458.

Reitzel, L. R. (2005). Best practices in corrections: Using literature to guide interventions. *Corrections Today*, 67(1), 42–45, 70.

Reyes, C. L. (2009). Corrections-based drug treatment programs and crime prevention: An international approach. *Journal of Offender Rehabilitation*, 48, 620–634.

Roberts, A. R., & Yeager, K. R. (eds) (2006). *Foundations of evidence-based social work practice*. New York: Oxford University Press.

Sackett, D. L., Straus, S. E., Richardson, W. S., Rosenberg, W., & Haynes, R. B. (2000). *Evidence based medicine: How to practice and teach EBM* (2nd ed.). Edinburgh, U.K.: Churchill Livingstone.

Seiter, R. P., & Kadela, K. R. (2003). Prisoner reentry: What works, what does not, and what is promising. *Crime & Delinquency*, 49, 360–388.

Sentencing Project, The (2008). *Reducing racial disparities in the criminal justice system: A manual for practitioners and policymakers*. Washington, DC: Author.

Serin, R. C. (2005). *Evidence-based practice: principles for enhancing correctional results in prisons*. Washington, DC: U.S. Department of Justice, National Institute of Corrections.

Sherman, L. W., Farrington, D. P., Welsh, B. C., & MacKenzie, D. L. (eds.) (2002). *Evidence-based crime prevention*. New York: Routledge.

Sherman, L. W., Gottfredson, D. C., MacKenzie, D. L., Eck, J., Reuter, P., & Bushway, S. D. (1998). *Preventing crime: What works, what doesn't, what's promising*. Washington, DC: National Institute of Justice.

Shlonsky, A., & Gibbs, L. (2006). Will the real evidence-based practice please stand up? Teaching the process of evidence-based practice to the helping professions. In A. R. Roberts & K. R. Yeager (eds.) *Foundations of evidence-based social work practice* (pp. 103–21). New York: Oxford University Press, Inc.

Thyer, B. A. (2007). Evidence-based social work: An overview. In B. A. Thyer & J. S. Wodarski (eds.) *Social work in mental health: An evidence-based approach* (pp. 1–28). Hoboken, NJ: John Wiley & Sons, Inc.

Thyer, B. A., & Wodarski, J. S. (eds.) (2007). *Social work in mental health: An evidence-based approach*. Hoboken, NJ: John Wiley & Sons, Inc.

U.S. Department of Justice (2011). *Second chance act adult mentoring grants to nonprofit organizations FY 2011 competitive grant announcement*. OMB No. 1121-0329. Washington, DC: U.S. Department of Justice, Office of Justice Programs, Bureau of Justice Assistance.

Webb, S. A. (2001). Some considerations on the validity of evidence-based practice in social work. *British Journal of Social Work*, 31(1), 57–79.

Weinbach, R. W., & Grinnell, R. M. (2007). *Statistics for social workers* (7th ed.). Boston, MA: Pearson Education, Inc.

Welsh, B. C., Sullivan, C. J., & Olds, D. L. (2010). When early crime prevention goes to scale: A new look at the evidence. *Prevention Science*, 11(2), 115–125.

Wheeler, D. P., & Goodman, H. (2007). Health and mental health social workers need information literacy skills. *Health & Social Work*, 32(3), 235–237.

Chapter 10

Council on Social Work Education (n.d.) *Advanced social work practice in the prevention of substance use disorders*. Retrieved from www.cswe.org/File.aspx?id=22249.

Council on Social Work Education (2008). *2008 educational policy and accreditation standards*. Alexandria, VA: Author

Ginsberg, L. H. (2001). *Careers in social work* (2nd ed.). Boston, MA: Allyn & Bacon.

Ivanoff, A., Smyth, N. J., & Finnegan, D. J. (1993). Social work behind bars: Preparation for fieldwork in correctional institutions. *Journal of Teaching in Social Work, 7(1)*, 137–149.

Koning, P. de, & Kwant, A. de (2002). Dutch drug policy and the role of social workers. *Journal of Social Work Practice in the Addictions, 2(3/4)*, 49–56.

McNeill, F. (2005). "Offender management" in Scotland: the first hundred years. Retrieved from www.cjscotland.org.uk/index.php/cjscotland/dynamic_page/?title=offender_management.

McNeill, F., Batchelor, S., Burnett, R., & Knox, J. (2005). *21st century social work: Reducing re-offending: Key practice principles*. Edinburgh, U.K.: Scottish Executive.

Pace, P. R. (2009). Social work and the Second Chance Act. *NASW News, 54(5)*, 4.

Ritter, N. M. (2006). Preparing for the future: Criminal Justice 2010. *National Institute of Justice Journal, 255*, 8–11.

Sarri, R. C., & Shook, J. J. (2005). The future for social work in juvenile and adult criminal justice. *Advances in Social Work, 6(1)*, 210–220.

Tonry, M. (2009). Explanations of American punishment policies: A national history. *Punishment & Society, 11(3)*, 377–394.

U.S. Department of Justice (2011a). *Attorney general Eric Holder speaks at the National Association of Counties Legislative Conference*. Retrieved from www.justice.gov/iso/opa/ag/speeches/2011/ag-speech-110307.html.

U.S. Department of Justice (2011b). *Second chance act adult mentoring grants to nonprofit organizations FY 2011 competitive grant announcement*. OMB No. 1121-0329. Washington, DC: U.S. Department of Justice, Office of Justice Programs, Bureau of Justice Assistance.

Whitaker, T., & Arrington, P. (2008). *Social workers at work*. NASW Membership Workforce Study. Washington, DC: National Association of Social Workers.

Wilson, M. (2010). *Criminal justice social work in the United States: Adapting to new challenges*. Washington, DC: NASW Center for Workforce Studies.

Index